# GREAT FRAMLINGHAM IN SUFFOLK AND THE HOWARD DUKES OF NORFOLK

A selection of 12 texts in English illustrating aspects of the History of Framlingham from the arrival of Thomas Howard in 1509 to the demolition of the Castle Interior during the later 17th century.

Edited by

JOHN RIDGARD

2009

ISBN 978 0 9555389 2 6

First published in 2009
by The Blaxhall Press

A catalogue record for this book is available from
the British Library

*Design and layout*
Rodney West Associates

This publication is printed on acid-free paper

Printed in Great Britain by
The Lavenham Press, Suffolk

*Front cover illustration: How a good huntsman hunts the reindeer
from the Hunting Book by Gaston Phoebus
Courtsey BNF*

# CONTENTS

|  |  | Pages |
| --- | --- | --- |
| Acknowledgements |  | iv |
| Introduction |  | vi |

The Wealth Behind the Castle Walls — 1
*The Last Will and Testament of Thomas Howard, 1520.*

Christmas Fare with the Howards, 1526 — 4
*An extract from the Book of Emptions.*

A Description of Framlingham Deer-Park — 13
*Ireland's Survey, 1662.*

Social and Economic Importance of the Park — 18
*The Keeper's Accounts, 1509-1517 (unabridged).*

Framlingham and the Last Great Medieval Funeral — 54
*Extracts from the Burial Rites of Thomas Howard, 1524.*

Aspects of 16th century Town Government — 57
*Framlingham Borough Court, Michaelmas 1520.*

Framlingham Manor Account Roll, Michaelmas 1543-4 — 62

The Survey of Framlingham, 1547 — 74
*Christopher Peyton's Terrar for Edward VIth (excluding Saxtead).*

The Inventory of Framlingham Castle, 1606. — 117

A Thriving Market Town — 121
*Framlingham Market Rental, c.1610.*

Constructing the Tomb of Henry Howard the Poet Earl — 126
*Griffith's Memorandum to Mr. Fuller, 1616.*

The Beginning of the Demolition — 129
*The Stones Account, 1656.*

Bibliography — 133

Index 1 - Keeper's Account - Chapter 4 — 135
Index 2 - The Survey of Framlingham, 1547 - Chapter 8 — 146
Index 3 - General Index — 152

*for*
Roger E. Ladd
whose ancestors lived and worshipped
in 17th and 18th century Framlingham.

# *Acknowledgements*

I wish to place on record my thanks to the following persons and institutions for permission to translate, transcribe and quote from their original manuscript sources and publications.

The Master and Fellows of Pembroke College Cambridge for permission to publish in whole or in part the following documents:
Pembroke College Archives Framlingham L 17.
Pembroke College Archives, Framlingham Court Rolls 1 for the year 1520.
Pembroke College Archives, College MS. Lz (zeta)
Pembroke College Archives, College MS. L theta
Pembroke College MS. 300.

His Grace the Duke of Norfolk and the Arundel Castle Trustees for permission to publish MS. A1610.

To Suffolk Record Office, Ipswich Branch, for their kindly and unfailing support and for permission to publish extracts from MS. HD88/6/1.

To the Priest-in-Charge of Framlingham Parish to publish an extract from FC101/A3/6/59 and to quote from other MSS. associated with it.

To Mrs Wendy Smedley for her article 'Fragment of a Daily Account Book' pub. Suffolk Institute of Archaeology and History and to Essex Record Office, Chelmsford, where the MS. was discovered.

I have enjoyed the highly professional assistance over many years of the Honorary Archivist of Pembroke College, Miss J. Ringrose of Cambridge University Library. I thank also Mrs. Heather Warne, Archivist at Arundel Castle and her team, for their kindness and hospitality. Finally, I thank my students for their enduring good humour and company.

# *Introduction*

First and foremost, this selection of translations and transcripts of original documents, each with its own short preface and comments, is intended to serve as an introductory source-book for Framlingham's future historians with interests in the period c.1500-c.1650. It should also be of some assistance to genealogists, landscape historians and students of food and drink, among others. Topics covered by books still in print, Mary Tudor's *coup d'etat* in 1553 for example, have here been avoided. With the exception of two texts discovered very recently, this selection therefore consists of those Framlingham-related documents from the Howard era which over the years have seemed to the author to be those most overdue for publication. Another editor would have chosen differently, placing more emphasis, perhaps, on the excellent and varied documents to be found in Framlingham's parish records kept at the Suffolk Record Office, Ipswich.

CHAPTER 1

# *The Wealth Behind the Castle Walls*
The Last Will and Testament of Thomas Howard, 1520

## Preface

Despite its illustrious connections, the surviving documentary sources for Framlingham are at best only 'good in parts'. The castle and town undoubtedly flourished when Thomas de Brotherton was lord in the early 14th century, for example, but the manuscript sources for this period are so few that it would be easy to assume that Framlingham was then in decline. This applies also to the very late 14th century when Margaret de Brotherton, Duchess of Norfolk, was in residence at the castle, even though she was one of the very wealthiest individuals in England. Documents written during the Mowbray era in the 15th century are in particularly short supply.

It is clear, nevertheless, that on several occasions large surges of money associated with a change in lordship or with a royal visit flowed into Framlingham. There is absolutely no reason to suppose the castle was in bad repair when, in 1509, the estate was restored to the Howards at the death of Henry VIIth and was further upgraded to provide a luxurious country residence for Thomas the 2nd Howard Duke of Norfolk in preparation for his retirement. Indeed, an obligation had been imposed on the Earl of Oxford, who acquired the estate in 1486 following the disastrous outcome (i.e. for the Howards) at the Battle of Bosworth Field, to keep the Castle in good repair. In 1521-2, after a long and distinguished career which ended almost literally in tears when he was compromised into pronouncing the death sentence on decidedly unsafe evidence of his old friend the Duke of Buckingham, Duke Thomas finally turned his back on London and retreated to Framlingham where he died two years later.

To demonstrate the enormous personal wealth which underpinned this high-point in the development of 16th century Framlingham, the best document is undoubtedly the Inventory of 1524 published in 1985 by the Suffolk Records Society. A useful second source, Thomas' will composed four years before his death, is here re-printed from the 1834 edition of Richard Green's History of Framlingham and Saxted.

1

# TEXT 1

## *The Last Will and Testament of Thomas Howard 31st May 1520*

'In the name of God, Amen. We, Thomas Duke of Norfolk, being hole of mind and of good memory etc.. My body to be buried in the Priory of Thetford. For levying £130 6s. 8d., for making of our tomb before the high altar of Thetford, as devised by us, Master Clerke Master of the Kinge's Workes of Cambridge, and Wassel Free- mason of Bury, and pictures of us and of Agnes our wife to be set together thereupon as well as may be for the said sum. I bequeath £300 each for the marrying of our daughters. To our sonne and heire apparent that shall be living at our decease, our great hangede bedde, palyd with cloth of golde, white damask and black velvet and bordered with these letters, T., A., and our hanging of Hercules made for our great chamber at Framlyngham. To our wife Agnes all manner of plate, jewels, garnyshed and ungarnyshed, with all our goods, that is to say, all our household stuff, beddings, hangings, sheets, fustians, blankets, pelows, cusheons, hanged beds of gold and silk, or whatever stuff that ever they be of, and all other stuffe belonging to bedding and apparelling of chambers. Item, we give her all our naprie, and all our chapel stuffe, with all maner of kechyn stuffe. Item we give and bequeath unto Agnes our said wife all our apparel for our body, with all the horses, geldings etc. We give and bequeath unto Agnes my said wyfe all our harness and other abilaments of warrys, with long-bowes, cross-bowes, and bendings, all our ringes, jewels of gold garnyshed and ungarnyshed, and all other plate of gold and silver, and all other our goods and chattels, all maner of detts owing to us as well as the revenues of our landes and their arrerage of the same, as other detts by specialties, obligaciones, bills or otherwise, due to us at the time of our decease, and she therewith to pay the charges of our burial and costs borne. We will that our said wife have and enjoy all our said goodes and of our bequest above written to hir own behove and use. And in our most humble wyse we beseech my lord Cardinal York good grace of his charitie to be good and gracious unto our said wife, in hir right that she may enjoy such things as we have given hir by this our last Will and Testament, and we beseech his grace that for a poor remembrance he will take our gift a pair of gilt pots we call Skotish pots.

In witness whereof, we the said Duke have subscribed our name and seale etc, this the last day of May, 12 Henry VIII.

And I constitute Agnes our said wife and Sir Thomas Blenerhassett our servant, our Executors.

All these other persons whose names be here subscribed were present at the subscribing and ensealing of this testament by the said Duke, and required specially by him to set their names hereunto, to the Intent they may be at all tymes hereafter witness the same.

T. Norfolk.

John Berners, per me John Jenny, Henry Eward, John Uvedale, William Ashebye.

## Comments

Several of the items mentioned in the will can be found in the Inventory compiled one week later by John Seintclere. ' Our great hangede bedde, palyd with cloth of golde, white damask and black velvet and bordered with these letters, T., A.', was there described by Seintclere as 'a large bed of state paned with clothe of gold, white damask and blak velvet Imbrodered with T and A king togidder with Seler and tester of the same containing in length six yards large and in depth three yards with A de valance of yelowe grene and red silke priced at £40'. The 'pair of gilt pots we call Skotish pots' given to Cardinal Wolsey were listed in the section dedicated to 'Seller, plate gilte'. 'Our hanging of Hercules made for our great chamber at Framlyngham' was bequeathed to Thomas' son and heir, who may have removed it to his favoured residence at Kenninghall in Norfolk.

For those interested in reconstructing the interior of the Castle *c.*1520, the reference in the will to the 'Great Chamber' and the History of Arcules' tapestry therein is a very useful starting-point. In 1524, the 'Great Chamber' indeed contained eight pieces of 'Counterfet Arras'. Another four pieces of an 'Arcules' in 'Counterfet Arras' were to be found in the 'chamber at the Great Chamber ende'. By 'counterfet' Seintlere perhaps indicated that it was of English rather than continental manufacture, a suggestion modestly reinforced by the evidence of the will that it was 'made for' the Great Chamber. Any claim that Arcules was made in East Anglia itself has to be tempered, however, by the knowledge that the Howard ménage at Tendring Hall in Stoke-by-Nayland, tended to buy their tapestries in London from import-export merchants.

# CHAPTER 2

# Christmas Fare with the Howards, 1526
## An extract from the Book of Emptions

## Preface

Expenditure on foodstuffs at Framlingham Castle was recorded on a daily basis in 'daily-diet' accounts for almost three centuries. At the end of the week, a summary was made which usually included in addition the consumption of alcoholic drinks and spices. A monthly total followed and at the end of the financial year (28th September) an annual account was prepared for audit and then approved. Almost all these types of documents for Framlingham have been lost or destroyed in fires, particularly in London where the Howards had a succession of town houses.

Until 2005, there was thought to be no surviving example of a daily-diet sheet. An exceptionally observant researcher then found a single folio of an account covering two days in 1428: it had been imperfectly catalogued and was being used as a wrapper for a gathering of post-medieval deeds. This solitary page has been translated and was published by the Suffolk Records Society in 2005 (Vol. 27). A miscellanea book attributed to the Castle treasurer, from the very end of the 14th century, has also been identified. There is a very real possibility that some of the hundreds of missing documents are sitting undiscovered in a private collection: they may resemble ledgers and so be on library bookshelves rather than rolls of vellum stored in chests or boxes in an attic. In order to illustrate the standard of living enjoyed by the Howard household at Framlingham, an excerpt from page 64 of the 'Book of Purchases' compiled at the family's equally palatial property at Stoke-by-Nayland has been substituted, of necessity.

Labelled 'The Book of Emptions, particular fare and expenses of the right high and mighty prince Thomas (3rd) Duke of Norfolk- 1st October 18 Hen VIII to 29 September 19 Hen VIII (1526-7), this beautifully bound volume (for which an un-named bookbinder was paid 18d. including materials) is deposited in Cambridge University Library and catalogued as 'Pembroke College MS. 300'.

## TEXT 2

*Tuesday the 25th Day of December 1526.*

| Item | | | |
|---|---|---|---|
| | 35 malards | 2½d a pece | 7s. 3½d. |
| | 55  wegyns | 2d. a pece | 9s. 2d. |
| | 38 Telles | 1½d a pece | 4s. 9d. |
| Emptions | | | |
| | 2 Corlewys | | 12d. |
| | 2 prevys | 2d. a pece | 4d. |
| | 3 plovers | 1d a pece | 3d. |
| | 8 woodcocks | 3d. a pece | 2s. |
| | 42 marlyngs | ½d. a pece | 21d. |
| | 22 redeshanks | ½d. a pece | 11d. |
| | 17 dusen and a half oppbyrds | 3d. a dusen | 3s. 4d. |
| | 40  grete byrds | ½d a pece | 20d. |
| | 40  smale byrdys | 4  a 1d | 10d. |
| | 11 pygges | | 3s. 4d. |
| | 200 eggs | 8 a 1d | 2s. 8d. |
| | 31 copple conyse at 4d the couple fett at Bery | | 10s. 4d. |

Item            present By Mr. Russhe

                10 cople telles
                3 cople wegyns
                8 dosen snyttes
                6 semewys
                4 copple sepyse
                5 dosen oxbyrdys
                                          Reward 3s. 4d.

Item            present by Mr. Bendysshe

                2 swannys
                                          Reward  10d.

Item            present by Mr. Debnam

                2 pecoks
                3 dosen oxbyrdys
                                          Reward 4d.

Item            present by Mr. Revett

                14 partryches
                4 woodcocks
                                          Reward 12d.

Item from Kennyggale

                5 doyse,  costs for bryngyng 7s.

Item from Ersam

|  | 3 doyse, costs for bryngyng 4s. |  |
| Item from Kelsale, | | |

|  | 6 doys, costs for bryngyng 6s. |  |

| Item | the hyre of a man and 2 horse to Bery to fetch conyes aforesaid, ther costs | 12d. |
| Item | 4 gallons crème | 16d. |
| Item | 6 gallons cord | 9d. |
| Item | 100 and half of wardyns | 14d. |
| Item | a bushell appells | 6d. |

£3  19s.  1½d.

Brekefast
To my ladyse grace        Braune and a capon stuyd
To 7 mese gentle          Braune
To 30 mese hows (hold)    Befe

Too my lords grace, my ladys grace and 23 persons to the same.

Dyner    first course
The Borys Hede
Brawne pottage
A stuyd capon
A bakemett with 12 byrds
Rostyd vele
A swane
2 rostyd capons
a custarde
stoke
fretter
Leche

second corse
gely
3 conyse
5 telles
a pecotcoke
12 redeshanks
12 smale byrdys
2 pastyse venyson
a tarte gynger
Brede

6    To the Borydys end
Brawne
A stysd capon
A bakyd cony
Rostyd vele

|               | Half a swane       |
|               | Custard            |
|               | Leche              |
| Reward        | gely               |
|               | 2 conyse           |
|               | 4  telles          |
|               | 12 smale byryds    |
|               | a pasty venyson    |
|               | a Tarte            |

To the House Gentle(men) (viz.) 28 yeomen, 60 gromes, and gent. Servants 44.

(Deiet) to the tresorer and the comp(t)roller

|               | Brawne             |
|               | A stuyd capon      |
|               | A Bakemett         |
|               | Half a swane       |
|               | A custerde         |
|               | Rost vele          |
|               | Leche              |

| Reward        | second porage      |
|               | 2 conyse           |
|               | 3 telles           |
|               | a pasty venyson    |
|               | a tarte            |
|               | gyngerbrede        |

| To the Marshall | Brawne                     |
|                 | Stuyd vele with a capon    |
|                 | A quarter pygge            |
|                 | Half a baked conye         |
|                 | A custard                  |

| Reward  second course | a cony             |
|                       | A pasty venyson    |
|                       | Leche              |

| To 3 mese gent(lemen) | Brawne                        |
|                       | Stuyd vele with half a capon  |
|                       | Rostyd vele                   |
|                       | Bakemetts                     |
|                       | A custard                     |

| Reward        | a cony             |
|               | A pasty of venyson |
|               | Leche              |

To 6 mese yeomen, 1 mese bakers and brewers, 1 mese portars and smethis, 3 mese ofycars, 2 mese strangers

> Brawne
> Stuyd vele
> Bakemetts
> Rostyd vele,

Rewards

> quarter pygge
> Gynger brede

To 3 mese gromes, 5 mese gent. Servaunts, 4 mese gromes of the kychyn, 2 cartars

> Sowse Brawne
> Stuyd vele
> Bakemetts
> Rost vele

To the Clarks, a yeoman cook of [........], cooks of the kychyn

> A quarter pygge
> Bakemetts and
> Leche

Reward

> a pasty of venyson
> A cony

To the gentle women and 12 persons to the same
To the first mese gentle women

> Brawne
> Stuyd vele with a capon
> A quarter pygge
> Half a bakyd conye
> A custard

Reward

> second porage
> A cony
> A pasty venyson
> A leche

To 2 mese gentle women Brawne
> Stuyd vele with half a capon
> Bakemetts and custerdis

Reward to 1 mese,
> a cony
> A pasty of venyson
> Leche

and to 1 mese,
> quarter pygge and gyngerbrede

To my lordys grace, my ladys grace and 24 persons to the same:

Soupper
First course
                                                 pottage
Befe
Slycyd motton boylled
Pettyte rostyd motton
2 malards
2 capons
2 conyse
2 pastyse venyson
8 dowsetts
Vautts

Second Course
                                                 gelyse
5 telles
2 corlewys
12 redshanks
5 plover
a Tarte of Corde
gyger brede

To the bordys Ende
                                                 pottage
Befe
Slycyd motton Boyllyd and
Rost motton
A capon
1 wegyns
7 dowsetts and
vautts

reward
                                                 2 conyse
4 telles
8 redeshanks
a pasty of venyson
a Tarte

To the gentle women and 12 persons to the same:

Soupper
Furst mese gentle women
                                                 befe
Slycyd motton Boyllyd
Rost motton
A capon
5 dowsetts

reward
                                                 a cony
a pasty of venyson
Leche

To 2 mese gentle women

befe
Slycyd motton Boyllyd
Rost motton
4 dowsetts to a mese

reward to 1 mese

a cony
a pasty venyson
Leche

To 1 mese a cony

To the Howse gentlemen: 28 yeman 60 gromes and 44 gentleman servants:

Sopper to the tresorer and to the comptroller:

befe
slycyd motton boyllyd
rost motton
a capon
2 mallards
5 dowsetts

reward

2 conyse
8 byrdys
a pasty of venyson
a Tarte

To the Marshalle

Befe
Slycyd rostyd motton
And Boyllyd motton
A capon
4 dowsetts

reward

cony
a pasty venyson
Leche

To 7 mese yeomen, 1 mese, portars and smethys, 3 mese offycers:

Befe
slycyd motton Boyllyd
Rost motton
dowsetts

To mese gromes, 6 mese gentlemen servaunts, 3 mese gromes of the kychyn, 2 carters:

Befe
Slycyd motton Boyllyd
And rost motton and
Leche

To 1 mese strangers              Befe
Slycyd motton boyllyd
Rost motton and
dowsetts

reward                       2 conyse

To the clarks and yeomen cooks of the kychyn:
Befe
Slycyd motton boyllyd
Rost motton
dowsetts
reward                       a cony
a pasty venyson
Leche

Expenses of the Day
Spent                      1 braune
And a rond befe
15 ronds whereof 5 rost
1 vele and a half
5 mottons
2 swannes
6 pygges
16 capons
48 conyse
a pekoke
4 mallards
2 wegyns
21 tellys
36 redshanks
4 dozen and 4 oxbyrdys
5 plovers
2 corlewys
in Butter, 23 dyshhes
300 eggs
in manchetts 46
in howse in 220
in trenchers 18
in Byere 5 and a half barrels
in Candyll 2 dosen and a half

delyvered into the pantry 27 cast manchetts
Remain                   in manchett 44
In howse 360
In trenchers 32
In byere 14 and a half barrels.

11

Strangers                                4 of Mr. Tylneys servants
                                         4 of Mr. Robarrts servants

## Comments

The cellarer at Stoke-by Nayland answered for his expenditure elsewhere and this explains the absence of wines from the above account. To estimate alcohol consumption at Framlingham Castle itself, the newly discovered membrane of 1428 is currently the best source. For present purposes, the entries for August 30th have here been abridged to illustrate the levels of personal consumption on that one day during the Mowbray era:

'To the janitor, 1 gallon of ale.
For the lord [John de Mowbray] during the day, 4 gallons of ale,
1 pitcher of wine
For the chamber of the lord John, 3 gallons of ale.
For the chamber of the lady [Catherine de Mowbray], 4 gallons of ale,
1 pitcher of wine for the lady and the chamber.
After the 9th hour, to the chapel, 2 gallons of ale.
To the kitchen, 1 gallon of ale.
To the Irish knights, 4 gallons of ale, 2 pitchers of wine.
Sir Robert de Wingfeld, 5 gallons of ale, half a pitcher of wine.
To Brandon, 4 gallons of ale.
To Norfolk, 2 and half gallons of ale.
To the lady's stable, 2 gallons of ale.
To the foreigner, 2 gallons of ale.
In drinks at the gate, 3 gallons of ale, 5 gallons allowed, half a pitcher of wine.
For the lord and lady at night, 7 gallons of ale, 1 pitcher of wine.
For the lord John, 3 gallons of ale.
To the F. chamber, 1 gallon of ale.
To the Hall, 30 gallons and a half of ale.

A 'pitcher' of wine was apparently another name for the 'pottle', half a gallon. The 'lord John' who was allowed only ale was probably John de Mowbray junior, the son and heir. It may well be the case that the Mowbrays themselves, particularly the Lady Catherine, took their food in their private chambers along with visitors of similar rank, while the household staff ate in the Hall. Two entries for the following day, 31st August, are of interest. A consignment of 36 gallons of ale was despatched to the Lodge, presumably to refresh a hunting party in the Park, and three gallons to the 'hospice' or guest accommodation. The general assumption that for persons of ducal status (and many of their employees) to consume a gallon of ale per day was 'normal' is in no way contradicted by the Framlingham data above. Wine seems to have been less liberally dispensed, but for selected adults to imbibe a pint of wine (predominantly French) per day in addition to the ale again seems customary.

# CHAPTER 3

# A Description of Framlingham Deer Park
## Ireland's Survey, 1662.

**Preface**

The significance of the Deer Park can barely be underestimated. Designed to enhance the approach to the Castle, the Park and the Mere within it advertised the noble status of the family in residence and provided a breathtakingly beautiful environment in which to entertain and impress high-ranking visitors. It also provided fuel and food, not all of it legally harvested, both for the castle and for the inhabitants of the town and local villages.

On present evidence, the Park was created in the first half of the 13th century. It brought about large-scale changes in the landscape, almost certainly eradicating one at least of the Domesday (c.1086) estates and causing the re-location of one of Framlingham's open-fields to Mapledale on the outermost, north-western limits of the parish, more than a mile from the town-centre.

Estimates of the Park's acreage differ considerably. According to the Survey of 1547, it contained about 400 acres. To this had been added, c.1520, a further 120 acres outside Framlingham manor (see below), which the Great Lodge was built as a luxurious, secluded retreat for important visitors. Robert Loder writing in 1798 believed the Park contained 600 acres and was about three miles in circumference. It was surrounded by the Park Pale, a substantial earthen bank with a timber fence on its summit: an impressive section of the bank still survives on the eastern fringe of the Park. The head parker originally resided in the 'proper' lodge, now Little Lodge. A number of disputes arose at the time of the 'dis-parking', c.1589. It was proposed, for example, that the 120-acre extension be sold back to the Cornwallis family who then effectively owned Oakenhill Manor in Badingham. This, it was argued, would have destroyed the 'very stately' appearance of the Park and greatly reduced the number of deer it could maintain. A herd of 2000 deer was considered appropriate for a park of '500' acres.

Although many of the medieval 'extents' provide useful information about both the Park and the Mere, the most detailed surviving survey remains 'Ireland's Terrar' compiled in 1662 and now catalogued as Pembroke College Cambridge MS L17.

## TEXT 3

A Terrar of the Lands in Framlingham Parke in lease to Francis Ireland howe circumferated, butted and bounded, made and delivered to be presented to the honourable Society of the Colledge of Pembrookhall in Cambridge the ....day of ...1662 as followeth viz.

The scituation of the Great Lodge howses and yards therto belonging abutting upon certeine inclosiers or peces of land called Kithing quarter and other called Dinnington quarter North, upon Baddingham quarter North East, Carthouse pightell full East, and upon other lands lately devided called Home Parke South, soe now following my intended way and method is to begyn at Dinyngton Gate and surround the whole parke by setting forth every outside inclosier upon whoselands abutting, begyneth as followeth-

Dinyngton quarter next the aforesaid gate abutteth on the kings hyeway which way is Triangular one way leading from the sayd gate towards Laxfield, an other of the sayd wayes called Coxes lane, and thother called Herings Lane which leadeth to Framlingham towne, the sayd wayes being North upon the sayd Dynnington quarter.

Buttons meadow abutteth upon an inclosier of land late Mr. Lemons called by the name of Herings, Norward, which said Buttons meadow conteineth aboute seaventeen acres.

Nuttalls Bottom lately devided into twoe inclosyers abutteth Norwest upon a pece of land late Edwards Alpe, gentleman, called Maltells, upon an other pece of land late aforesaid Mr. Lemons, upon the lands late Jeames Buttons and upon another pece of land of the said Mr. Alpes late Gilberts, North; the said Nuttalls Bottom conteineth aboute twenty acres.

Smock Pightell abutteth Westward upon twoe peces of land of the aforesaid Mr. Alpes thone called by the name of Clayland, thother a pece late Gilberts aforesaid conteineth about fower acres.

A pece of land called Thirty Acres lately devided into thre severalls abutteth Westward upon the foresaid pece of land of Mr Alpes called Clayland, upon a small pece of land late Jeames Buttons aforesaid called by the name of the Harrow and alsoe upon the hyway and Durrants Brige leading from Dinnington to Framlingham: the said thre inclosiers conteyne aboute 30 acres.

14  Gravellpitt Close abutteth upon the aforesaid kings hyway Southwesterly, conteineth aboute fourteen acres.

A percell of Diggins lately called Brickell Close lately devided into twoe severalls abutteth upon part of the lands of John (Castor) and of a pece of land late Edmond Smyths and upon an other pece of land called (Catllsclose) being Philip Bucks Southwest; both peces of the said Diggins conteyn aboute 15 acres.

Towne Parke of late devided in thre severalls abutteth upon a pece of Glebe belonging to Framlingham Rectory, Southerly, and upon the foresaid highway leading from Dinnington to Framlingham; all thre peces conteyn aboute fower and thirty acres.

Stableyards as in twoe severalls abutteth upon the sayd hyway one side theroff Southerly and one end thereof Southeasterly.

That called part of the Stableyard wheron the Almshowses lately built abutteth on the foresaid hyway and Mylbridge Eastwardly conteineth aboute one acre and halfe.

The Easterly end of the Meermeadow in lease to Francis Ireland abutteth upon the ortchard of Ralph Beart and upon the ortyard of Thomas Clarck and upon an other pece of the said Meermeadow which was late in lease to Francis Ireland but is now in the use and occupacion of John Kerich.

Little Paddox sideing upon the Castlelands called Vyneyards Southerly and upon the kings hyway leading from Baddingham to Framlingham Easterly conteineth aboute six acres.

Great Paddox abutting upon the landes of Mr. Maidston on the East.

Ashing Groave lately devided into twoe inclosiers abutting upon the lands of the sayd Mr. Maidston Eastward in the occupacion of Matthew Skynner.

An other pece of land in the occupacion of John Baker abutting upon the lands of the sayd Mr. Maidston and of land late Thomas Saverns.

An other pece of land called Rettingpitclose abutting Eastward upon the land of Martha Smyth and in the occupacion of Thomas Sewell, upon the lands of Nicholas Browne, Joseph Morse and of the aforesaid Mr Maidston.

Another inclosier lately devided from out of the said Rettingpit Close abutting Easterly upon the lands of the said Mr. Maidston.

An other inclosier called called Hersclose lately devided into three inclosiers abutteth upon the lands of the said Mr Maidston East.

An other pece of inclosier called Newlaidclose conteineth aboute twenty acres abutteth East upon the lands late Mr. Edward Dunstons.

An other pece called Hommeadow abutting upon the lands lately purchased by John Bence Esquire called Saltfield full East.

An other pece of inclosyer called Carthowse Pightell abutting upon the aforesaid Salt Field East.

An other pece of inclosyer called Badingham quarter conteineth aboute eleaven acres some part wherof abutteth Salt Fields aforesaid and other some part from the gate called Baddingham Gate towards a watering called Wynsell upon lands late Mr. John Waldgraves nowe Mrs. Elizabeth Allexanders widdow full East.

Winsell Meadow lately devided into twoe inclosiers thone end wherof abutteth upon the foresaid Mrs. Allexanders lands full East and the one side therof stretcheth besideth along Coxes Lane first above mentioned Northet.

## Comments

Perhaps the most valuable pieces of information this Terrar provides are the exact location of the medieval vineyard, east of the castle near Little Paddocks, and Brickell (Brick Kiln) Close, the source of many of the bricks used in the 16th century building programme both inside and outside the castle.

Also situated within the Park, the Mere was consistently described as a fishery for over three centuries. No surviving document gives details of the fish species caught there, despite the important contribution freshwater fish made to the Pre-Reformation diet of all social classes. Both the 'daily-diet' entries of 1428 (above) referred to days on which meat ruled the menu. Recourse must again be made, therefore, to the kitchen accounts of other first-class Howard residences in order to guess which species were netted in the Mere for consumption on Fridays and the other fleshless days of the year.

An outstanding document in this respect from the Howard 'Palace' at Kenninghall near Diss in Norfolk has survived as part of Rye MS 74 in Norfolk and Norwich Record Office:

Friday September 1st 1525:
13 Saltfish, 5s. 2d.
4 peykys ( pikes), 2s. 11d.
2 tenches, 8d.
A gret ele, 14d., 3 elys, 11d., small elys 16d., 3s.5d.
27 perchys 2s. 10d.
100 rochys, 3s.
A samon trowt, 20d.
25 playse, 12d.
Butere, 3s.4d.
100 eggs, 7d.
Yeste 2d.
15 whytyng, 4d.
30 plays, 12d.
2 solys, 8d.

A 1000 oysters, 20d.

A cod, 4d.

Total 28s. 5d.'

The freshwater fish purchased that day (pike, tench, perch, eels, roach and salmon trout) cost fractionally more than the salt-water species, an astonishing statistic.

The dinner menu of a fish-day at Stoke-by-Nayland (Cambridge University Library Pembroke College MS.300), Friday 28th December 1525, can again be taken as a reliable guide to what would have been served at Framlingham Castle itself:

'Diner

First course:

Oysters, rysc pottage, Bottar, rede heryng, white heryng, Lynge, a Saltfish, salt salmon, 2 salt ells, podryd code, a peke, stuyd ells, 8 place, a custarde, Leche.

Second course:

2 dyshes gely, half a brete, 2 carppys, 6 floundes fyde, a rost ele, a tenche, a balyd gornarde, stuyd prynys, a Tarte of Pruynys and gyngerbrede.'

From the Mere, the fish caught there were stored until required in the three small holding ponds which still exist below the castle walls. Unlike Clare Castle, Framlingham has no record, as yet, of an 'aquarium' where, within easy reach of the kitchens, fish were starved and cleaned ready for the table. The three 'vivaria' were in need, at 'small charge', of being 'scoured and restored' *c.*1589. The Mere was then described as a 'greate poole of water of the content of tenne acres at the least'. Without a systematic rota for scouring, it too would have disappeared beneath rushes and other marginal plants until it became water-meadow.

CHAPTER 4

# Social and Economic Importance of the Park
The Keeper's Accounts, 1509-1517 (unabridged).

## Preface

Venison was a form of currency. It was given as presents by those wealthy enough to own a park, to reinforce their social and political relationships. Live deer were also given or exchanged for the same purposes. It was beyond price: no cash equivalent was ever put on venison whether in whole carcases or in joints until a much later date. As already demonstrated, it was a regular feature of the Howardian diet. It also occupied a special place in the hearts and minds of poachers.

This group of Park-Keeper's accounts are among the rarest and most interesting of all the documents in Framlingham's archive. Although they have been published in part before, this appears to be the first occasion on which they have been transcribed in full. Three separate manuscripts (B.L.Add.27451, ff.11-25inc., B.L.Add. Ch. 16654, Bl.Add. Ch. 17745 ) have been amalgamated to form one almost continuous document covering the period August 1508 to August 1517. To assist future researchers, the word 'item' in the original MSS has been replaced by an identification number to aid indexing and the organisation of biographical details. Additional numbers have been added where appropriate, without affecting the contents of the original text.

Richard Chamber had been appointed parker for life in 1493-4. The bequests in his will clearly indicate that he died a comparatively wealthy man. His accounts were written up by a number of different clerks and begin when he had already been in office for 15-16 years. He rubbed shoulders with some of the most influential individuals not only from Suffolk but also from the highest levels of Tudor society excluding Henry VIII but including Cardinal Wolsey (see nos. 858 & 859) and Henry's sister Mary 'the French Queen' (659).

*Glossary:*

| | |
|---|---|
| *buck* | male fallow deer, *c.*32-36 inches high at shoulder, weight 125-140lbs. |

| | |
|---|---|
| *doe* | female fallow deer, *c.*32-34 ins.at shoulder, 80-90lbs, after gutting. |
| *prickett* | male fallow deer in second year |
| *sorell* | male fallow deer in third year. |
| *sore* | male fallow deer in fourth year. |
| *fawn* | young of fallow deer in first year |
| *fawynyngtyme* | June & early July. |
| *tegg* | female deer in second year. |
| *rascalle* | young deer, not yet 'warrantable', i.e. not ready to be hunted |
| *maille* | male |
| *morkyn* | diseased, abortive. |
| *garget* | inflammation, in females usually of udder. |
| *root* | rut, mating season, end of October. |
| *course* | pursuit of deer. |
| *quick* | alive. |
| *moren* | murrain, unspecified, often fatal disease. |
| *gres(se)* | 'in the grease', fat. A term used to denote when an animal was in prime condition for the chase or slaughter. |

## TEXT 4

[MS heading defective]

| | | |
|---|---|---|
| 1. | mastrys  Drure | 1 buk |
| 2. | the towne of Harleston | 1 buk |
| 3. | my Lord Wyleby ys brethern | 1 buk |
| 4. | mastyr Antony Wyngfelde | 1 buk |
| 5. | the pryor of Seynt Peters | 1 buk |
| 6. | the pryor of Cryst  Churche | 1 buk |
| 7. | the pryor of Hoxon | 1 buk |
| 8. | the pryor of  Heye | 1 buk |
| 9. | the towne of Ipswyche | 1 buk |
| 10. | the towne of Woodebrege | 1 buk |
| 11. | the pryor of Dodreysche | 1 buk |
| 12. | John Henyngham | 1 buk |
| 13. | Edmond Gelgate | 1 buk |
| 14. | Edmond Jenney | 1 buk |
| 15. | the vicar of Sypton | 1 buk |
| 16. | Thomas Wolverston | 1 buk |
| 17. | William Latymer | 1 buk |
| 18. | the mastyr of Metyngham | 1 buk |
| 19. | Jorge Ayschfelde and William Cheke | 1 buk |
| 20. | John Ichyngham | 1 buk |
| 21. | John Tersylle | 1 buk |
| 22. | Cristofer Harman and Matthew | 1 buk |
| 23. | the vicar of Debnom and Edward Reve | 1 buk |
| | As wyche Edward Reve fet hys part and the vycar of Debnom ded nat and I gave yt to | |

19

Herry Evered and Bryan mastyr Chasy ys clarke.

| | | |
|---|---|---|
| 24. | my Lord Wylleby ys brodyr law | |
| 25. | Raffe (Enyrs) cam and kyllyd a | 1 do. |
| 26. | Thomas Terelle schulde hav had a do the last wyntyr and he preyd me that shuld go with me tylle he fet yt. | |
| 27. | Thes be the lossys of thys somer dede of the moren be myelmes: | |
| | | 4 buks |
| | | 7 sowrells |
| | | 5 prekets |
| | | 14 doys |
| 28. | also yong Robert Colvylle cam rydyng be the paille and brake yn and kyllyd a sowrell on Seynt John's day in Crystmas. | |
| 29. | Crystofer Wylloby | 1 do |
| 30. | (the Prior ) of Pentney | 1 do |
| 31. | the pryor of Seynt Peters | 1 do |
| 32. | be the commandemet of my Lord Howard to Lambeth | 6 doys |
| 33. | be the commandemet of mastyr Stuard to Lambeth | 6 doys |
| 34. | mastyr Stuard | 1 do |
| 35. | by the commandemet of mastyr Chafy, William Buckler the towne clarke of Ypswych | 1 do |
| 36. | by the commandemet of Mr. Tylney, the parker of Framlyngham | 1 do |
| 37. | by the commandemet of Mr. Chafy, the vycar of Stooke a do and she went wyth me tylle thys yere and now he hath her | 1 do. |
| 38. | thes be the lossys now syn myelmes: | |
| | in primis | 3 buks |
| | sower | 1 |
| | sowrells | 59 |
| | pryket | 1 |
| | doys | 17 |
| | fawnys | 18 |
| 39. | at the awdyt | 1 do |
| 40. | to my lady to London | 1 do. |
| 41. | the Pryor of Butley | 1 do. |
| 42. | Abbas of Brosyard | 1 do |
| 43. | John Goldyngham | 1 do. |
| 44. | Jorge Mannok | 1 do |
| 45. | My lady Wyngfelde | 1 do. |
| 46. | The Pryor of Hey | 1 do. |
| 47. | Thomas Sampson | 1 do. |
| 48. | Terrelle | 1 do |
| 49. | The parson of Kelsale | 1 do |
| 50. | My lady Bowser | 1 do |

20

| | | |
|---|---|---|
| 51. | Wyllyam Rowse | 1 do |
| 52. | My lady Wylleby | 1do |
| 53. | For mastyr Stuard | 1 do [deleted] |
| 54. | To mastyr Pryor of Pentney | 1 do |
| 55. | To Herry None and Rambery | 1 do |
| 56. | My lady Arundelle | 1 do |
| 57. | To Olyveor of the barony of the chekyr by the commandement of my Lord Howard | 1 do. |
| 58. | by commandment of my Lord Howard, my lady Sowtwelle | 1 do. |
| 59. | By the commandement of Mastyr Stuard, the Pryoresse of Camsey | 1 do. |
| 60. | Mastyr Tylney | 1 do |
| 61. | Be a warrant of my lords, Mr Kylle and he gave her to my lady Debnom and to Worsepe and he deyryd me to go with me tylle he fette yt and sche hath go with me there 3 yer or more and now this yer he hath feett herr | 1 do |
| 62. | Also be a warrant of my lord cam from Cales to herry Garrson and Geffery Wood | 1 do |
| 63. | Be a warrant of dormant of my lords to kyng's celester a do and he gave her to Richard Joly and sche goeth with me tylle | |
| 64. | Thes be the lossys thet I have syns the audyt | |
| 65. | Fyrst be a warrant of my lordd, 6 doys to mastyr Wysman[?] | 6 doys |
| 66. | Be a warrant of my lords to Antony Hansart | [....] |
| 67. | Lost of bukkys | (5) |
| | of sowers | [ ] |
| | of sowrells | 10 |
| | of preketts | 14 |
| | of doys | 3 score and (5?) |
| | of fawnys | 205 |
| | be five score the hondryd and thys were dede be Seynt Jeorge day these be the lossys afterward | |
| 68. | ther cam a dog of Thomas Peersys and kyllyd me a do | 1 do |
| 69 | Also ther duye | |
| | sowrell | 1 |
| | fawnys | 5 |
| 70. | In the first yer of our sovereyn lord kyng Henry the VIII and yn the 17th yer of Rychard Chambyr parker of Framlyngham | |
| 71. | These be the lossys that I had yn fawnyng tyme | |
| | A sowrell | 1 |
| | Doys | 2 |
| | Fawnys | 27 |
| 72. | Thees be the lossys that I have kyllyd thys gresse seson of buckys | |
| 73. | My lord Wyllebye | 1 buk |
| 74 | Be a warrant of my lordys mastyr of the rollys | 1 buk |

21

| | | |
|---|---|---|
| 75. | Mastyr urstwyke | 1 buk |
| 76. | Be a warrant of my lords mad the 3 day of August delyveryd a buk I wot not tylle hom | 1 buk |
| 77. | by warrant of my lords, Syr Wyllyem Hedge | 1 buk |
| 78. | by a warrant of my lords, Rycharde Warton | 1 buk |
| 79. | by a warrant of my lords, Herry Kook | 1 buk |
| 80. | by a warrant of my lords, Thomas Sampson and John Wysman | 1 buk |
| 81. | by a warrant of my lords, Willyem Wyngfeld of Spexalle | 1 buk |
| 82. | by a warrant of my lords, Edward Jernyngham | 1 buk |
| 83. | by a warrant of my lords, the dene of Powlys (Paul's) | 1 buk |
| 84. | by a warrant of my lords, Herry Thafy | 1 buk |
| 85. | mastyr townys End | 1 buk |
| 86. | John Melket, clarke | 1 buk |
| 87. | be a warrant of my lord's, Syr Rychard Hastyngs | 1 buk |
| 88. | be a warrant of my lord's, Humfrey Wyngfelde | |
| 89. | Edward Cornwalese | 1 buk |
| 90. | John Glemham | 1 buk |
| 91. | The towne of Donwyche | 1 buk |
| 92. | Be a warrant of my lord's, Syr John Jacobe | 1 buk |
| 93. | Syr Robert Cheeke | 1 buk |
| 94. | My lady Pryores of Camsey | 1 buk |
| 95. | The Abbot of Derham | 1 buk |
| 96. | John Tasborow and John Jenney | 1 buk |
| 97. | The parson of Woolpet | 1 buk |
| 98. | Mastyr Steward | 1 buk |
| 99. | Anthony Wyngfelde | 1 buk |
| 100. | Robert Brewsse | 1 buk |
| 101. | Wyllyem Rowse and Robert Wylmer | 1 buk |
| 102. | Humfrey Everton | 1 buk |
| 103. | Jorge Mannok | 1 buk |
| 104. | Wyllyem Playter | 1 buk |
| 105. | the parson of Framlyngham | 1 buk |
| 106. | Syr Jamys Hobberd | 1 buk |
| 107. | Humferey Wyngfelde | 1 buk |
| 108. | Mastyr Hopton | 1 buk |
| 109. | Robert Brown servaunt with my Lord of Norwyche | 1 buk |
| 110. | my Lord of Norwyche | 1 buk |
| 111. | Mastyr Burdy the mayr of Lyne | 1 buk |
| 112. | Edmond Bedynfeld | 1 buk |
| 113. | By commandement of my lord Howard, I took Thomas Roosch | 1 buk |
| 114. | John Iechyngham | 2 buks |
| 115. | By commendement of my lady Any's grace I | |

|  |  |  |
|---|---|---|
|  | took Thomas Revet | 1 buk |
| 116. | Edmond Jacob and Robert Calle | |
|  | for hys maryage | 1 buk |
| 117. | Edmonde Dawnde and Wyllyem Halle | 1 buk |
| 118. | be commandement of my lord Howard, | |
|  | Heryy Cook and the servaunts of Stooke | 1 buk |
| 119. | my lady Elyzabethe of Boleyne | 1 buk |
| 120. | Waslyngton servaunt of armys | 1 buk |
| 121. | mastyr Talmage | 1 buk |
| 122. | my lady Brame | 1 buk |
| 123. | Edward Grymston | 1 buk |
| 124. | John Blenerhasset | 1 buk |
| 125. | mastyr Russche | 1 buk |
| 126. | Chananer was with me and hys wyff and he had | 1 buk |
| 127. | the porter ys wyffe went to chyrche of a chyld | |
|  | and sche had | 1 buk |
| 128. | mastyr Tylney | 1 buk |
| 129. | the pryor of crist cherche | [ ] |
| 130. | the pryor of seynt Peters | [ ] |
| 131. | the pryor of Woodbrege | [ ] |
| 132. | the abbas of Brosyyerd | [ ] |
| 133. | the pryoress of Flyxtone and the pryoress | |
|  | of Bongey | (1) buk |
| 134. | the pryor of Fylstow | [ ] |
| 135. | Syr Rychard Wentforthe | 1 buk |
| 136. | Syr Edmond Geney | 1 buk |
| 137. | Syr John Awdeley | 1 buk |
| 138. | John Henyngham | 1 buk |
| 139. | My lady Wyllebye | 1 buk |
| 140. | My lady Wyngfelde | 1 buk |
| 141. | Reyner Hamerton and Rychard Southhawys | 1 buk |
| 142. | To Colveeke | 1 buk |
| 143. | The pryor of Dodnysche | 1 buk |
| 144. | The abbot of Sypton | 1 buk |
| 145. | John Mychylle | [ ] |
| 146. | My lord's servaunts of Thorpe | 1 buk |
| 147. | the baly of the towneschyppe of Harlston | 1 buk |
| 148. | to John Tasborow and John Jenney | 1 buk |
| 149. | the parson of Woolpet | 1 buk |
| 150. | mastyr Stuard | 1 buk |
| 151. | Anthony Wyngfelde | 1 buk |
| 152. | Robert Brewsse | 1 buk |
| 153. | Wyllyem Rowsse and Robert Mylmer | 1 buk |
| 154. | Humfrey Everton | 1 buk |
| 155. | Jorge Mannok | 1 buk |
| 156. | Wyllyem Playter | 1 buk |
| 157. | The parson of Framlyngham | 1 buk |
| 158. | The Gylde of Framlyngham | 1 buk |

| | | |
|---|---|---|
| 159. | the parson of Kelsale | 1 buk |
| 160. | the townshepp of Bonggey | 1 buk |
| 161. | the mastyr of Metyngham | 1 buk |
| 162. | Robert Wyngfeld | halffe 1 buk |
| 163. | The pryor of Hey | 1 buk |
| 164. | Thomas Banyerd and mastrys Throgmorton | 1 buk |
| 165. | Thomas Fastalle of Pettare | 1 buk |
| 166. | Crystofer Harman | 1 buk |
| 167. | Herry Everord | 1 buk |
| 168. | To my lord Howard to Berry | [ ] |
| 169 | To my lord Howard to Norwyche | [ ] |
| 170. | Mastyr Cawndyche | 1 buk |
| 171. | To Nicholas Calle for hys maryage | 1 buk |
| 172. | Thosse be the lossys that I have had thys somer | |
| | Ded of the lax | bukkys 2 |
| | Sour | 1 |
| | Doys | 11 |
| 173. | my lord Wyllebye | 1 doy |
| 174. | John Mychyllys dowtrys maryage | 1 doy. |
| 175. | the pryor of Butley for hys stallyng | 1 doy |
| 176. | be commaund of mastyr Stwrd to London | 6 doys |
| 177. | to the audyt | 1 doy |
| 178. | Syr Robert Brandon | 1 doy |
| 179. | Syr John Tymperley | 1 doy |
| 180. | Syr Jamys Hubbard | 1 doy |
| 181. | Syr Fylyppe Caltrope | 1 doy |
| 182. | mastyr Hasseet | 1 doy |
| 183. | my lady Wyngfeld | 1 doy |
| 184. | mastyr Antony Wyngfeld | 1 doy |
| 185. | John Glemham | 1 doy |
| 186. | mastyr awdyter | 1 doy |
| 187. | the Pryor of Seynt Peters | 1 doy |
| 188. | John Hevenyngham | 1 doy |
| 189. | the mastrys Germyn | 1 doy |
| 190. | the pryor of Hey | 1 doy |
| 191. | Humfrey Everton | 1 doy |
| 192. | Jamys Revet | 1 doy |
| 193. | Robert Cheeke | 1 doy |
| 194. | the prioress of Campsey | 1 doy |
| 195. | the pryor of Buttley | 1  doy |
| 196. | Thomas Aylmer | 1 doy |
| 197. | my lord of Oxforth | 2 doys |
| 198. | for mastyr Stuard | 1 doy |
| 199. | be warrant of my lord's, the pryor of Buttley | 1 doy |
| 200. | At 3 tymys syn the audyte | 18 doys |
| 201. | Syr Fylyppe Tylney | 1 doy |
| 202. | the parson of Framlyngham | 1 doy |
| 203. | mastyr Thomas Roosche | 1 doy |

204.  These be my lossys be warrant of my lord
      to John Glemham 6 quyk doys as wyche 2 of
      them brake ther neeke in the cart and
      another brake bothe her hyndyr leggs yn the
      takyng as wyche I partyd on betwyxt Wyllyem
      Rowsse Robert Aylmer and me than he had
      a whey 4¾ quylke doys.

205.  Also by commaundement of mastyr Garnyshe
      that he schulde have 12 Qyuk deer as wyche he
      a sowrelle and an dogge brake his morelle and
      kyllyd a do and I gave to mastrys Garnyshe
      and hur gentylwoman and to hys son and heyr
      Houge Poley maryed hys dowtyr and Houg Grymston
      and anothyr agayn a tre kyllyd hyr selfe so he
      had a whey than hys sowrell and 9 doys and a fawne.

206.  Thesse be the lossys of malle dere;

      | | |
      |---|---|
      | bukks | 14 |
      | sowers | 10 |
      | sowrells | 7 |
      | pricketts | 20? |
      | doys | [ ] |
      | fawnys | 3 score. |

207.  Also on good Fryday yn the stabylle a
      dog of Robert Aldered bet a buk and aftyr died.

208.  These be the lossys that hath dyye syn good Friday, of morren;

      | | |
      |---|---|
      | bukks | 4 |
      | sowrells | 2 |
      | morkyn preketts | 14 |
      | teggs of the same yere. | 9 |
      | doys Lost this fawnynge tyme | 4 |
      | of fawnys of thys yer lost | 35 |

209.  In the second yer of our soferen lord Kyng Herry the 8 and yn the
      18 yer of Rychard Chambyr, parker of Framllyngham

210.  doctor Terryman the mastyr of the chapel
      of the feld                                    1 buk

211.  Syr John Betson                                1 buk

212.  mastrys Hottoffe                               [ ]

213.  Syr Doctyr Breget                              1 buk

214.  mastyr Chek and hys company                    1 buk

215.  my lord Wylleby                                1 buk

216.  by a warrant of my lord's, Willyam Lytton      1 buk

217.  my lord Barnes                                 1 buk

218.  be a warrant of my lord Howard to Ypswyche     3 buks

219.  Also Danyelle commaynded me to delyver
      yn my lord Howard's name delyver Thomas
      Halle of Ypswyche                              1 buk

220.  mastrys Hasset                                 1 buk

| | | |
|---|---|---|
| 221. | my lady Brame | 1 buk |
| 222. | mastyr Hyham | 1 buk |
| 223. | mastyr Humfrey Wyngfeld | 1 buk |
| 224. | Mastrys Burton for the maryage of a kinsman of hyrs | [ ] |
| 225. | the pryor of Dod Nysch | [ ] |
| 226. | the convent of Buttley | [ ] |
| 227. | Mastyr Stonwey and Peche | [ ] |
| 228. | the pryor of Hey | 1 buk |
| 229. | Loveday and Hamerton | 1 buk |
| 230. | Robert Wyngfeld and Warton | 1 buk |
| 231. | the mastyr of Metyngham | 1 buk |
| 232. | the parson of Wherlyngworthe | [ ] |
| 233. | Thomas Taylor | 1 buk |
| 234. | Thomas Wooverstone | 1 buk |
| 235. | my lord Wylleby | 1 buk |
| 236. | the abbas of Brosyerd | 1 buk. |
| 237. | the prioress of Campsey | 1 buk |
| 238. | Lewes and John Gernard | 1 buk |
| 239. | Artur Hopton | 1 buk |
| 240. | John Henyngham | 1 buk |
| 241. | Edward Grymston | 1 buk |
| 242. | John Wyssman | 1 buk |
| 243. | Rychard Colvylle | 1 buk |
| 244. | Humfrey Everton | 1 buk |
| 245. | the prior of Woodbreg | 1 buk |
| 246. | Thomas Roosche | 1 buk |
| 247. | the abbot of Berry | 1 buk |
| 248. | John Woodows | 1 buk |
| 249. | the parson of Kelsalle and the mastyr of Carlton | 1 buk |
| 250. | the prioress of Bongey | 1 buk |
| 251. | my lady Wylleby | 1 buk |
| 252. | Rychard Caundysche | 1 buk |
| 253. | Cristofer Harman | 1 buk |
| 254. | be a commaundement of my Lord Howard, Wyndbusher | 1 buk |
| 255. | be a warrant of my lady's grasse | 1 buk |
| 256. | Anne Howard, the parson of Ketylberghe | 1 buk |
| 257. | Lyonell Talmage | 1 buk |
| 258. | be a warrant of my lord's grace, Dame Anne Cursunn | 1 buk |
| 259. | be a warrant of my lord's, mastyr | [ ] |
| 260. | be a warrant of my lord's, mastrys Fastalle | 1 buk |
| 261. | be warrant of my lord's, Robert Payton | 1 buk |
| 262. | be warrant of my lord's, Thomas Ganelle | 1 buk |
| 263. | be a warrant of my lord's, Waltyr Hubard | 1 buk |
| 264. | James Revet | 1 buk |

| | | |
|---|---|---|
| 265. | the byschope of Norwyche | 1 buk |
| 266. | be a warrant of my lord's, John Smythe | 1 buk |
| 267. | be a warrant of my lord's, Robert Southwelle | 1 buk |
| 268. | Thomas Spoorne | 1 buk |
| 269. | John Garnysshe | 1 buk |
| 270. | be a warrant of my lord's, mastrys Petyte | 1 buk |
| 271. | be a warrant of my lord's, Thomas Wysman | 1 buk |
| 272. | John Gray and Wylyem Clowthe | 1 buk |
| 273. | be a warrant of my lord's, John Goldyngham | 1 buk |
| 274. | the pryor of Fylstow | 1 buk |
| 275. | be a warrant of my lord's, Syr Robert Wyngfelde | 1 buk |
| 276. | be a warrant of my lord's, Thomas Terelle | 1 buk |
| 277. | be a warrant of my lord's, Edward Gernyngham | 1 buk |
| 278. | be a warrant of my lord's, Syr Wyllyem Clopton | 1 buk |
| 279. | mastyr Antony Wyngfelde | 1 buk |
| 280. | Mannok | 1 buk |
| 281. | mastyr Spylman | 1 buk |
| 282. | the townschyp of Bongey | 1 buk |
| 283. | Thomas Wyndam | 1 buk |
| 284. | mastyr Tylney | 1 buk |
| 285. | the Guylde of Framlyngham | 1 buk |
| 286. | the parson of Framlyngham for tythe | 1 buk |
| 287. | Pryor of Seynt Peters | 1 buk |
| 288. | the Pryor of Buttley | 1 buk |
| 289. | Syr Jamys Hubbard | 1 buk |
| 290. | my lady Wylleby | 1 buk |
| 291. | Cristofer Wyllebye | 1 buk |
| 292. | Humfrey Done and John Lancastyr | 1 buk |
| 293. | the towneschyp of Ippwyche | [ ] |
| 294. | be a warrant of my lord's, the parson of Framlyngham and Thomas Hulle | 1 buk |
| 295. | be a warrant of my lord Cursum and he desyryd me he schuld goo with me stylle and have a doo for yt but I saw not the warrant | 1 buk |
| 296. | be a warrant of my lord's, John Sharpe and he desyryd me yt schuld go with me stylle and have a doo for yt | 1 buk |
| 297. | Herry Everard | 1 buk |
| 298. | Thees be the lossys that I have had this somer of malle deer; | |
| | of bukkys | 17 |
| | of sowers | 4 |
| | of sowrells | 6 |
| | of prekets | 7 |

27

|  |  |  |
|---|---|---|
|  | of dooys | 15 |
|  | of fawnys | 13 |
|  | All the lost before Myelmes. |  |
| 299. | Thes be the dere that I Have kyllyd syn myelmas; |  |
| 300. | agayne my lords comyng | 2 doys |
| 301. | my lord wan he cam on the lawn and kyllyd | 3 doys |
| 302. | my lord Howard and my lord Wylleby | 1 doy |
| 303. | for mastyr Townysend | 1 doy |
| 304. | the poor of Ely for the stallacyon | 1 doy |
| 305. | Cristofer Harman | 1 doy |
| 306. | To London for the sargeantsfest | 8 doys |
| 307. | Thes be the lossys syn Mychelmes; |  |
|  | buk | 1 |
|  | of sowrells | 2 |
|  | of dooys | 5 |
|  | of fawnys | 2 |
| 308. | Now to my lord to London | 6 doys |
| 309. | be a commaundement of my lord to Dowe of Stratbrook | 1 doy |
| 310. | to the awdyt | 1 doy |
| 311. | be a warrant of my lords, John Sharpe and he browt me the warrant desyryd me yn wyntyr to have do for yt | 1 doy |
| 312. | my lord Wyllebye | 4 doys |
| 313. | my lord to London | 6 doys |
| 314. | my lord at another tyme to London | 6 doys |
| 315. | to mastyr Steward to London | 1 doy |
| 316. | mastyr Tylney | 1doy |
| 317. | my lord Howard to Kennynghalle | 4 doys |
| 318. | to the parson of Framlyngham | 1 doy |
| 319. | Willyem Jenye | 1 doy |
| 320. | mastyr Dawndye | 1 doy |
| 321. | be a warrant of my lord, the pryoy of Buttley | 2 doys |
| 322. | my lady Wyllebye | 1 doy |
| 323. | my lord of Oxforth | 2 doys |
| 324. | mastyr Antonye Wyngfeld | 1 doy |
| 325. | my lady Wyngfeld | 1 doy |
| 326. | John Henyngham | 1 doy |
| 327. | The pryor of Seynt Peters | 1 doy |
| 328. | The abbot of Leyston | 1 doy |
| 329. | The abbot of Sypton | 1 doy |
| 330. | Sir Edmund Jeney | 1 doy |
| 331. | Robert Cheek | 1 doy |
| 332. | thes be the lossys that I have had thys wyntyr; |  |
|  | of bukkys | 290 |
|  | of sowers | 89 |
|  | of sowrells | 132 |
|  | of prekets | 230 |

|  |  |  |
|---|---|---|
|  | of doys | 46(..) |
|  | of fawynys | 4(.) 3 |
| 333. | These be the that ded that we have fownd wythyn the palle and with-owt |  |
| 334. | The sum of thys losse 15 (16) hundryd and 5 score and 7 |  |
| 335. | in the 3rd yere of soveren lord kyng Henry the VIII and yn the 19 yere of Rychard Chambyr parker of Framlyngham, thes be the lossys that I had yn the fawnyng tyme ded of the r(.......); |  |
|  | of fawnys | 28 |
|  | of bukks | 6 |
|  | a sowrell | 1 |
|  | of doyys | 7 |
| 336. | my lady Bedyngfeld | 1 buk |
| 337. | Jorge Mannok | 1 buk |
| 338. | mastyr Herry Nowne | 1 buk |
| 339. | be a warrant of my lord, Syr Thomas Knyvet | 1 buk |
| 340. | be a warrant of my lord, Rychard Warton | 1 buk |
| 341. | be a warrant of my lady, Willyem Bucknam | 1 buk |
| 342. | Watyr Blyant and Rychard Jeney | 1 buk |
| 343. | the towschyppe of Woodbrege | 1 buk |
| 344. | the abbes of Brosyerd | 1 buk |
| 345. | mastyr pryor of Buttley | 1 buk |
| 346. | be a warrant of my lord, Syr Jamys Hobbard | 1 buk |
| 347. | Antonye Hansard | 1 buk |
| 348. | Syr Jamys Framymgham | 1 buk |
| 349. | be a warrant of my lords, Syr Robert Curson | 1 buk |
| 350. | Jorge Hevenyngham | 1 buk |
| 351. | Rychard Cawnedysche | 1 buk |
| 352. | Jamys Revet | 1 buk |
| 353. | The pryor of Ely | 1 buk |
| 354. | Dowty and Cooke | 1 buk |
| 355. | be a warrant of my lords, Mary Denys | 1 buk |
| 356. | My lord of Norwyche | 1 buk |
| 357. | Mastyr comyssarye | 1 buk |
| 358. | Mastyr Lannse | 1 buk |
| 359. | The mastyr of Metyngham | 1 buk |
| 360. | The mastyr of the chapelle of the field | 1 buk |
| 361. | Lionelle Talmage | 1 buk |
| 362. | Be a commaundement of my lord Howard, Wyllyam Tymperley | 1 buk |
| 363. | Be a warrant of my lord Howard, Thomas Wyngfelde | 1 buk |
| 364. | Be a warrant dormant, mastyr Lucas, | 1 buk |
| 365. | Dam Margery Bacon | 1 buk |
| 366. | My lady Jeney | 1 buk |
| 367. | My lady Tylney | 1 buk |
| 368. | The pryor of Woodbrege | 1 buk |
| 369. | John Echyngham and Edward hys sonne | 1 buk |

| | | |
|---|---|---|
| 370. | The pryor of Hey | 1 buk |
| 371. | John Hevenyngham | 1 buk |
| 372. | Arthur Hopton | 1 buk |
| 373. | Antonye Wyngfelde | 1 buk |
| 374. | Willyam Rowsse and Aylmer | 1 buk |
| 375. | Thomas Sporre | 1 buk |
| 376. | Robert Kempe | 1 buk |
| 377. | The Abbot of Sypton | .1 buk |
| 378. | The parson of Kelsale and John Wodous | 1 buk |
| 379. | My lady Wyllebye | 1 buk |
| 380. | Robert Cheke | 1 buk |
| 381. | My lord Howard's servauntys | 1 buk |
| 382. | Crystofer Wyllebye | 1 buk |
| 383. | Thomas Terelle | 1 buk |
| 384. | The townshepe of Harlyston | 1 buk |
| 385. | On owr lady day night, the last the parson of Ketylbergh cam yn to the parke wyth Willyam Smyth the luter and Thomas Cosyn of ketylnergh and sta (…) and ther and had yt a whey | |
| 386. | and then he cam agayn the Thursday followyng the same folk with dyverse othe and kyllyd a nother buk and had hym a whey. | |
| 387. | ther was a buk drownyd yn the goot (sic?) and last | 1 buk |
| 388. | agayn my lord's comyng | 1 doy |
| 389. | to the maryage of Johnn Mychyll's doutyr | 1 doy |
| 390. | the pryor of Sent Peters schuld have had a buk yn somer and he desyryd to have a do and he hath her | 1 doy |
| 391. | the awdyt | 1 doy |
| 392. | mastyr Tylney | 1 doy |
| 393. | Rychard Chambyr | 1 doy |
| 394. | My lord Wyllebye | 2 doys |
| 395. | My lord of Oxforthe | 2 doys |
| 396. | The pryor of Seynt Petyrs | 1 doy |
| 397. | Mastyr Antonye Wyngfeld | 1 doy |
| 398. | The parson of Framlyngham for tythe | 1 doy |
| 399. | My lady Bowser | 1 doy |
| 400. | Mastrys Hevyngham | 1 doy |
| 401. | Thomas Baldre and Edmund Gylgate a buk and he desyryd me to have a do for yt | 1 doy |
| 402. | be commaundement of my lord Howard, Syr Jamys Danyelle | 1 doy |
| 403. | Edmund Howard | 1 doy |
| 404. | These be the lossys that I had thys wyntyr; | |
| | of buks | 1 |
| | of sowrells | 7 |

30

|  |  |  |
|---|---|---|
|  | of preketts | 6 |
|  | of doys | 18 |
|  | of fawnys | 15 |
| 405. | In the 4 yere of our soferen Lord King Henry 8 and the 10 yere of Rychard Chamber Parker of Framlyngham, the be the lossys that I had lost in fawnyng tyme; |  |
| 406. | There cam yn a bygche of Robert Catyr of Badyngham and kyllyd me a do |  |
| 407. | Also lost of fawnys | 45 |
| 408. | These be the bukks that I have kyllyd this yer; |  |
| 409. | mastyr Corrector | 1 buk |
| 410. | Rychard Prat, baly of Stow | 1 buk |
| 411. | to Corpus Christi Gylde of Norwych | 1 buk |
| 412. | Mastyr Herry None | 1 buk |
| 413. | to Pryor of Penteney | 1 buk |
| 414. | my lord abbot of Sypton | [  ] |
| 415. | be a warrant of my lord's, Edmund (.........) |  |
| 416. | A buk hyng hym selfe yn the parke and thee on halfe I gave to John Rosyngton's wyffe chytche goying and the other among good felaws |  |
| 417. | Herry Pope | 1 buk |
| 418. | be the commaundement of my lord Howard, John Sadeler | 1 buk |
| 419. | the pryor of Buttley | 1 buk |
| 420. | the Abbot of Lestyon | 1 buk |
| 421. | the Pryor of Woodbrege | 1 buk |
| 422. | the Pryor of Seynt Petyrs he desyryd me to have a do for hys buk |  |
| 423. | the Pryor of Hey | 1 buk |
| 424. | Anthony Wyngfeld | 1 buk |
| 425. | My lady Wyllebeye | 1 buk |
| 426. | Willyam Rows and Regnold Rows | 1 buk |
| 427. | Anthony Hansart | 1 buk |
| 428. | Everton and Robert Haylmer | 1 buk |
| 429. | Nycholas Calle for hys maryage | 1 buk |
| 430. | The Sellerer of Berye | 1 buk |
| 431. | Be the commaundement of my lord Barnes, Cristofer Wyllebye, | 1 buk |
| 432. | John Teye | 1 buk |
| 433. | John Thetforthe | 1 buk |
| 434. | Jamys Hylle and Rychard Peveralle | 1 buk |
| 435. | Robert Kempe | 1 buk |
| 436. | Sir Robert Brandon | 1 buk |
| 437. | Mastyr Garnysshe | 1 buk |
| 438. | Rafe Everard | 1 buk |
| 439. | Doctor Coolle | 1 buk |
| 440. | Matthew Harman and Nycholas Game | 1 buk |
| 441. | Jorge Bukynham | 1 buk |

31

| | | |
|---|---|---|
| 442. | My ladye Catysbe | 1 buk |
| 443. | The mastyr of Metyngham | 1 buk |
| 444. | The prioress of Flexton | 1 buk |
| 445. | Be a warrant of my lord, my lade Luce | 1 buk |
| 446. | My lady Bowser | 1 buk |
| 447. | Thomas Roysche | 1 buk |
| 448. | Robert Payton | 1 buk |
| 449. | Mastyr Dene of the chapelle of the Felde | 1 buk |
| 450. | Mastyr mayr of Lyn | 1 buk |
| 451. | Robert Cheke | 1 buk |
| 452. | Be warrant of my lord, John Barker | halfe a buk |
| 453. | Robert Brewse | 1 buk |
| 454. | John Danyelle | 1 buk |
| 455. | The parson of Orforth | 1 buk |
| 456. | The towne of Donwyche | 1 buk |
| 457. | My lord of Norwyche | 1 buk |
| 458. | Thomas Sporne | 1 buk |
| 459. | Mastyr Haryson | 1 buk |
| 460. | My lord pryor of Elye | 1 buk |
| 461. | Syr Rychard Caundysche | 1 buk |
| 462. | My lord's servaunts and sowgyors at Framlyngham | 1 buk |
| 463. | Mastyr Myche | 1 buk |
| 464. | The towne of Bongeye | 1 buk |
| 465. | Mastyr Tylneye | 1 buk |
| 466. | The towne of Glemham | 1 buk |
| 467. | Masteyr Jeorge Wylleby and masteyr Thomas Wyllebye | 1 buk |
| 468. | Mastyr Mannok | 1 buk |
| 469. | The gylde of Framlyngham | 1 buk |
| 470. | Mastyr Geldyngham | 1 buk |
| 471. | Mastyr Chase | 1 buk |
| 472. | Mastyr Wodows | 1 buk |
| 473. | The parson of Framlyngham | 1 buk |
| 474. | On the Monday at nyght aftyr Seynt Bartylmewys daye cam hunters yn to the parke and stalled a buk | |
| 475. | Also the dyyd of the garget | 3 buks |
| 476. | Yn the root seson a buk fawt and dyd breke hys lege | |
| 477. | Also then dyed of the gargett | 3 doys |
| 478. | the Pryor of Seynt Petyrs deseryd me a do for hys buk and now he hathe hyr. | |
| 479. | to the audyte | 1 doy |
| 480. | mastyr Tylneye | 1 doy |
| 481. | the Pryor of Framlyngham for hys Tythe | 1 doy |
| 482. | my lord Wyllebye | 2 doys |
| 483. | mastyr Goldyngham | 1 doy |

Parson
32

| | | |
|---|---|---|
| 484. | the Pryor of Seynt Petyrs | 1 doy |
| 485. | my lord Howard's servaunts | 1 doy |
| 486. | be a warrant of my lords, | |
| | mastyr Willyem Rowse | 1 doy |
| 487. | Syr John Jacobe | 1 doy |
| 488. | Crystofer Hewat and Jamys Kynge | 1 doy |
| 489. | the Pryor of Hey | 1 doy |
| 490. | These be the lossys syn the audyte; | |
| | of bukks | 7 |
| | of sowrells | 3 |
| | of preketts | 4 |
| | of dooys | 10 |
| | of fawynys | 3(..) |
| 491. | of ded now syn Estyr of morkyn fawynys | 3 |
| | of malle and rascalle | 14 |
| 492. | In the 5 yer of Kyng Herry and the 21 of Rychard Chambyr | |
| 493. | Thes be the dere I have kyllyd this somer; | |
| 494. | mastyr Edmund Howard | 2 buks |
| 495. | mastyr Tylneye | 1 buk |
| 496. | be commaundement of my lord Howard, | |
| | the towne of Yarmowthe | 1 buk |
| 497. | the balys of Yermowthe | 1 buk |
| 498. | mastyr Savage, John Hunt, Newton | |
| | and John Cheke | 1 buk |
| 499. | Framlyngham Parke Richarde Chambre sworne | |
| | The certificate of richard Chambre keper there | |
| | of all dere  and ded of mureyn Anno 7, Regis Henrici VII. | |
| | Richard Chambre sworn Anno VI (1514-1515 ) | |
| 500. | Item in primis for the awdyte  (Anno V1) | 1 do. |
| 501. | abbot of bery | 1 do. |
| 502. | the prior of Seynt Petyrs schuld have a buk | [MS defective] |
| 503. | my lord Wyllebye | 1 do |
| 504. | abbot of Leyston | 1 do |
| 505. | Syr Anthony Wyngfeld | 1 do |
| 506. | Syr William Rowse | 1 do |
| 507. | Cristofer Harman and Matthew Harmane | 1 do |
| 508. | my lady Vere | 1 do |
| 509. | mastyr Lane | 1 do |
| 510. | Syr Cristofer Wyllebye | 1 do |
| 511. | Roger Aldred for his marriage | 1 do |
| 512. | (…….) of (…)neyn (….)…[MS defective] | 1 do |
| 513. | mastyr Latymer | 1 do |
| 514. | mastyr Lowthe | 1 do |
| 515. | the parson of Framlyngham for hys tythe | 1 do |
| 516. | mastrys Fastalle of Ypswyche | 1 do |
| 517. | mastyr Foorthe of Hadley | 1 do |
| 518. | for my lord of Norfolk at to tymys to London | 12 dois pro |
| | hospicio domini. | |
| 519. | Nicholas Joly and my lords servaunts | 1 do |

33

520. John Fox maryed John Tendyrlovys dowtyr
and oftyntymys the dere pasture upon ther
grownd, therfor they had to ther maryage ......... 1 do
521. mastyr corrector ......... 1 do
522. Edmund Jacob for his brothers maryage ......... 1 do
523. my lord of Surrey had to Wyndferdyng parke
of quyk dere;
524. To Wyndferdthyng Parke;

| | |
|---|---|
| of sowers | 2 |
| of preketts | 2 |
| of doys | 16 |
| | 20 dere |

525. for lord Wylleby took quyk dere for my
lord of Norfolke for to have to Hersham;
To Ersham Parke;

| | |
|---|---|
| a preket | (1) |
| doys | 18 |
| a fawne | (1) |
| And kyllyd 2 doys and a fawne | 23 dere |

526. Thes be the lossys ( of moreyne ) synse the awdyte;

| | |
|---|---|
| of buks | 17 |
| of sowrs | 12 |
| of sowrells | 10 |
| of prekets | 48 |
| of doys | 90 |
| of fawnys | 115 |
| | 292 dere |

527. (marginal note 'dede of moreyne before
Candelmas anno 6th, regis Henrici VIIIth.)
Thes wher ded by candyllmes
528. Nycholas Callys wyffe a do and sche desyryd
me thatt yt go stylle tylle sche fett yt
529. Thes be ded syn candylmaes;

| | |
|---|---|
| of buks | 6 |
| of sowers | 2 |
| of prekets | 5 |
| doys dyed of fawnyng | 2 |
| of fawnys ded in fawnyng tyme | 33 |
| | 48 |

530. (marginal note: dede of moreyne aftyr in
fawnyng tyme candelmes).
531. the 7th yere of our soferen lord kyng Herry the VIII in the XXIII
yere of Rychard Chambyr , parker of Framlyngham (1516-17).
532 . my lord of Norwyche ......... 1 buk
533. my lord of Wylleby ......... 2 bukks
534. by commaundment of my lord Wylleby,
Sir Lyonelle Demok ......... 1 buk
535. my lady Vere ......... 1 buk

34

| | | |
|---|---|---|
| 536. | the abbot of Sypton | 1 buk |
| 537. | Sir William Rows | 1 buk |
| 538. | the Abbas of Brosyyrd | 1 buk |
| 539. | the mastyr of Metyngham | 1 buk |
| 540. | John Hevyngham | 1 buk |
| 541. | Sir Arthur Hopton | 1 buk |
| 542. | Sir Edmond Jeney | 1 buk |
| 543. | Sir John Wylleby | 1 buk |
| 544. | Sir Anthony Hansert | 1 buk |
| 545. | Colton | 1 buk |
| 546. | Sir Thomas Lovelle | 1 buk |
| 547. | the Prior of Hey and the Scoolle mastyr. | 1 buk |
| 548. | for John Teye | 1 buk |
| 549. | the balys of Ypswyche | 1 buk |
| 550. | Robert Cheke | 1 buk |
| 551. | the gyld of Framlyngham | 1 buk |
| 552. | the abbot of Bery | 1 buk |
| 553. | the prior of Butley | 1 buk |
| 554. | the prior of Seynt Petyrs | 1 buk |
| 555. | the prior of Woodbrege | 1 buk |
| 556. | the prior of Elye | 1 buk |
| 557. | Mastyr Edmond Wyngfeld and William Jeney | 1 buk |
| 558. | Crystofer Harman | 1 buk |
| 559. | Edmond Gelgatt | 1 buk |
| 560. | Robert Forthe thelder | 1 buk |
| 561. | Doctor Calle | 1 buk |
| 562. | the parson of Framlyngham for his tythe | 1 buk |
| 563. | my lord Cursonn was here and kyllyd a buk and a sowrell and I gave he sowrelle to lord Cursoun's servants and Sir Rychard Wentworthys servants | 1 buk |
| 564. | Sir Rychard Wentforthe | 1 buk |
| 565. | Sir Anthony Wyngfeld | 1 buk |
| 566. | Sir Rychard Cawndyshe | 1 buk |
| 567. | Sir John Awdeley | 1 buk |
| 568. | Sir John Glemham | 1 buk |
| 569. | Sir James Framyngham | 1 buk |
| 570. | the townshepe of Ypswyche | 1 buk |
| 571. | mastyr Lane | 1 buk |
| 572. | the towne of Wodbrege | 1 buk |
| 573. | the pryoress of Campsey | 1 buk |
| 574. | mastyr commysary | 1 buk |
| 575. | be a warrant of my lord's, John Draper gentleman | 1 buk. |
| 576. | be a warrant of my lord's, John Mascalle of the Chancerey | 1 buk |
| 577. | be a warrant of my lord's, Rychard Warton | 1 buk |
| 578. | the parson of Orforthe and John Garlond | 1 buk |

35

| | | |
|---|---|---|
| 579. | be a warrant of my lord's | 1 buk |
| 580. | Sir Edward Ichyngham | 1 buk |
| 581. | Regnold Lytylprow | 1 buk |
| 582. | John Rychers of Bongey | 1 buk |
| 583. | Sir Crystofer Wyllebye | 1 buk |
| 584. | Herry Kooke | 1 buk |
| 585. | my lady Bowser | 1 buk |
| 586. | be a warrant of my lord's, mastyr Chauncy (Chasye) | 1 buk |
| 587. | mastyr Lucas | 1 buk |
| 588. | Thomas Benet and Robert Mells | 1 buk |
| 589. | mastyr Thomas Fyncham | 1 buk |
| 590. | William Mekylfeld | 1 buk |
| 591. | Mastyr Prior of Thelforthe | 1 buk |
| 592. | Robert Browne | 1 buk |
| 593. | Thomas Sporne | 1 buk |
| 594. | the towne of Harleston | 1 buk |
| 595. | Sir Thomas Tyrelle | 1 buk |
| 596. | Thomas Coole for hys dowtyr's maryage | 1 buk |
| 597. | for mastrys Marget Hasset | 1 buk |
| 598. | Edmond Rookwood | 1 buk |
| 599. | Nycholas Calle | 1 buk |
| 600. | be warrant of my lord's, William Crane gentylman | 1 buk |
| 601. | Humfrey Everton | 1 buk |
| 602. | Thomas Rushhe | 1 buk |
| 603. | Sir Thomas Wyythe | 1 buk |
| 604. | Syr Phylyppe Tyllneye | 1 buk |
| 605. | the abbot of Leyston | [  ] |
| 606. | Lossys thys somer ded of the wyppys; | |
| | of bukks | 3 |
| | of sowers | 5 |
| | of prekets | 1 |
| | of dooys | 8 |
| 607. | a dog cam in and kyllyd a do. | |
| 608. | Geffrey Dallyng of Laxfeld mercer, (two) dogs of hys cam in and kyllyd a doo. And a fawne. | |
| 609. | on Holy Rood even I fond in the parke Sir John Bowse paryshe pryst of Tanyngton with hys bow bent and an arrow in yt betyng att the herde. | |
| 610. | These be the doys that I have kyllyd thes seson: | |
| 611. | my lord Wyllebye | 2 doys |
| 612. | for the awdyt | 2 doys |
| 613. | to my lord's grace to Lambethe | 8 doys |
| 614. | afty that the second tyme | 6 doys |

36

| | | |
|---|---|---|
| 615. | at the 3rd tyme | 6 doys |
| 616. | at the 4th tyme | 6 doys |
| 617. | my lord Wylleby | 1 doe |
| 618. | the prior of Buttley | 1 doe |
| 619. | the prior of Seynt Petyrs | 1 do |
| 620. | the prior of cryst chyrche | 1 do |
| 621. | Sir Antony Wyngfelde | 1 do |
| 622. | the pryor of Fylstowe | 1 do |
| 623. | Crystofer Harman | 1 do. |
| 624. | mastyr Robert Cheke | 1 do |
| 625. | my lady Vere | 1 do |
| 626. | the prior of Letheryngham & the parson of Badyngham | 1 do |
| 627. | John Roysngton for hys wyfys chyrche goyng | 1 do |
| 628. | Thomas Lowthe | 1 do |
| 629. | my lady Catysbe | 1 do |
| 630. | mastyr Chauncy | 1 do |
| 631. | be a warant of my lord's grace, Sir Willyam Rows | 2 doys |
| 632. | Bryaunt had a do gyvyn hym and he deseyryd me she schald go with me tylle he fete hyr and thys yeere he hathe hyr | 1 do |
| 633. | Thomas Grymston schuld have a do the last yer and thys yer he hath her | 1 do |
| 634. | Nicholas Calle and John Pulham | 1 do |
| 635. | my lady Berneys | 1 do |
| 636. | Sir Fylype Calthorpe | 1 do |
| 637. | Nycholas Cally's wyffye schuld hav had a do last yer and now sche hathe yt | 1 do |
| 638. | Frances Calthorpe | 1 do |
| 639. | Syr John Wellebye | 1 do |
| 640. | Sir Crystofer Heydon | 1 do |
| 641. | Anthony Hanserth | 1 do |
| 642. | my lady Calthorpe | 1 do |
| 643. | be a warrant of my lord's grace, Jermyn of Mettfeld | 1 do |
| 644. | mastyr Steward | 1 do |
| 645. | mastyr Tylneye | 1 do |
| 646. | Jeorge Buknom | 1 do |
| 647. | the parson of Blaxshalle and Matthew Harman | 1 do |
| 648. | be the commaundement of my lorde Edmonde Howard, Symon Oldryng yermowthe | 1 do |
| 649. | mastyr Corrector | 1 do |
| 650. | My lord Wylleby cam from London and he schewyd me that my lord's grace was content that he schold kyll doys her and for as many doys as he kyllyd heer he scholde put quyke | |

|  |  |  |
|---|---|---|
|  | doys in Hersham parke for them, as wyche he had | 10 doys |
| 651. | Also he seyd my lord's grace was content thatt my lord Byrsschope schulde have | 2 doys |
| 652. | He seyd that my lord's grace schuld have to putt in Hersham parke | 6 doys |
| 653. | Also he schewyd me that my lord's grace was content that Syr John Hevyngham schud have 4 doys and he schulde put in Hersham Parke for them | 8 doys. |

654. Thes be the lossys that I have had thys wynter ;

|  |  |
|---|---|
| of bukks | 7 |
| of sowrells | 4 |
| of preketts | 10 |
| of dooys | 17 |
| of fawnys | 71 |

655. Thes be dede be candylmes

656. Thes  be the lossys sythe candylmes;

|  |  |
|---|---|
| of  bukks | 3 |
| A buke dyed drownyd in the moot |  |
| of sowrells | 2 |
| a sower | 1 |
| of prekets | 4 |
| of doys | 5 |
| of the last yer fawnys morkyns | 49 |

657. These be ded syn Wython day
the 8 yer of our sovereyn lord kyng Herry the 8th and in the 24th
yer of Rychard Chambyr, parkyr of Framlyngham (1517-8)
Losses thys fawnyngtym

|  |  |
|---|---|
| of fawnys | 45 |

658. Thes be the bukks I have kyllyd thys yer

|  |  |  |
|---|---|---|
| 659. | the frenshe quene | 1 buk |
|  |  | 2 fawnys |
| 660. | She sent to me for a fawne |  |
| 661. | the duke sent to me for a buk | 1 buk |
| 662. | the quene cam agayn and kyllyd | 4 buks |
| 663. | be a warrant of my lord's grasce | 1 buk |
| 664. | be a warrant of my lady's grace, Sir Herry Gylforthe | 1 buk |
| 665. | mastyr prior Seynt Petyrs | 1 buk |
| 666. | my lord Wyllebye | 1 buk |
| 667. | Sir Anthony Wyngfelde | 1 buk |
| 668. | mastyr Robert Cheke | 1 buk |
| 669. | the prior of the black fryers Donwyche | 1 buk |
| 670. | Syr John Awdeley | 1 buk |
| 671. | my lord Cursom | 1 buk |
| 672. | Nicholas Calle and John Pulham | 1 buk |
| 673. | my lord Edmond Howard was her and kyllyd | 4 buks |

| | | |
|---|---|---|
| 674. | my lord Edmond kyllyd | 1 sowrell |
| 675. | Sir Thomas Booleyn | 2 buks |
| 676. | the seyd Sir Thomas | 1 sowrell |
| 677. | with him cam the prior of Seynt Overas | |
| | And he had | 1 buk |
| 678. | my lord Dacres | 1 buk |
| 679. | Thomas Lucas | 1 buk |
| 680. | John Teye | 1 buk |
| 681. | be the commandement of my lord Surrey, | |
| | Nicholas Joly and hys company | 1 buk |
| 682. | mastyr prior of Thetforthe | 1 buk |
| 683. | mastyr parson of Norwolde | 1 buk |
| 684. | mastyr parson of Woolpete | 1 buk |
| 685. | be the commandement of my lady's grace, | |
| | lady Capele | 1 buk |
| 686. | be a warrant of my lord's grace, | |
| | Nicholas Jackesson sergeaunt | 1 buk |
| 687. | be a warrant of my lord's grace, | |
| | Robert Sampson, clarke of the privy sealle | 1 buk |
| 688. | be a warrant of my lord's grace, | |
| | Syr Thomas Lovelle | 1 buk |
| 689. | mastyr Mannoke | 1 buk |
| 690. | Mastyr Mannoke sent to me in gresse seson | |
| | was twelmonthe and desyryd me that hys | |
| | buk schuld go with me tylle he send for hym | |
| | and thys yer he atthe hym. | |
| 691. | Herry Pope | 1 buk |
| 692. | mastyr doctor Malbard | 1 buk |
| 693. | Herry Cooke | 1 buk |
| 694. | mastyr selerer of Berrye | 1 buk |
| 695. | William Mekylfellde | 1 buk |
| 696. | mastyr Thomas Fyncham | 1 buk |
| 697. | mastyr parson of Stonham | 1 buk |
| 698. | for the gylde of Framlyngham | 1 buk |
| 699. | for mastyr parson of Framlingham for hys tythe | 1 buk |
| 700. | mastyr Tyneye seyd he wolde have no buk | |
| | and hope to have yt another tyme. | |
| 701. | Thomas Baldrye of Ypyswyche | 1 buk |
| 702. | mastyr Jackessone | 1 buk |
| 703. | be commandement of my lord Edmond | |
| | Howard, mastyr Kemp | 1 buk |
| 704. | be commandement of my lord Edmond | |
| | Howard, Houg Gyrlyng | 1 buk |
| 705. | be a warrant of my lady's grace, | |
| | Thomas Wyngfelde | 1 buk |
| 706. | be a warrant of my lord's grace, Surry's grome | |
| | of my lord of Suffolk's chambyr | 1 buk |
| 707. | John Woodwalle | 1 buk |

| | | |
|---|---|---|
| 708. | Edmond Rookwode | 1 buk |
| 709. | mastyr Kent | 1 buk |
| 710. | be a warrant of my lady's grace | 1 buk |
| 711. | be a warrant of my lord's grace | 1 buk |
| 712. | George Henyngham | 1 buk |
| 713. | mastyr Forthe | 1 buk |
| 714. | mastyr Gelgate | 1 buk |
| 715. | mastres Hasset | 1 buk |
| 716. | Marget Hasset | 1 buk |
| 717. | the towne of Donwyche | 1 buk |
| 718. | William Henne kepere of the Castelle for hys maryage | 1 buk |
| 719. | be a warrant of my lord's grace, Andrew Wyndysssore | 1 buk |
| 720. | my lord of Norwyche | 1 buk |
| 721. | the abbot of Berey | 1 buk |
| 722. | the abbot of Sypton | 1 buk |
| 723. | the abbot of Leyston | 1 buk |
| 724. | the prior of Butleye | 1 buk |
| 725. | the prior of Woodbrege | 1 buk |
| 726. | the prior of Fylstowe | 1 buk |
| 727. | the abbas of Brosyarde | 1 buk |
| 728. | Rychard Wentworthe | 1 buk |
| 729. | Syr Arthur Hopton | 1 buk |
| 730. | Syr Edmond Jeney | 1 buk |
| 731. | Syr Wyllyam Rowsse | 1 buk |
| 732. | Syr John Wyllebye | 1 buk |
| 733. | Syr Thomas Wyndham | 1 buk |
| 734. | Syr John Glemham | 1 buk |
| 735. | to the fryers of Norwyche | 2 buks |
| 736. | mastyr Stward | 1 buk |
| 737. | Robert Hogon and his companye | 1 buk |
| 738. | the prior of Letheryngham | 1 buk |
| 739. | John Hevyngham | 1 buk |
| 740. | Anthony Hanserth | 1 buk |
| 741. | Frauncys Calthorpe | 1 buk |
| 742. | William Jeney | 1 buk |
| 743. | William Playtere | 1 buk |
| 744. | Crystofer Harman and Matthew | 1 buk |
| 745. | my lady Rowsse and mastrys Fastolfe of Pettaw | 1 buk |
| 746. | the towne of Bungey | 1 buk |
| 747. | the towne of Walton and Trymley | 1 buk |
| 748. | my lady Catesby | 1 buk |
| 749. | my lord of Suffolke cam yn and wyth hym cam my lords Fwatyr and my lord Corsoun and they kyllyd | 4 buks a sower and 2 sowrells |

a preket

2 doys

and a fawne

| | | |
|---|---|---|
| 750. | they strake yn the hede a buk and aftyr | |
| | I kyllyd hym and servyd a warrant with hym | 1 buk |
| 751. | Thes be the lossys thys somer of the garget; | |
| | of buks | 9 |
| | of sowers | 3 |
| | of sowells | 4 |
| | of prekets | 1 |
| | doys dyed of fawnyng and the garget | 11 |
| 752. | Thes be the dere that I ghave gon to kyll thys seson; | |
| 753. | Sir John Wyllybyee | 1 doy |
| 754. | for Edward Caltrolpe maryage | |
| | and Marget Foxe | 1 doy |
| 755. | be my lord's grace to London | 6 doys |
| 756. | mastyr Stward | 1 doy |
| 757. | for the audyte | 2 doys |
| 758. | to my lord's grace to London before the awdyt | |
| | and aftyr | 36 doys. |
| 759. | my lord Wylleby | 2 doys |
| 760. | Robert Taylor and hys company, servaunts of | |
| | my lord of Surrey | 1 doy |
| 761. | Fraunces Calthorpe | 1 doy |
| 762. | Robert Kempe | 1 doy |
| 763. | Edmonde Rookwoode | 1 doy |
| 764. | Robert Mellys | 1 doy |
| 765. | the parson of Borowe | 1 doy |
| 766. | Sir Thomas Wyndham | 1 doy |
| 767. | be a warrant of my lord's grace, Herry Nowne | 1 doy |
| 768. | John Germyn of Metfelde | 1 doy |
| 769. | Nycholas Calle for hys wyffy's chyrche goyng | 1 doy |
| 770. | to pryor of Letheryngham and the parson | |
| | of Badyngham | 1 doy |
| 771. | George Tompson of Kelsalle for hys maryage | 1 doy |
| 772. | John Lancastre | 1 doy |
| 773. | the prior of Fylstow | 1 doy |
| 774. | mastyr Tyllneye | 1 doy |
| 775. | Edmond Hylle | 1 doy |
| 776. | the prior of Buttley | 1 doy |
| 777. | the parson for the tythe | 1 doy |
| 778. | Sir Edmond Jenneys | 1 doy |
| 779. | Sir Wyllyam Rowse | 1 doy |
| 780. | Sir Anthonye Wyngfelde | 1 doy |
| 781. | mastyr Henyngham | 1 doy. |
| 782. | These be the lossys that I have had thys yere; | |
| | quyk dere sent to Hersham | |
| | of buks | 1 |

|                       |     |
| --------------------- | --- |
| of sowers             | 4   |
| of sowrells           | 2   |
| of preketts           | 2   |
| A maille fawne        |     |
| of doys               | 20  |
| A rascalle fawne      |     |
| of fawnes             | 31  |

783. These be the dere thatt be ded in the same place;

|                |    |
| -------------- | -- |
| of bukks       | 7  |
| of sowers      | 3  |
| of sowrells    | 5  |
| of preketts    | 8  |
| of doys        | 23 |
| of fawnys      | 59 |

784. John Pulham thelder cam rydyng be the wey and found a do with owt and hys doge kyllyd hym and he hyng hys doge.

785. Also Watyr Warner the sone of Anes Warner of Denyngton for stallyd my lord's dere and browt hyr in to the parke and lyeth wan I was fetyng them home and put hys byche to hyrr: also on Seynt Mark's day, John Foxe and yonge Thomas Hylly's ladds and William Tendyrlove they went forthe to the releysing of the hare and had a cowrse and browt hyr in to the parke and kyllyd a do with fawne and another fawne.

786. In the 9th yere of owre soferen Lorde kyng Henry the VIII and in the 25th yere of Rychard Chambre parkere of Framlyngham (1518-19).

787. Lossys in fawnyng tyme;

|             |    |
| ----------- | -- |
| of fawnys   | 73 |

788. Thes be the deere that I have kyllyd thys somer;

| | | |
| --- | --- | --- |
| 789. | my lord Wyllebye | 2 buks |
| 790. | the abbot of Berry | 1 buk |
| 791. | the abbot of Sypton | 1 buk |
| 792. | the abbot of Leyston | 1 buk |
| 793. | the prior of Woodbrege | 1 buk |
| 794. | the prior of Fylstow | 1 buk |
| 795. | the abbas of Brosyerd | 1 buk |
| 796. | the prior of Letheryngham | 1 buk |
| 797. | Sir Anthony Wyngfelde | 1 buk |
| 798. | Sir Edmond Jeney | 1 buk |
| 799. | Sir William Rowse | 1 buk |
| 800. | Sir John Wyllebye | 1 buk |
| 801. | the prior of the black fryers of Donwyche. | 1buk |
| 802. | Henyngham | 1 buk |
| 803. | Wylliam Jeney | 1 buk |
| 804. | the grey fryers of Norwyche | 1 buk |

| | | |
|---|---|---|
| 805. | mastyr Tylneye and the surveyor | 1 buk |
| 806. | mastyr Tylneye and the surveyor for my lord's counselle to Bongey | 1 buk |
| 807. | Thomas Baldre | 1 buk |
| 808. | the parson of Blaksalle and Matthew Harman | 1 buk |
| 809. | mastyr Fastolle of Pettow | 1 buk |
| 810. | mastrys Fastalle of Ypswyche | 1 buk |
| 811. | the towne of Harlystone | 1 buk |
| 812. | the towne of Sowolde | 1 buk |
| 813. | Nicholas Calle and John Pulham thelder | 1 buk |
| 814. | Robert Mellys | 1 buk |
| 815. | Robert Cheke | 1 buk |
| 816. | Robert Gosnalle | 1 buk |
| 817. | Framlyngham gyllde | 1 buk |
| 818. | the parson for hys tythe | 1 buk |
| 819. | be a warrant of my lord's grace, Elizabeth Kempe | 1 buk |
| 820. | be a warrant of my lord's grace, Edward Knyvet | 1 buk |
| 821. | be a warrant of my lord's grace | 1 buk |
| 822. | be a warrant of my lady's grace, Robert Hogone | 1 buk |
| 823. | to Robert Tayler and my lord of Surrey's Servaunts | 1 buk |
| 824. | mastrys Brewsse | 1 buk |
| 825. | the parson of Orforthe and John Garland | 1 buk |
| 826. | Jeorge Bakar a kuk, a he had the haunche And the one syd and to a systyrlaw of myn the other syd at Nedom and so he carryed Alle together | 1 buk |
| 827. | be warrant of my lord's grace, Dame Margaret Blenerhasset | 1 buk |
| 828. | to my lady Barnes | 1 buk |
| 829. | William Sabeon | 1 buk |
| 830. | the prior of Castlaker | 1 buk |
| 831. | the mastyr of Carleton | 1 buk |
| 832. | be a warrant of my lord's grace, Edward Broket | 1 buk |
| 833. | be warrant of my lady's grace | 1 buk |
| 834. | the pryor of Thetforthe | 1 buk |
| 835. | Edmund Tylneye | 1 buk |
| 836. | Thomas Tylney | 1 buk |
| 837. | be a warrant of my lord's grace, Rychard Roberts dene of the chapelle | 1 buk |
| 838. | the parson of Kelsalle | 1 buk |
| 839. | Thomas Sporne | 1 buk |
| 840. | mastyr Wyythe | 1 buk |
| 841. | the prior of Romborow | 1 buk |
| 842. | Rychard Warton | buk |
| 843. | for the convent of the priory of Thetforthe | |

|  |  |  |
|---|---|---|
|  | and John Thyrkylle | 1 buk |
| 844. | Nicholas Calle and Herry Cook | 1 buk |
| 845. | William Mekylfelde | 1 buk |
| 846. | be the commaundement of my lord of Surrey,<br>Nicholas Joly for hys maryage | 1 buk |
| 847. | my lord Edmond Howard | 6 buks |
| 848. | my lord Edmond | a preket and a fawne |
| 849. | Sir Thomas Bulleyn | 3 buks and a fawne |
| 850. | ther cam a XI (eleven) of my lord's servaunts<br>to Ypswyche and they sent to me for a buk<br>and I kyllyd a buk and sent them to the to<br>Mowneyes and ther company | 1 buk |
| 851. | to grey fryers of Ypswycche | 1 buk |
| 852. | Sir Phylype Tylney | 1 buk |
| 853. | the prior of Mendham | 1 buk |
| 854. | to a warrant of my lord's grace,<br>Sir Robert Wyngfelde | 1 buk |
| 855. | John Fyncham | 1 buk |
| 856. | be the commawndement of my lord<br>Edmond Howard delyveryd to a frynd of hys<br>I wot not to whom gyffne to Dasttey chapellen<br>to M… comit……[MS cut] | (1 buk) |
| 857. | the prior of Pentney | 1 buk |
| 858. | for the comyng of my lord Cardenalle | 1 buk |
| 859. | he cam trow the parke and kyllyd | 1 buk and a do. |
| 860. | on the next day I was sygned to kylle for hym | 12 buks. |
| 861. | in the kyllyd a sowrelle the on halfe I gave to<br>Regnold Rowse and the other I had my selfe. |  |
| 862. | Nicholas Calle and mastrys Hamerton<br>and John Pak | 1 buk |
| 863. | my lady Bouser | 1 buk |
| 864. | Ther be ded of the garget thys yer; |  |
|  | of buks | 6 |
|  | of sowers | 6 |
|  | of sowrells | 7 |
|  | of preketts | 43 |
|  | of doys | 67 |
|  | of fawnys | 55 |
| 865. | Thourisdey after Mycholmes daye at nyght<br>I toke the parson off ketylberggys biche<br>in the parke |  |
| 866. | on the moroue after at nyght I had a doo<br>byttyne in the Parke and kyllyd |  |
| 867. | for the audytyr | 2 doys |
| 868. | my lady Echyngham | 1 doy |
| 869. | the town of Donwyche | 1 doy |
| 870. | mastyr parson of ketylbere | 1 doy |
| 871. | the prior of Seynt Peters | 1 doy |

| | | |
|---|---|---:|
| 872. | parson of Framlyngham for tythe | 1 doy |
| 873. | John Henyngham | 1 doy |
| 874. | Sir Edmund Jeney | 1 doy |
| 875. | Fraunsys Calthorpe | 1 doy |
| 876. | Robert Harvye's maryage | 1 doy |
| 877. | for Anne Toppyng's maryage | 1 doy |
| 878. | Robert Cheke | 1 doy |
| 879. | John Garnyssche | 1 doy |
| 880. | Crystofer Harman | 1 doy |
| 881. | mastyr Kent | 1 doy |
| 882. | for Barbor maryage | 1 doy |
| 883. | mastyr Bryant | 1 doy |
| 884. | John Pulham | 1 doy |
| 885. | Wylliam Gardener | 1 doy |
| 886. | Nycholas Calle | 1 doy |
| 887. | my lady Rowse | 1 doy |
| 888. | the abbess of Brosyerd | 1 doy |
| 889. | These be the lossys that I had of quyk deere to Wyndferdyng for my lord of Surreye; | |
| | of bukks at the first takyng | 3 |
| | of sowers | 2 |
| | of doys | 7 |
| | of malfaunys | 2 |
| | of rascalle faunys | 2 |
| 890. | At the second tyme: | |
| | buks | 1 |
| | sowres | 1 |
| | preketts | 2 |
| | doys | 4 |
| | malfawnys | 5 |
| | Rascallfawnys | 3 |
| 891. | At the thred tyme: | |
| | buks | 3 |
| | sowers | 1 |
| | preketts | 4 |
| | doys | 10 |
| | malefawnys | 2 |
| 892. | a do was kyllyd in the takyng | |
| 893. | At the fowrt tyme: | |
| | bukks | 2 |
| | sowers | 1 |
| | sowrells | 1 |
| | doys | 10 |
| | mallfawnys | 1 |
| | rascalle fawnys | 2 |
| 894. | and a do was kyllyd in the takyng | |
| 895. | At the fyfte tyme: | |
| | bukks | 1 |

45

|  |  |  |
|---|---|---|
|  | sowrells | 1 |
|  | doys | 1 |
|  | male fawnes | 2 |
|  | rascalle fawnes | 3 |
| 896. | At the syxt tyme: |  |
|  | bukks | 1 |
|  | sowrells | 1 |
|  | preketts | 6 |
|  | doys | 16 |
| 897. | a do was kyllyd in the takyng |  |
| 898. | At the VII tyme: |  |
|  | preketts | 2 |
|  | doys | 6 |
| 899. | Sum to the hundred 6 score and on quikdere |  |
| 900. | These be the dere that was had to Hersham for my lord of Norfolk |  |
| 901. | At the fyrst carryage; |  |
|  | of bukks | 1 |
|  | of sowelle | 1 |
|  | preketts | 8 |
|  | doys | 14 |
|  | mall fawnys | 3 |
|  | rascalle fawnys | 5 |
| 902. | and a do kyllyd in the takyng |  |
| 903. | At the second tyme: |  |
|  | of bukks | 5 |
|  | of sowers | 2 |
|  | of sowrell | 1 |
|  | preketts | 5 |
|  | doys | 15 |
|  | malfawnys | 1 |
|  | rascalle fawnys | 4 |
| 904. | At the thred tyme: |  |
|  | bukks | 7 |
|  | of sowere | 1 |
|  | of sowrells | 2 |
|  | of preketts | 3 |
|  | doys | 13 |
|  | malle fawnys | 2 |
|  | rascalle fawnys | 3 |
| 905. | On the fowrte tyme: |  |
|  | preketts | 2 |
|  | doys | 23 |
| 906. | Summ of the quyk dere 6 score and on |  |
| 907. | The be the lossys that be dede thes wynter in Framlyngham Parke; |  |
|  | of buks | 44 |
|  | of sowers | 19 |

|  | of sowrelles | 28 |
|---|---|---|
|  | of preketts | 54 |
|  | of doys | 4 score and 9 |
|  | of fawnys | 8 score and 5 |
| 908. | In the 10th yer of our coferen lord kyng Henry the VIII and in the 26th yer of Rychard Chambre, Parker of Framlyngham | |
| 909. | Thes be the dere that I have kyllyd this somyr; | |
| 910. | the abbot of Siptone | 1 buk |
| 911. | the prior of Butley | 1 buk |
| 912. | the prior of Wodbryge | 1 buk |
| 913. | the prior of Filstoue | 1 buk |
| 914. | the prior of Ele | 1 buk |
| 915. | the prior of Sente Petris | 1 buk |
| 916. | the prior of Cristichurche of Ipswiche | 1 buk |
| 917. | the abbas of Brisyard | 1 buk |
| 918. | the priores of Cansey | 1 buk |
| 919. | my lord Wilbenyghbe | 2 buks |
| 920. | my lord Corsome | (1) buk |
| 921. | Sir Rychard Wentwoyrth | 1 buk |
| 922. | Sir Antonye Wyngfelde | 1 buk |
| 923. | Sir Artur Hoptone | 1 buk |
| 924. | Sir John Wilbenyghbe | 1 buk |
| 925. | Sir Edmonde Jeney | 1 buk |
| 926. | Siyr Humferey Wyngffylld | 1 buk |
| 927. | William Jeney | 1 buk |
| 928. | John Henyngham | 1 buk |
| 929. | Cristover Harman | 1 buk |
| 930. | Thomas Rusche | 1 buk |
| 931. | Matthew Harman and the parsone off Blaksalle | 1 buk |
| 932. | masteres Fastale off Pettawe | 1 buk |
| 933. | masteres Hasset | 1 buk |
| 934. | Nocoles Calle | 1 buk |
| 935. | the parson of Orforde | 1 buk |
| 936. | Fraunces Calthorpe | 1 buk |
| 937. | Edmond Gelgate | 1 buk |
| 938. | the Toune Donwich | 1 buk |
| 939. | the Lordschipe off Collnes | 1 buk |
| 940. | my lady Bouser | 1 buk |
| 941. | Sir Willyam Rous | 1 buk |
| 942. | Master Comissarie | 1 buk |
| 943. | Sir Edward Itchingham | 1 buk |
| 944. | Robard Cheke | 1 buk |
| 945. | Thomas Tylney | 1 buk |
| 946. | my lady Boyeth and master Bedyngffylld and master Crane and mastyr Thomas Raycleffe | 1 buk |
| 947. | Sir philipe Tylney | 1 buk |
| 948. | Sir Robard Huggone and Roger Appilleyarde | 1 buk |
| 949. | Sir Thomas Wyndham | 1 buk |

| 950. | Framlyngham Gylde | 1 buk |
| 951. | Roger Collome | 1 buk |
| 952. | Humfrey Hevertone | 1 buk |
| 953. | the dene of my lord of Norfolk's chapell | 1 buk |
| 954. | the parsone of Framingham's Tyethe | 1 buk |
| 955. | John Pullam the elder | hauffe buck |
| 956. | [deleted] Elizabeth Greye | 2 buks |
| 957. | [deleted] ( Mary) Gernyngham | 1 buk |
| 958. | Humfrey Dune | 1 buk |
| 959. | my lady Ichyngham | 1 buk |
| 960. | my lady Arnedelle | 1 buk |
| 961. | be a warrant of my lord's grace, John Worsop | 1 buk |
| 962. | Thomas Belynforyth | 1 buk |
| 963. | be a warand off my lord's grace, Mary Gerningham | 1 buk |
| 964. | be a warand off my lord's grace, Elizabeth Grey | 1 buk |
| 965. | for Thomas Lucase | 1 buk |
| 966. | for Willyam Bucus | 1 buk |
| 967. | for John Jarmyne | 1 buk |
| 968. | for John Reynolde and Robard Taylyar and Cristofer Heyward and Thomas Melis | 1 buk |
| 969. | be a warand of my lord's grace | 1 buk |
| 970. | be a warand of my ladi's grace | 1 buk |
| 971. | for master Jakson | 1 buk |
| 972. | for Thomas Nauntone | 1 buk |
| 973. | for Doctor Calle | 1 buk |
| 974. | for Thomas Bakone | 1 buk |
| 975. | for Robard Mells | 1 buk |
| 976. | for Sir John Temperley | 1 buk |
| 977. | Edmomd Tilney | 1 buk |
| 978. | by the commandimet off my lorde of Surrey to masterdyshryff off Norwich | 1 buk |
| 979. | Thes be the lossys that dyed off the garget and off the reterbak thys somare; | |
| | of bucks | 15 |
| | of souers | 6 |
| | of sorarells | 9 |
| | of prikettis | 4 |
| | of doyes | 11 |
| 980. | Thes be the lossis of faunys in faunynge tyme and this somare; | |
| | of fonnys | 31 |
| 981. | be a warrand of my lord's grace sent to Lambethe | 6 doyes |
| 982. | be the same warand of my lord's grace | 6 doyes |
| 983. | to parker's douther was maried and shee hade a doo | |
| 984. | by the comadimet off my lord's grace | |

|  | John Borneman | 1 doo |
|---|---|---|
| 985. | for the hawdite | 1 doo |
| 986. | for my lord of Norfolk's grace to Lambethe after the audite and senyt | 30 doyes |
| 987. | be the same warand of my lord's grace | 6 doyes |
| 988. | to parker's douther was maried and shee hade a doo |  |
| 989. | by the commaundymet of my lord of Surrey's to Kennyggahelle | 5 doys |
| 990. | Sir Antone Wyngffylde | 1 doy |
| 991. | Sir Antone Wyngffyllde would a haude a doo the laste yere and he prayede me for to lett hyr goo tyll he hete hyr and this yer he hayth her | 1 doy |
| 992. | Sir Edmunde Jeney | 1 doy |
| 993. | the prior of Buttley | 1 doy |
| 994. | the abot of Leistone | 1 doy |
| 995. | the prior of St. Petrys | 1 doy |
| 996. | the prior of Wodbryge | 1 doy |
| 997. | Thomas Tylney | 1 doy |
| 998. | the Priores of Campsey | 1 doy |
| 999. | Cristofer Harman | 1 doy |
| 1000. | the parson of Blaksalle and Matthew Harman | 1 doy |
| 1001. | the parson of Orforde and John Garlunde | 1 doy |
| 1002. | Nicholas Calle desyeryd me for to lett hyr tyll he fette her |  |
| 1003. | William Gardyner and John Pulham | 1 doy |
| 1004. | John Garnyche | 1 doy |
| 1005. | the towne of Glemham | 1 doy |
| 1006. | Thomas Fayerweyther | 1 doy |
| 1007. | John Stannard baly of Dychyngham | 1 doy |
| 1008. | the parson of Framlyngham for tytthe | 1 doy |
| 1009. | the Abbot of Bery sente to me for a dou upon seynt John's daye in Cristismas and I kyllyd her and delyveryd hyr to John Crispe and to John Chyrete and in the whey homeward they toke a corse in Holfereth and broute a soverell into the parke and kyllyd hyme there as wich I toke up the one doge in the parke and keppyd hym they made labor to Syr Willyam Rowces for the dog and I delyveryde the dog to hym. |  |
| 1010. | Sir Thomas Wyndome | 1 doy |
| 1011. | Sir Fraunces Caltheprope | 1 doy |
| 1012. | my lady Rows | 1 doy |
| 1013. | the steward of Letheringham and the prior | 1 doy |
| 1014. | the vicar of Laxtffylde | 1 doy |
| 1015. | Robert Gosnold | 1 doy |
| 1016. | Thomas Reve | 1 doy |

49

| | | |
|---|---|---:|
| 1017. | the baly of Hallsworthe | 1 doy |
| 1018. | for Doctor Car | 1 doy |
| 1019. | for John Wodiwarde | 1 doy |
| 1020. | masteresse Fastalle of Ipswiche | 1 doy |
| 1021. | Humfrey Wyngfyad | 1 doy |
| 1022. | my lady Temperley | 1 doy |
| 1023. | my lady Barnes | 1 doy |
| 1024. | mastres Aylmer | 1 doy |
| 1025. | be a warand of my lord's grace for Robert Frounceys | 1 doy |
| 1026. | Item Thomas Naunton | 1 doy |
| 1027. | Item Robert Mylls | 1 doy |
| 1028. | by awarande of my lady's grace for Master Richard Robardys | 1 doy |
| 1029. | by a warand of my lady's grace the parsone of Erle Soham | 1 doy |
| 1030. | Sir Phillipe Caltherope | 1 doy |
| 1031. | masteres Hogone | 1 doy |
| 1032. | my lady Blander Hasset | 1 doy |
| 1033. | John Lancaster | 1 doy |
| 1034. | for Thomas More | 1 doy |
| 1035. | by accomaundyment of my lord of Surrey Robert Taylor on doo and he deieryd me for to lette hyr goo tylle he fette hyr | |

1036. Thes be the lossys that I have had this winter in Framlyngham Parke;

| | |
|---|---:|
| of buks | 23 |
| of soures | 16 |
| of souerrelys | 9 |
| of prickets | 16 |
| of doyes | 38 |
| of faunys | 95 |

1037. upon oure Lady daye in lent at nyght cam in a greunde and a begle of Thomas Burels of Denyngtone and kyllyd a doe and 9 fawnys.

1038. At the 9th yere of owere sufferende lorde kyng Herry the VIII and in the 27th yere of Richard Chaumber parker of Framlyngham

1039. Thes be the losses I have had this fownyngetyme;

| | | |
|---|---|---:|
| | dyeyd this fownyngetyme | 52 fownys |

1040. Thes be the bucks I have be kyllyd this somer

| | | |
|---|---|---:|
| 1041. | In primis my lord of Surrey came to Framlyngham and kyllyde | 3 buks |
| 1042. | my lord of Norwich | 2 buks |
| 1043. | my lord Cursome | 1 buk |
| 1044. | Sir Thomas Wyndome | 1 buk |
| 1045. | Sir Rychard Wentworth | 1 buk |
| 1046. | Sir Antone Wyngfelde | 1 buk |
| 1047. | Sir Artur Hoptone | 1 buk |

| | | |
|---|---|---|
| 1048. | Sir Edmunde Jeney | 1 buk |
| 1049. | Sir William Rows | 1 buk |
| 1050. | Sir John Glemham | 1 buk |
| 1051. | John Willoube | 1 buk |
| 1052. | John Wyseman | 1 buk |
| 1053. | be a warante of my lord's grace, Sir Edwarde Ickeyngham | 1 buk |
| 1054. | Sir Philip Bothe | 1 buk |
| 1055. | the abbas of Brysyarde | 1 buk |
| 1056. | the Prioress of Cansey | 1 buk |
| 1057. | my lady Bouser | 1 buk |
| 1058. | my lady Arendelle | 1 buk |
| 1059. | mastres Fastolfe of Ipswiche | 1 buk |
| 1060. | mastres Bacone | 1 buk |
| 1061. | the Abbot of Bery | 1 buk |
| 1062. | the Prior of Ely | 1 buk |
| 1063. | the Abbot of Sipton | 1 buk |
| 1064. | the Abbot of Leystone | 1 buk |
| 1065. | the Abbot of Seynt Jonis | 1 buk |
| 1066. | the Prior of Butley | 1 buk |
| 1067. | the prior of Wodebrygge | 1 buk |
| 1068. | the prior of Crystechurche | 1 buk |
| 1069. | the prior of Seynt Peturs | 1 buk |
| 1070. | the prior of Snape | 1 buk |
| 1071. | the prior of Letheryngham | 1 buk |
| 1072. | the parson of Badingham | 1 buk |
| 1073. | the parson of Orforde | 1 buk |
| 1074. | master Kent | 1 buk |
| 1075. | John Rows for syngyng of his fyrst mase | 1 buk |
| 1076. | John Henyngham | 1 buk |
| 1077. | Fransis Caltrope | 1 buk |
| 1078. | Robard Cheke | 1 buk |
| 1079. | Thomas Russhe | 1 buk |
| 1080. | Thomas Nawntone | 1 buk |
| 1081. | Humfrey Wyngefelde | 1 buk |
| 1082. | Reynold Rows and John Packe | 1 buk |
| 1083. | John Pullome | 1 buk |
| 1084. | the parson of Chelisworth and John Garlonde | 1 buk |
| 1085. | Nicholas Calle | 1 buk |
| 1086. | Cristofer Harman | 1 buk |
| 1087. | Edmunde Gelgate | 1 buk |
| 1088. | the gylde | 1 buk |
| 1089. | master Jacsone would have had a bucke and he disired to have a doo for a  [blank] | |
| 1090. | to Nicholas Joly and my lord of Surrey's servants | 1 buk |
| 1091. | the towne of Ipswich | 1 buk |
| 1092. | the towne of Downewich | 1 buk |

| | | |
|---|---|---|
| 1093. | the towne of Sowthwolde | 1 buk |
| 1094. | the lordship of Collanes | 1 buk |
| 1095. | the prior of Bery | 1 buk |
| 1096. | the parson for his tyethe | 1 buk |
| 1097. | John Fayrechillde and the vecar of Sypton | 1 buk |
| 1098. | the parson of Holsiley and Edmunde Jacobe | 1 buk |
| 1099. | doctor Mowor | 1 buk |
| 1100. | master Edmunde Tylney | 1 buk |
| 1101. | master doctor Hare | 1 buk |
| 1102. | Reynold Gelone and Robard Smythe | 1 buk |
| 1103. | be warande of my lord's grace, the deane of his chapell | 1 buk |
| 1104. | by waraunte of my ladys grace to the deane of her chapell | 1 buk |
| 1105. | master Lege | 1 buk |
| 1106. | mastres Aylmer | 1 buk |
| 1107. | by a warante of my lord's grace, Elizabeth Janney | 1 buk |
| 1108. | mastress Lucas | 1 buk |
| 1109. | George Baker for his mariage | 1 buk |
| 1110. | Robard Mellis | 1 buk |
| 1111. | the prior of Bromhill | 1 buk |
| 1112. | master Sir Belyngeford | 1 buk |
| 1113. | Robert Hogon | 1 buk |
| 1114. | master Godsalf | 1 buk |
| 1115. | Ralff Cantrell | 1 buk |
| 1116. | be a warent of my lord's grace | 1 buk |
| 1117. | Robard Wyngefelde | 1 buk |
| 1118. | Richard Warton | 1 buk |
| 1119. | Sir Cristofer Heydon | 1 buk |
| 1120. | Thomas Reve | 1 buk |
| 1121. | John Fynchome | 1 buk |
| 1122. | be a warontar of my lord's grace, Sir Edward Boleyne | 1 buk |
| 1123. | he cam thorowe the Parke agayne the next daye and his dogges coler slypte and kyylyd me a sory soure | |
| 1124. | my lady Ichyngham | 1 buk |
| 1125. | Thomas Godfferey | 1 buk |
| 1126. | warante my lady's grace, Richard Hogone | 1 buk |
| 1127. | and he gave it mastres Baldre, Edmunde Rows and Robard Gosnolde | 1 buk |
| 1128. | Thomas Fastoff | 1 buk |
| 1129. | master doctor Car [    ] | 1 buk |
| 1130. | William Gardener and John Reynowe | 1 buk |
| 1131. | Humfferey Evertone | 1 buk |
| 1132. | John Boreman | 1 buk |
| 1133. | mastress Blanderharsete | 1 buk |
| 1134. | Thes be the lossys that I have had this somer | |

in Framlyngham Parke;

| | |
|---|---|
| of buckes | 3 |
| of sowre | [ ] |
| of sourellis | [ ] |
| of dooes | 9 |

1135.  the mundaye afore Mychelmas daye cam in a
dogge of Johnson of Denyngtone the
schoe maker and kyllyd 2 dooes. And there
the dogge was take up and I sende to hym
to wete whether he wold have the dogge
agayne and he sende me word naye: then
I hynge hym upon a tre.

## Comments

Richard Chamber's responsibilities seem to have ended with the dispatch of the deer, quick
or dead. It seems likely that the venison was salted or dried, possibly smoked, before it was
despatched, for example, to the Howard's favoured town house in Lambeth next-door to
the Archbishop's Palace. The list of non-recipients would make almost as intriguing a study
as of those actually on the 'gift-list'.

One of the most interesting poaching incidents came to court in Framlingham in July
1471. Seven years previously, Simon Cole of Worlingworth, farmer, together with others
associated with him, had entered the Park with greyhounds and taken away two does and
a buck to the guest-house of Sir Roger Aylmere in Tannington, where they were received
and entertained. This took place during the night of Monday the fourth day after the Feast
of Corpus Christi. This coincided almost to the hour with major incidents at Tannington
and Dennington during the Great Rising of 1381, when, at Tannington , the freedom of the
countryside and the right to take wild food were an issue of contention.

Of the many lines of research which it is hoped this Text will generate, the presence of
musicians in the hunting party, particularly lute-players, should provoke further investigation.
The court-rolls of Framlingham contain at least one other example of this custom to match
entry no. 385 above.

An apartment within the Great Lodge (see also text 3, p14), long after its prime in *c.*1530,
has survived in the probate inventory of Sir Robert Hitcham of 1636:
'In the Great Lodge
Item one feather bedd, Boulster and twoe pillows  forty shillings
Item twoe blanketts and an ould dornix Coverlid fower Shillings
Item one paire ( deleted) peece of Tantarides for a coverlid
three shillings fower pence.
Item one bedsted and Wallens and Curtens with Matt and Lyne fortie shillings.
Item one Turkywork Cupboard Cloth sixe shillings.
Item ould hangings about the Chamber tenne shillings.
Item one paire of Andirons and Fyer Shovell three shillings.
Item one little table and twoe ould Chaires nyne shillings.
Summa five pounds fifteene shillings fower pence'.

53

# CHAPTER 5

# Framlingham and the
# last Great Medieval Funeral
## Extracts from the Burial Rites of Thomas Howard, 1524.

## Preface

Thomas the second Howard Duke of Norfolk died at home in Framlingham Castle on 21st. May 1524. The inventory of his goods at Framlingham was compiled a week later on May 28th. Because the 'Iuellis and apparelle perteyning to my Lord's Aune body' were listed in the inventory immediately before the chapel itself (and not in his chamber), it seems he was by then lying in state there, presumably embalmed. This section of the inventory was divided between two groups, his personal ornaments and his outer clothing. The five personal ornaments were valued at over £55 and a collection of gowns and coats at just over £51. The gowns and coats were apparently placed near his corpse and intriguingly included one item 'sore worn' worth only 5s.. It was probably these garments which were used to great dramatic effect later on in his funeral ceremony. It took a month to organise the burial, considered by some historians to be the last great medieval funeral in England.

The following extract borrowed from Thomas Martin's *History of Thetford*, Appendix No. 8, describes the departure of the Duke's corpse from Framlingham on June 22nd. 1524 until its arrival at Diss on its way to Thetford Priory for burial.

## TEXT 5

'First of the order and manner of decking and garnishing the Castle of Framlingham where the noble prince died: the chamber of state, the great chamber of the hall, the chapel and the choir, were hung with black clothe, garnished with escutcheons of his arms; in the midst of the choir was a place ordained with four great principals, bearing certain lights, which burned day and night, and were made with bars about them, hung with black cloth, garnished with escutcheons of his arms, in which place the noble corpse was to lie, until such time as all things might be in readiness for his removal thence to the place where he was to rest. The black cloth, which was hung in the place before mentioned, the great court, the porter's gate etc., decked with his arms, were four hundred and forty yards. When all things were in readiness, the noble corpse was brought from his chamber into the chapel, which his grace kept prince like, for he had great pleasure in the service of God; and whilst there, three solemn masses were daily sung, and nineteen mourners kneeling about the hearse during the singing of the mass; the principal mourner, the earl of Surry, being with the king's grace on business, he appointed lord William his brother to be his deputy, who was at the head alone, and the other mourners at the sides; and about the noble corpse every night was a watch of twelve gentlemen, twelve yeomen, two yeomen ushers, and two gentlemen ushers'.

*On the twenty-second of June:*

'the body was brought forth out of the chapel, in order to its interment at Thetford and laid in a chariot, and the horses that drew the chariot were finely decked, each having four escutcheons, and on his forehead a small escutcheon beaten in oil with fine gold. Besides mourners' attendants, there were six gentlemen waiting on the chariot, to attend on the noble corpse as time required: and six knights were appointed in every town to be assistants; also attending on the chariot were four hundred staves with torches burning, bowing and every one of the bearers had a gown and hood. The order and procession to the town of Diss, in the way to Thetford, was very magnificent; first went three coaches of friars, then the minister of the church, followed by his chaplain, then the standard borne by [   ] Windham esquire, followed by knights, esquires, gentlemen of the household, treasrer, and comproller, with their staves in their hands, their horses trapped etc., then his banner borne by Sir Edward Bray, knight, and his coat of arms by Carlisle herald, the helmet and crest by Windsor herald, the target of his arms by the Clarenceux king of arms, and the coat of arms which was to be offered, borne by Garter king of arms, all of whom rode in their liveries of black, their hoods on their heads, their horses trapped, and on every one of them four escutcheons of his arms. Then came the chariot, wherein the noble corpse lord lay garnished, followed by the chief mourner alone, and in a space behind him the other mourners two and two, riding together in their long gowns of black cloth, their hoods on their heads; next after them followed the chamberlain, with his staff etc., then came the master of the horse, leading a sumpter horse, trapped in fine cloth of gold, garnished with escutcheons of his arms etc., then all the other lords, knights and gentlemen in black, according to their degree, which were to the number of nine hundred. In this order and manner they came to the town of Diss, twelve miles from the Castle of Framlingham, where they rested at night. They were met on the way by all the ministers of the towns and villages between the Castle and Diss, singing such service as thereunto belonged; and every church in towns and villages had six shillings and eight-pence, with five escutcheons of his arm, three in colours and two in metal. In the town of Hoxne, the bishop of Norwich met them in his pontificalibus, with all the procession of the place, singing the service appointed....'

The funeral itself was a masterpiece. By 6 a.m., the mourners were assembled in the Priory church to hear the first of the masses sung by the prior of Butley. Perhaps the most potent image of the entire ceremony came when Carlisle herald:

'wearing the coat of the duke deceased, went to the door of the abbey, where he conducted a knight up to the offering, wearing the armour of the duke departed, riding on a warhorse trapped with fine cloth of gold, garnished with his arms, bearing in his hands the said duke's axe, with the point downwards, and so riding to the choir door, the horse led between the son and heir of the said Fitzwalter, and the son and heir of Rice ap Thomas, then came to the sexton of the abbey, challenging the horse for his fee, on which the knight alighted, and was led up to the offering by the two who led his horse: and Carlisle herald going before him he offered his axe to the bishop with the point downwards, who delivered it to Carlisle, who stood and held the said axe on the right hand of the bishop, by Garter king of arms'.

The image of the Duke returning from the dead, followed by the subject of the hour-long funeral sermon which followed, 'Behold the lion of the Tribe of Judah triumphs', so terrified the congregation, according to the Duke's great grandson (Henry, d.1614), that 'all ran out of the church with haste' leaving the preacher Dr. Mackerell of Whitby alone in the pulpit.

## Comments

Account books to which Thomas Martin had access recorded that on the day of the internment, there was a 'magnificent entertainment, consisting of four hundred meals served', and 'liveries of gowns and coats of black cloth given to nineteen hundred persons'. The total cost of the funeral was put at £1,340. Translating this into GBP is almost a meaningless venture and would require a very large basket of carefully selected items to produce a serious figure for the purpose of price-comparison. The exercise is nevertheless entertaining. With eggs costing 1.5d per dozen at Tendring in 1526, £1 sterling could then have bought 1920 eggs, presumably of the highest quality. At a well-known high-end UK supermarket in September 2008, the £1 would have purchased 3 eggs of similar class. The difference between the two figures, 640:1, would, if applied to the figure (above) of £1340, produce an up-dated total cost for the Duke's funeral of c. £858,000. This figure is not unbelievable.

Two schools of thought surround the fate of the Duke's cadaver and of his tomb in Thetford Priory after it closed its doors in 1540. Blomefield (*History of Norfolk*, Vol. 2, p.125) believed that the Duke's bodily remains were removed (together with the freestone monument enclosing them to Framlingham church and were placed on the south side of the altar. Thomas Martin said that at the dissolution of Thetford Priory, the Duke's remains were taken to Framlingham 'and his tomb destroyed'. The two statements are not wholly incompatible. To remove the tomb from its brick plinth at Thetford necessarily entailed dismantling the monument before carting it elsewhere for reconstruction. Even if the monument which still stands south of the altar is accepted without serious doubt as that of Thomas the 3rd Howard Duke, there remains the enigma concerning Hitcham's tomb c.1636 having been placed adjacent to it, when the logical sequence might have been that Thomas the 2nd Duke should have been entombed next to the altar and Thomas 3rd Duke south of him, instead of Hitcham.

# CHAPTER 6

# Aspects of 16th Century Town Government
Proceedings of the Borough Court at Framlingham
held on October 1st 1520

## Preface

The prime documentary source for the social and economic history of life outside the walls of the Castle are the records of the proceedings in Framlingham's various courts, 'the court-rolls'. The bounds of the Manor of Framlingham appear to have followed roughly the same route as the Parish boundary although they were completely separate institutions. Within the Manor, the Borough originally consisted of the properties abutting on the market-place and Church Street, the commercial core of the town. The burgesses, owners of these premises had their own court, held upstairs in the Toll-house or Market Cross usually on Saturdays. By the 17th century, the borough had extended its limits west of the river into the suburbs or Uplands. The inhabitants of both the Manor and Borough were also regulated by the Leets, subdivisions of Loes Hundred. The verdicts and bye-laws passed by the Leet courts were frequently written up on the same rolls as the other courts, but the Leets were, again, separate organisations from both the manor and parish. Some of the Leet business appears to overlap with that of the other courts: brewers and bakers, for example, could be amerced (fined) in both the manor and leet courts within the same year. Much depended on the efficiency of the steward (the representative in court of the lord of the manor) and the zeal of the 'capital pledges', in effect the leading townsmen, as to who and what appeared on the agenda of any of the courts.

Compared with similar townships, the 16th and 17th century court-rolls of Framlingham are no better than average for the quality of their penmanship and state of preservation. The series of borough courts in particular contains several gaps and some of the manor court-rolls have strayed into other manuscript collections or have been lost altogether. That said, they remain a mine of information unobtainable from any other source.

The specimen borough court translated below was chosen solely for its legibility.

The original MS is in the Pembroke College Cambridge Archive (ref: court rolls, 1-12 Henry VIII).

## TEXT 6

Framlingham Borough - A Court General held there on Monday next after the Feast of St.Michael the Archangel in the year written above
(12th Henry VIII) Monday October 1st 1520.

Absentees:
Thomas Baldwewyn on a common plea, vouched for by George Roke.
John Pulham junior on a similar plea (vouched for) by John Pulham senior.

Members of the inquisition-

John Pulham senior
Robert Smyth
John Shymmyng
John Saye
William Saxe
William Irelond
George Roke
William Savage
Walter Spynke
Nicholas Cole
Robert Ebbys
Robert Collys
(all) sworn in as jurors.

Amerced (2s.) 6d.
Who say on oath that:
John Pulham Junior (12d.),
Nicholas Joly (2d.),
Adrian Culterman (2d.),
Thomas Hakon (2d.),
(matheus) (Harman), (2d.),
the Guardians of the Guild of the Blessed Mary (2d.),
Thomas Tye (2d.),
John Saye (2d.),
the Tenants of the tenement recently held by John Fulmerston (2d.),
and Joan Hille widow (2d.), have not cleaned out that part of the common ditch called the Towndyshe against their own lands as they ought to do, therefore etc..
And they were ordered to put things right before the next court under penalty, each of them, of 12d..

Amerced 6d. And that John Alfeld (3d.) and John Moyse (3d.) encroached on the public street there by laying down logs to the nuisance of the king's lieges. Therefore they are at mercy etc. And they were ordered to put things right before the next Feast of the Purification of the Blessed May the Virgin under penalty, each of them, of 12d.

Amerced 3d. And that the same John Alfeld deposited his excrement in the Guyldehalle yarde and caused damage to the same with his faulty gutter. Therefore he is at mercy. And he was ordered to put things right before the next court under penalty of 12d.

Amerced 3d. And that Robert Calle wasted his bond tenement called Lokyngtons by letting its buildings fall into disrepair. Therefore, etc.. And he was ordered to repair it sufficiently before the next court under penalty of 12d.

Amerced 3d. And that Ida Goldsmyth let her horse go at large in the public market-place of Framlingham to the great danger of children there. Therefore she is at mercy. And she was ordered not to do it again under penalty of 40d.

Amerced 6d. And that Robert Calle (3d.) and Joan Shemmyng (3d.) let their pigs and boars go out at large and these animals often visit the common pastures of Framlingham. Therefore they are at mercy. And they were ordered not to do it anymore under penalty of 12d..

Amerced 12d. And that Thomas Kenred did likewise against the order he had at the last court under penalty of 12d.. Therefore he is at mercy. And he was ordered not to do it again under penalty of 12d.

Amerced 18d. And that Joan Hille (6d.), Joan Alfeld (6d.) and Alice Sterkewether (6d.) are common brewers of ale and bakers of bread for sale and they sold it in breach of the king's assize. Therefore they are at mercy.

Amerced 3d. And that John Mey brought bread into the borough for sale and sold in breach of the lord's assize.

Amerced 12d. And that Margaret Joly (3d.), Margaret Calle (3d.), Agnes Pulham (3d.) and Joan Roke (3d.) are common ale-sellers and they sold it in breach of the king's assize. Therefore they are at mercy.

Sale. And that Nicholas Joly outside the court sold to Reginald Irelond the burgage tenement formerly belonging to Robert Laughter [......].

## Comments

Despite its routine appearance and content, this court nevertheless introduces several topics of interest. It lists, for example, the brewers, bakers and alehouse-keepers: their careers can be traced by reference to earlier and later rolls. Seven brewers and retailers of ale were named, most of them trading in the northeast corner of the Market-place near the junction with Church Street. Because neither the court-rolls nor the surveys of Framlingham are abuttal-rich, locating precisely the various inns and pubs of 16th century Framlingham is abnormally difficult compared with many other towns and villages. The Joly family seem to be most associated with the inn, formerly the White Hart, later re-named the Crown and Anchor. The Pulhams had several business interests including, very probably, the inn now called The Crown. The Alfeld's premises, as Text 6 illustrates, was situated up-hill from the Guildhall Yard (unless sewage defied gravity) near which, as other courts recorded, the school was then held. One of their predecessors in this property, Joan Breghouse, had been charged with running a very noisy bordello there and loudly abusing her husband by day and by night. How her activities affected the delivery of the school curriculum is not on record. Framlingham's oldest inn still trading under its original name was the White Horse (c.1617).

Before 'Merry' England was allegedly subdued by austere religious forces in the 17th century, Framlingham was indeed a lively place. Some of the inns were promoting illicit gaming, mostly cards and dice, and two or three at least had illegal 'Tennis Yards'. A few private individuals possessed a tennis court of their own: in 1507, John Staynger was fined 3d. for 'playing tennis in his mansion' and frequently climbing over the walls between himself and Richard Chamber (presumably to get his ball back) and in doing so damaged the said Richard's walls. At the southernmost tip of the Fairfield, in a meadow later called Pin Meadow, the 'Popynplayers' performed. Opinions differ as to whether this was a Puppet theatre or a quoits pitch. It may be significant that this meadow was glebe land belonging to the parish church. On present evidence, Framlingham did not have a pitch for 'camp-football', the fore-runner of soccer , but Saxtead's football ground was situated, as was often the case, on glebe land, between the church and the present A1120.

Despite this link between glebe land and recreational use, information from the court-rolls seriously challenges the tradition that it was the parish church which directed and was the engine driving Framlingham's social life. Enterprising inn-keepers such as Nicholas Joly (husband of Margaret above) were significant contenders for this role and there was also the Guild of the Blessed Mary which, although originally church-based, became a significant community organisation in its own right. There is not one single reference to a church ale being held in Framlingham church, unlike, for example, Bungay. Church 'Gatherings' were held fairly regularly, however, and seem to have been a subdued version of the large-scale 'Ales' seen elsewhere.

Framlingham Guild was a remarkable organisation. Almost at the end of its existence before it was dissolved in 1549, it was led by an alderman, in effect a mayor. It is greatly to be regretted that no example of its annual accounts of expenditure have survived. It clearly had social meetings of its own, including the Annual Feast with venison courtesy of the Duke of Norfolk (see Text 4, e.g. no.158). Extremely deft foot-work by leading parishioners appears to have kept the former guild lands from falling into the hands of state after the Guild was compulsorily wound up by Henry VIII. A parish document of 1608 listed the ways in which the Guild had employed its profits for the use of the community:
'...to the use of the Feaste of the said Guylde as also to the keepinge and releife of certen lunaticke persons and other pore people inhabytinge within the saide Towne and to the settyng forth of souldiers and other charges within the saide Towne'.

These 'other' charges were later said to include the repairing and mending of the bells, the payment of the Tax, the repairing of the church and steeple and yet more unspecified charges.

A notable absentee from the list of 'charges' was any mention of support for education. A possible explanation may be that the school at Framlingham had ceased to exist. This is unlikely. Both a grammar school and, on court-roll evidence, a school for choirboys attached to the chapel in the castle, had been active during the later Middle Ages.

Framlingham's most illustrious ex-pupil, however, was John of Lancaster (1389-1435). The son of Henry IV, brother of Henry Vth, created John Duke of Bedford in 1414, Regent of France, patron and collector of the arts (viz. The Bedford Hours), governor and, at one point, heir to the throne of England, young John received expert teaching while staying at the Castle in the household of Margaret Duchess of Norfolk in late 1397 and 1398. The state of education in the town during the Howard era seems to have slipped somewhat from these heights: the remarkably poignant will of Thomas Waller dated 1560 perhaps describes the situation most accurately:
' … the said Alice my wife shall fynde George my sonne three yeres to Gramer Schole in case there be anye kept within the toune of Framlynham or else that he maye lerne to wryte and reade such as be to be hadde within the sayd toune so that he lose not hys tyme'.

The 15th and 16th century court-rolls of Framlingham contain many examples of local government in its early stages of development. Regulation of the consumption of alcohol, the control of large domestic animals and the struggle to dispose of human sewage hygienically have already been noticed in Text 6. Food purity was another such issue: nothing quite compares in this category with the charge brought against the Framlingham butcher Robert Gleve by the court of the medieval borough of Earl Soham. Rather than leading his pack-horse to market laden with flesh for sale, he sat on it and he had 'snuffled on our meat from his nose'. Although Framlingham had several excellent wells, clean water for much of the population was taken from the Riverside. Pollution was a constant threat adding substantially to the courts' business. There was industrial effluent from tanneries, hemp (cannabis) and flax retting to contend with, not to mention the 17th century rector who dumped his night-soils upstream of the Riverside rather than carting it across town to the Common Dunghill east of Fore Street.

An excellent example of a building-permission bye-law survives from 1585:
'It is ordained that no-one shall make from new or erect any buildings to be situated on the public roads within the precinct of this (Framlingham) leet, unless it be with the assent and consent of all the inhabitants, under penalty of 5s.each'.

Framlingham had a fire in common with other 17th century towns despite its fire-regulations. Margery Harold was found to have let her chimney become decayed but lit fires on her hearth. Katerina Chamber, widow (of Richard the Parker) burned straw with fire in the common street to the grave nuisance of her neighbours… and 'allowed her pigs to go at large in the common streets (and cemetery) without rings in their snouts'.

# CHAPTER 7

# The Manor of Framlingham
# Account Roll 1543 – 4

## Preface

At Michaelmas (29th September), the officers responsible to the lord of the manor for the efficient administration of the manor were required to undergo an audit. The document which emerged from this process was known as a 'compotus' or Account-Roll. The usual format for all types of medieval and Tudor accounts began with the dated heading. The 'compotus' then divided itself into three parts, Income, Expenditure and Stock Account. By the 16th century, the inclusion of a Stock (or Grange) section was unusual, because of changes to the manorial system caused largely by the 'Peasants' Revolt' of 1381.

The income section was divided between a number of 'panels' giving details of different sources of revenue received by the manor, the 'expenses' section by 'panels' detailing the cash released for the different types of expenditure. Modern accountants have frequently expressed their admiration for the sophistication of these documents. 'Arrears' from the previous year were treated as income, for example, on the assumption that the arrears had actually been collected although they could be seen as a cash 'float' should similar arrears be carried forward to the following year. Cash released to the lord of the manor was treated as 'expenses'. To calculate the real profitability of a manor therefore involved taking a careful look at the arrears and not counting money released as an expenses. Simply deducting expenditure from income gives a false impression.

Such considerations apart, it is the contents of some of the panels that Account-Rolls are useful to historians. The 'cost of buildings' panel in the 'expenses' section, for example, can provide invaluable data to architectural historians, the 'sales of wood' in the income side to those with environmental interests.

Framlingham is, again, not well supplied with 16th century Account-Rolls. The Arundel Castle archive of the Duke of Norfolk is the most prolific source from which Text 7 is taken (ref. A1610).

## TEXT 7

*Framlyngham ad Castrum*
The account of Nicholas Joly, bailiff, Thomas Shymmyng deputy of Richard Cole, reeve, Thomas Burton, collector, and John Spynke deputy of John Erlond, hayward there, as also of Thomas Burton deputy of Robert Smythe, hayward on the part of Saxtead (viz.) from the feast of Michaelmas in the 35th year of the reign of King Henry VIII until the feast of Michaelmas next following in the 36th year of the reign of the same lord King, viz. for one whole year.

As below;
Arrears
The same (officers) render account for 26s. 8d. for the arrears of their last accounts from the preceding year as is more fully entered up at the feet of the said accounts.

Total 26s. 8d.

Fixed Rents
And for £30 16s. 8¾d. from rents of various of the lord's tenants both free and as customary tenants there to be paid at five terms of the year viz., on the Feast of St. Andrew the Apostle, £6 11s. 6d., the Annunciation of the Blessed Virgin Mary, £6 11s. 3d., Easter 13s., the Nativity of St. John the Baptist, £6 15s 3d¾., and Michaelmas £10 15s.7d. as is contained in detail in the account of Nicholas Calle formerly the bailiff there, ending at the Feast of Michaelmas in the 22nd year of the reign of the late King Henry VIIth. And for 5s.1¾d. from new rents per annum as appears on the court rolls from the time of the reigns of Edward IIIrd., Henry VIth and as is contained in detail in the account of the said Nicholas Calle ending at the aforesaid feasts at the aforesaid terms as is contained in various preceding accounts.

Total £31 22½d.

Small Leases in Framlyngham
And for £4 12s ¾d. from the leases of various lands and tenements there per annum as is contained in detail on the aforesaid account at the aforesaid terms falling within the aforesaid time.

Total £4 12s.¾d.

Small leases in Saxsted
And for 27s. 6d. from rents and leases there per annum as let to various of the lord's tenants as is contained in detail on the account aforesaid to be paid at the usual terms there, viz., for the same terms falling within the aforesaid time.

Total 27s. 6d.

Leases of Demesne Lands

And for 36s. 8d. from the lease for various lands lying in separate pieces viz.,

At Fayrefeld, 9 acres,

At Leveryngstok, 19 acres,

At Sowterswente, 19 acres,

leased to various tenants there by renting or paying for each acre 8½d less in total 2d., yet the rent used to be for each acre 10d. as is contained in the preceding account.

And for 10s. from the lease of Holegatehille leased to Joan Warde widow viz., for each acre 6d.

And for 2s. from the lease of 4 acres of land leased to theaforesaid Joan Warde per annum.

And for 8s. from the lease of 16 acres of land there per annum recently in the tenure of John Brody, leased [ MS. blank.] one counted there this year.

And for 26s. from the lease of 52 acres of land lying at Grymescrofte recently in the tenure of John Caponn by paying for each acre 6d., now leased to various of the lord's tenants there.

And for 46s. from the lease of 92 acres of land lying at Mapuldawe recently in the tenure of John Albrede by paying for this for each acre 6d., now leased per annum.

And for 36s. from the lease of 52 acres of land there lying at le Stubbyng leased to William Irelond and others of the lord's tenants there by paying for each acre 6d.

And for 5s. from the lease of 4 acres of land there for a certain parcel of meadow joined to it beneath the wood called Bradhawe leased per annum yet it recently paid 6s. per annum.

And for the lease of 26 acres of land lying in Ketylbergh recently let to John Hokestowe and others by paying for each acre 6d.

And from the profits of 43 acres of pasture newly enclosed at Bradelhawe recently in the tenure of John Bynowe which used to pay 33s. 4d. per annum viz. for the aforesaid time, but he does not answer for it here on the grounds that it is accounted for below under the heading of grazing, as is contained there.

And for 32s. 4d. from the lease of 52 acres of land lying at Saxtedewente recently let to John Eme, Roger Wyarde and others of the lord's tenants by paying for each acre 7½d. less in total 2d.

And for 11s. 8d. from the lease of 14 acres of lying at Watlyngeswente recently leased to Edmund Balle and Walter Caponn per annum viz. for each acre 6d.

And for 17s. 6d. from the lease of 26 acres of land at Vyneyarde and no more because one acre lies in the hands of the heir of John Wynter as above as leased to John Barow and others paying for each acre 6d.

And for 16d. from the increase of rent for a parcel of land called Hallefelde over and above the 12s. from ancient rent of the same charged above in the heading [MS. blank] as recently leased to Joan Warde widow by the rolls of court for the 18th year of the late King Henry VII.

And for 20d. recently received for the lease of a certain parcel of land and pasture near le Fludyate as it is enclosed with hedges and ditches recently in the tenure of William [MS blank] but for the 6s. 8d. recently received similarly for the lease of the pasture of the site of the manor recently in the tenure of Roger Banham formerly the rector of the church there of Framlyngham viz, for the whole time of this account, nothing is received here because it is charged below with other pastures, as is contained in various previous accounts.

Nor is anything received from the le Mounteys of the Castle which used to render in rent 5s. per annum or for the 2s. recently received from the lease of the ditch between the Castle and the rectory there viz. for the aforesaid time not received here on the grounds that the said pastures are leased with other lands to Alexander Drewry under the annual lease of £6 13s. 4d. for which a response was made to the lord for the aforesaid time as in the second heading following as appears more fully. Nor does he answer for the 12d. recently received for the lease of the meadow called Oldefreth viz. for the said period on the grounds that it was charged below with pasture and woodlands there as is contained in the preceding account.

Total £12 8s..

Lease of Buildings with Profits from the Stalls

From certain profits arising from the lease of the great barn there which used to render 20d. and afterwards 12d. per annum, he does not answer because it remained in the hands of the lord for his own private use throughout the aforesaid time.

Nor does he answer for the 5s. formerly received for the lease of a building within the manor next to the mere nor for the 3s. for the lease of the great Stable at the Barnes viz. for the whole time of this account, for which he does not answer for the aforesaid reason.

Nor does he answer for the lease of a stable with another building joined to it within the manor aforesaid, viz. for the same time, he does not answer for the aforesaid reason.

Nor does he answer a profit arising from the stalls of the butchers, tanners and other craftsmen there this year because an answer was given to the lord afterwards under the heading of profits of the Fairs.

Nor does he answer for the lease of a shop in the marketplace there which used to render 3s. 4d, formerly let to Thomas Symonde mercer, on the grounds that it remained in the hands of the lord for lack of a tenant.

Nor does he answer for the lease of another shop in the market-place aforesaid which used to be let for [MS. blank] per annum for the aforesaid reason.

Nor does he answer for the lease of a room in the end of the Toll-house viz. for the aforesaid time for the aforesaid reason, yet it used to render 2s. per annum and afterwards 12d., as is contained in preceding accounts.

Total nothing.

Rent of Escheated Lands

From the rent of a messuage or burgage lying in Framlyngham market-place in the lands of the lord seized in the name of an escheat, formerly John Stoke's and others', which used to render 5d. and before that 10d. viz. for the aforesaid time, he does not answer on the grounds that it was charged above under the heading of Fixed Rents within the total 5s. 1¾d. as is contained in detail in the account of the bailiff there ended at Michaelmas in the 17th year of the reign of King Henry 7th. Nor does he answer for the 4d. formerly received for the rent of a parcel of land lying in the market street there next to the Tenement Gilbert viz. for the same time on the grounds that it remained unoccupied in the hands of the lord for lack of a hirer on the oath of the accountant. But he does answer for 53s. 4d. from the rent of a place of land formerly Thomas Lokyngton's with 17 acres of meadow and pasture in the hands of the lord seized in the name of an escheat as let to various persons for an annual rent.

Total 53s. 4d.

New Rents

And for 2d. from new rent of a parcel of vacant land lying in Framlyngham market-place as it is let to William Holande by rolls of court etc.

And for 2d. from the new rent of another parcel of land containing by estimate in length 7 perches and in breadth 14 perches lying next to the riverbank and the Maneryarde as it is let to Richard Owles by rolls of court from the 18th year of the late King Henry 7th.

And for 2s. 8d. from the new lease of three and a half acres of land in Parham recently in the tenure of William Rameshulte per annum.

And for 4s. 8d. from the new lease of a certain meadow in Parham called Lokyngton's Mede recently Thomas Ramshult's abutting on the meadow belonging to the Priory of Campsey towards the north, falling into the hands of the lord in the name of escheat for lack of an heir of the said Thomas, over the 2s. from the ancient rent of the same meadow charged above under the title of Fixed Rents as let to Robert Godwyn for the term of 60 years this year ending being the 11th as appears more fully set out in the indenture.

And for 2d. for a new rent in the charge of the reeve there per annum.

And for 2d. from the new rent of William Nuttelle for a piece of waste land there per annum.

And for 12d. from the new rent of Alexander Gylbert for the site of the mill called the Myllhill per annum.

And for 4d. from the new rent of Robert Gylbert for a piece of waste and vacant land and pasture per annum.

And for 21½d. for the new rent of various parcels of land in the tenure of various of the lord's tenants there per annum.

And for 17s 6d. from the increase of rent for the three demesne closes called Sowterswent, Fayrefelde and Newclose as let to Nicholas Joly over and above the 35s. 10d from the ancient rent of the same closes as appears by a certain bill for this, shown and examined in the 30th year of the present king Henry 8th.

Total 28s.7½d.

Works and Custumary Services.

And for £22 11s.1½.,¼d., 1/8d., arising from the rents and works and various customary services of the lord's custumary tenants there, at various prices valued between them as appears in the details contained in the bailiff's account there ending at Michaelmas in the 20th year of the reign of King Henry 7th, to be paid at the usual terms there viz. for the same terms falling within the aforesaid time.

Total £22 11s. 1d., ½d., ¼d.,1/8d..

Lease of Pasture
And for 53s. 4d., from rent of a pasture called Braddelhawe as recently let to Nicholas Joly by [MS. blank] the lord Duke's supervisor for the term of [MS. blank] years with [MS. blank] from the increase in the annual rent over that which used to be paid at the terms of the Annunciation of the Blessed Mary the Virgin and Michaelmas in equal portions viz. for the two terms falling within the time for this year of his term [MS. blank].

Grazing of the Park
For the various sums of money received from annual grazing within the lord's park there, viz. for the time of this account, he does not answer on the grounds that the grazing of this park was not sufficient for the wild animals being in the same park, if there had been any grazing to be had during this same time, for which reason no grazing was had for this same time on the oath of the said accountant.

Total Nothing.

Profits of the Fair and Market
But he does answer for 16s. from the profits of a Fair held there this year at Michaelmas, at the close of this account, in the charge of the bailiff there, as appears in a certain gathering of paper for this purpose, on this account shown and examined.

Total 16s.

Sale of Brick
And for 7s. 9d. for the price of 300 bricks, and for the price of 18 combs of coals price per comb, 4d., as sold to various persons by the said accountant this year as appears on the aforesaid paper gathering on this account shown and examined. And for 27s. received for the price of 14 cartloads of thatch and 500 tiles sold there this year as appears in the aforesaid gathering in greater detail.

Total 34s.9d.

Waifs and Strays
And from a certain profit arising from waifs and strays or from the goods and chattels of felons and fugitives in any part or parts of this demesne this year viz. for the aforesaid time, he does not answer on the grounds that nothing of this casual nature came in there on the oath of the accountant.

Total Nothing

Sales of Wood.
But he does answer for the 14s. 4d. for the price of 12 cartloads of wood or underwood sold there this year sold as appears on the aforesaid paper gathering account shown and remaining on this account.

Total 14s. 4d.

Perquisites of Court.

And for £17 2s. 5d. from the perquisites of a leet and [blank] court held there this year with 6s. 8d. from the common fine and with £15 2s. 5d. from land fines as appears by the rolls of the same, shown on this account. And for 3s. 5d. from the perquisites of a court held at Ashe as appears by the rolls of the same, shown and examined on this account. And for 10s.6d. from the perquisites of a court held within the borough of Framlyngham this year as appears by the rolls of the same, shown and examined on this account. And for 113s. from the perquisites of a leet and of a court held at Saxted with 3d. from the common fine and with 13s. land fines as appears by the rolls of the same shown and examined on this account.

Total £23 9s. 4d.

## TOTAL OF RECEIPTS WITH ARREARS
£115 16s. 11d, ½d, ¼d, 1/8d..

Rents Paid Out

The same (officer) accounts in annual rents paid out to various persons written below, viz. to Ketylberghe Hall 12d., to the heirs of Lord John Ketylberghe 19d., to the heirs of John Holbroke 12d., to John Gaunte 6d., to Robert Drane 1d., to the Church of Framlyngham for a lamp to burn before the high altar, 5s., and to the same church for wax-scot 13½d., viz. in payment of this rent resolute for the aforesaid time as allowed on the preceding account, 10s. 5½d.

Total 10s. 5½d.

Tithes Paid

And in money paid out to the rector of Framlyngham Church for tithes of grazing in the park there this year at the rated value of the same charged above, after all expenses in the hunting season there each year, 20s.4d.

Total 20s. 4d.

Loss and Reductions in Rents.

And in the loss of rents from various lands and tenements in Framlyngham and Saxted being in the hands of the lord on the grounds that each of the lands and tenements remain in the hands of the lord for lack of notice and each of the same lands and tenements are being let for lesser sums than those for which they used to be let, of which the parcels and reasons more clearly appear in the 7th year of Edward 4th viz. in the allowance of this type of loss during the said time as was allowed in the preceding accounts, 52s.7d., ½d. ¼d.

And in the allowance of works and customs of lands and tenements being likewise in the hands of the lord in Saxted as appear similarly in greater detail in the parcels and reasons on the aforesaid account viz. in the allowance of all types of loss as were allowed in various preceding accounts, 4s.

And in the allowance of rent of two acres of demesne land charged above at 15s per annum and [ ]acre(s) recently in the tenure of the Rector of the church of Framlyngham charged above at 2s. per annum on the grounds that they are within the lord's precinct there for enlargement of the same as is contained in the preceding account, 2s.

And in the loss of rent of a piece of land with a barn and other buildings built on it formerly in the tenure of Thomas Lokyngton charged above at 14s per annum on the grounds that they are now leased to John Stoge paying for this only 20d. per annum on the grounds that it could not be let for a higher sum and thus there was a loss of rent for the aforesaid term of 12s. 4d.

And in the loss of rent of a meadow in Parham called Wydderleys formerly held by Thomas Lokyngton charged above at 5s. per annum on the grounds that it is let to William Rameshulte for only 2s. per annum because also the greater part of it is flooded with water and in no way could it be let for a higher price, on the oath of the accountant, and thus there is a loss of 3s..

And in the decrease of rent of a close containing by estimate 5 acres and a half charged above at 6s. 8d. per annum on the grounds that it was let to John York for life by the annual payment of only 4d. and because also the lord of the manor shall have the reversion of the said John's tenement in which he lives immediately after the death of the said John , which same John has died, as is testified  on this account, and thus there is an allowance of rent during the aforesaid term of 6s. 4d.

And in the decrease of rent of a parcel of land formerly in the tenure of Thomas Lokkyngton charged above at 2s. 6d. per annum because it remains in the hands of the lord and no profit came from it on the grounds that it is not known where this land is situated, for which reason it is not known how any person or persons can be distrained, as he says on oath, 2s. 6d.

And in the decrease of rent of a certain pasture called Oldefryth charged above at 40s. per annum because it remains in the hands of the lord over the 20s. raised from this from John Gabone this year because no-one wanted to take this pasture for a higher price during the said term on the oath of the accountant and so there is a loss of 20s..

And in the loss of rent of four and a half acres of land lying within the said lord's park there charged above under the heading of Assised Rents at 6s per annum because it remains in the hand of the lord as the said accountant says on his oath at 6s.

Total 118s. 9¾d.

Bailiff's Fee

And in the fee of Nicholas Joly Bailiff there receiving 60s.10d. per annum by reason of his exercising and occupying this same office, viz. in the allowance of this fee for this aforesaid term as used to be allowed for similar fees to the same Nicholas or others holding or occupying the same office in various previous accounts, 60s.10d.

Total 60s.10d.

Costs and Making of Hay

And in the allowance made to the hayward of Saxsted for 12 custumary mowing-works about the mowing in the lord's meadow on the part of Saxsted, price of each mowing-work 1½d. in total 18d.

And in the allowance made to the same Hayward for 52 summer works in the same meadow by estimation on the part of Saxted about the preparation of the same hay, price of each work 1d. ½d, ¾d., in total 2s.2d.

And in the allowance made to the Hayward of Framlyngham for 8 custumary mowing-works about the mowing of the lord's meadow there, price of each mowing-work, 1½d., in total, 12d.

And in the allowance made to the bailiff there for the mowing, tossing and making of the hay from the lord's meadow there called Newmedew within the park there and for the carriage of the same to the lord's grange there for the expenses of the wild deer, horses and other of the lord's animals and those of his officers as appears on a gathering of paper shown for this on this account and examined, 21s.

And in the allowance made to the reeve there for carriage of 27 loads of hay from a certain meadow of the lord called le Hallmede to the same grange of the lord, taking for each cartload 3d. as appears in the preceding account, similarly the allowance made of 12d. for le goldyng of the same hay as appears on a certain gathering of paper shown on this account and kept in he hands of the auditor, 7s. 9d.

And in the allowance made to the bailiff there for the carriage of 18 cartloads of hay from the said grange to the park there to various places in the same park for the sustenance of the deer in winter, strewing and dividing it, taking for each cartload 8d. as appears in the same gathering of paper yet there was once only an allowance of 6d. per cartload as appears more clearly in the preceding accounts, 12s.

And in the allowance made to the same bailiff for the cutting out and clearing of the water-channels within the park there this year as appears by the aforesaid paper shown on this account and examined, 5s. 4d.

Total  49s. 4d.

The Expenses of the Steward and Expenses of the other officers.

And in the expenses of the steward, other officers and tenants of the lord at Framlyngham, 26s., Asshe, 2s., and Saxted, 8s. 8d.,  as much for the holding of courts there this year as for having and maintaining good governance on this demesne., 37s.

And in the stipend of the auditor's clerk writing this account and all the sections of the same, just as the similar allowance was made for the same clerk in various preceding accounts, 6s. 8d.

And in the expenses of the said  accountants, viz. the collector, 20d., the reeve, 20d., and the hayward of Framlyngham 20d., and the hayward on the part of Saxted, 2s. 8d., coming from their homes to Keninghale for the hearing and completing of this account in the presence of the auditor, 5s. 8d.

Total 49s. 4d..

Repairs.
And in money paid on the said account for various repairs made there this year, viz., the making of a ditch at Sowterswente, 13s. 4d., the firing or manufacture of (20000) tiles ordered for the repair of the castle there at 2s. per thousand, 40s., for carriage of clay from the park to the kiln, 18s., for carriage of under-wood from Snell's Pightelle to the kiln, 9s., and for the felling of wood and under-wood ordered both for the Tyle kyllne and for timber ordered for the repair of the castle and for the making of shingles, 16s. 1d., for the hewing and sawing of 7 trees in Snell's aforesaid., 10s., 3d., for the splitting and manufacture of 5000 shingles ordered for the repair of the castle, 5s., for the purchase of nails called lath nayle, 8s., for mending of the park pale there, 18d., for the purchase of 3 locks and staples for the park gates there, 3s. 2d., in total as appears on the gathering aforesaid on this account. Exhibited and retained in the hands of the lord's auditor, £6 4s. 4d.

Total  £6  4s. 4d.

Releases of cash.
And in money released to Robert Holdyche, armiger, the receiver of the almighty Prince Thomas Duke of Norfolk there at various times, viz., on one occasion by the hands of Thomas Shimmyng the deputy of Richard Cole the reeve there,  on the 3rd  May in the 36th year of King Henry 8th, 100s., on another occasion by the hands of the same reeve at the completion of his account, £9 12s. 4d., on another occasion by the hands of Thomas Burton the Collector there on the said 3rd May in the same 36th of the aforesaid king, £8 10s., on another occasion by the same collector at the completion of his account, £15 7s. on another occasion by the same Collector likewise released after the completion of his account £6 4s. 8¼d., on another occasion by the hands of John Spynke deputy of John Erlonde the hayward there on the aforesaid day and year, £6, on another occasion by the hands of the same John at the completion of his account, £14 16s. 5¼d., on another occasion by the hands of the said John after the completion of his account aforesaid, 26s. 8d., on another occasion by the hands of Thomas Button, deputy of Robert Smythe the Hayward on the part of Saxted on the said May 3rd and 36th year of the aforesaid king, 100s., and on another occasion by the hands of the aforesaid Thomas at the completion of his account, £13 7s. 7d.,  in total as appears both on the 8 bills in the hands of the said receiver signed on this account, made good and remaining in the memoranda of the account for this year and by 2 other bills by the acknowledgement of the same receiver on his account in the hands of the lord's auditor.

Total £85 4s. 8¼d.

## TOTAL OF ALL ALLOWANCES AND RELEASES
£106 9s. 6d. 1/2d. 1/4d.

And there is owed £9 7s. 5d. from certain allowances of the hayward of Framlyngham, 4s. 2½d., from uncollectable court fines imposed on various persons in the court-rolls of this year for various trespasses committed by them within this demesne because some of these persons are paupers and of no value and others of them are resident outside this demesne and in no way can their fines be collected, on the oath of the said Hayward on this account. And there is owed £9. 3s. 2½d. From which

(Charged) against the heir of Arthur Russhe armiger for the profit of his lands as appear in the rolls of court of this year because the said lands are in the hands of the lord King during the minority of the same heir , therefore it appears here as above until it can be raised from his arrears £6 13s 4d. (which is charged on the account of the receiver there this year as is detailed there).

(Charged) against the occupier of the lands and tenements formerly belonging to the Priory of Butley called [.......], 7s. per annum on the grounds that all the lands and tenements belonging or pertaining to the said former priory are in the hands of the lord king by reason of the dissolution of the same priory, therefore it appears here as above until it be known whether the lord Duke should be charged with payment of the same rent or not this year from his arrears, 7s.

(Charged) against the heir of Thomas Baldrey for the rent of certain lands in Ketylberghe at 14½d. per annum because all the lands and tenements are in hands of the lord King during the minority of the same heir therefore it appears here as above until it can be raised for this year from his arrears, 14½d.

(Charged) against the heir of Arthur Russhe armiger for the profit of his lands as appear in the rolls of court of this year because the said lands are in the hands of the lord King during the minority of the same heir therefore they appear here as above until it is possible to raise the money from his arrears, 20d.

(Charged) against John Pereson for part of his 50s. fine as is more clearly laid out in the rolls of court for the 32nd year of the present King, therefore it appears here until a scrutiny can be had in the court rolls or surveys for a true appraisal of who holds these lands.

(Charged) against Thomas Button for part of his 73s. 4d. fine this year as appears in the court-rolls of this year over the 53s. 4d. paid to the receiver there this year and the remainder to be paid at the next account this year from his arrears, 20s. (charged in the receiver's account there this year as is detailed there).

(Charged) against the accountants themselves, viz. Nicholas Joly bailiff there, nil, Thomas Shymmyng deputy for Richard Coole the reeve, nil, Thomas Burton the Collector, nil, John Spynke the deputy of John Erlonde the hayward there, nil, as also Thomas Button the deputy of Robert Smythe the Hayward on the part of Saxted, nil, this year for their arrears, nil.

And it (the account) is cleared.

## Comments

Although in no way extraordinary, this account nevertheless contains a wide variety of information useful to local historians in particular. It establishes beyond all reasonable doubt that the original Manor House and associated buildings were sited between the church and the Mere: there is presumably a late-Saxon manor house and farmstead waiting to be excavated in what is now the Rectory Garden. If it were needed, the evidence that the Park was overstocked with deer is implied by the attention paid to the gathering and storage of hay for their consumption. The brick-kiln in the Park is nicely documented: the pit within the Park which supplied the clay was later to be used as a swimming-pool. That 20,000 tiles and 5000 locally-sourced shingles were among the building materials expended on the maintenance of the castle demonstrates that it was being kept in a reasonable state of repair by Thomas the 3rd Howard Duke. This helps to explain why Queen Mary chose Framlingham Castle from which to launch her *coup d'etat* in 1553, nine years after this account was drawn up.

As could have been predicted, the large sum of £85+ in cash released to the Duke' treasury is the largest item in any section of the account. Borrowing, with utmost caution if not outright scepticism, the ratio of £640:£1 from Text 5, this figure translates to a sum in excess of *c.* £50,000. This manor was immensely profitable: about three-quarters of its income was from rents.

# CHAPTER 8

# The Survey of Framlingham, 1547

Christopher Peyton's Terrar for Edward VIth
(excluding Saxtead).

## Preface

Two versions of Sir Christopher Peyton's Survey of Framlingham have survived. The earlier volume, very much a 'working' document containing many contemporary and later amendments with marginal notes, is now Bodleian Library Oxford MS. Gough Suffolk 2. The 'fairer' copy here translated, became Pembroke College Cambridge MS. Lz (zeta). Both versions are dated 1547 when the Framlingham estate became a crown possession following its forfeiture on the charge of treason by Thomas Howard 3rd Duke of Norfolk.

The two versions differ substantially in the way they collate the data gathered for the survey. In the finished (Pembroke) version, Peyton listed the tenants according to their tenurial class, viz. freeholders, burgesses, copy-holders and others. Some individuals therefore appear several times under different headings throughout the survey. This creates additional difficulties in ascertaining, for example, where an individual tenant actually lived. The Bodleian version, on the other hand, tended to collect together most or all of the various pieces of property held by an individual, whatever the status of the land or buildings involved, and then leave it in a rough and, sometimes illegible, pile. With caution therefore, Pembroke MS. Lz (zeta) was preferred here for use as Peyton's standard text, with annotations from the other manuscript sources added as appropriate.

In this translation from the Latin, individual entries have been numbered by the editor to facilitate research. Unfortunately, this survey was largely constructed from the evidence of court-rolls rather than by precise measurement on site of lands and tenements. There are therefore few abbutals given, making reconstruction of the town and manor that much the more difficult.

## TEXT 8

*The domain or Manor of Framlingham ad Castrum with the members in the county of Suffolk*

*The survey made there by Sir Christopher Peyton the king's surveyor of all and singular the possessions of the court of augmentations and of the worshipful crown royal in the county of Suffolk on the 21st day of November in the year of the reign of the Lord Edward by the grace of God King of England, France and Ireland, Defender of the Faith and on earth the supreme head of the Anglican and Irish church after the conquest of England the first (1547)*

Part of the possessions of Thomas recently Duke of Norfolk attainted of high treason.

The free tenants in Framlingham aforesaid.

1. William Dowsing holds freely certain lands lying in Framlingham aforesaid formerly Grenes and he pays for this at the feasts of the Annunciation of the Blessed Mary the Virgin and of St. Michael the Archangel equally per annum:
   viz: in  the charge of the collector　　　　　　　　3s. 10d.

2. The aforesaid William Dowsing holds freely various lands formerly Fulmerstones and pays for this at the aforesaid feasts equally per annum:
   viz: 2s. 2d.[deleted] in the charge of the collector 3s. 2d.

3. Nicholas Stebbing holds freely certain lands there formerly Edward Newmans and pays for this at the aforesaid feasts per annum:
   viz: in the charge of the collector　　　　　　　4d.

4. The same Nicholas holds freely various lands there formerly Masons and pays for this per annum:
   viz: in the charge of the collector　　　　　　　4d.

5. John Chamber holds freely there a piece of land called Stoffers (8½d.) and pays for this at the aforesaid feasts equally per annum:
   viz: in the charge of the collector　　　　　　　8½d.

6. The same John holds freely a pightle called Hulver Pigthle and pays for this per annum:
   viz: in the charge of the hayward
   one hen worth 2d.

7. Katherine Chamber holds freely there a tenement called Maughtells Tenement paying for this at the aforesaid feasts equally per annum:
   viz: in the charge of the collector　　　　　　2s. 2d.

8. The same Katherine holds freely there a pightle called Peris pigthle (12d.)

75

alias Coterowe Rente, and a parcel of land (3d.) formerly Nutthille(s) and a croft called Kings Croft (6d) and three roods of land (3d.) formerly John Tendisloves, paying in total at the aforesaid feasts equally:
viz: in the charge of the collector      2s.

9. Anna Hill widow holds freely various (3s. 8d.) lands there formerly [ ] and for various lands formerly David Carter's (2d.) and for a small close called Oldewayes (8d. ) Closse paying for this in total at the aforesaid feasts equally
viz: in the charge of the collector      4s. 6d.

10. John Smithe holds freely certain lands there and pays for this at the aforesaid feasts per annum:
viz. in the charge of the collector      15½d.

11. Robert Colles holds freely a close called Newmarketclose (6d.) and another close called Sturmyns (12d.) and another close called Watlyngs and two acres and a half of land lying between the lands formerly John Wright senior (5d.), paying in total at the aforesaid feasts equally per annum:
viz: in the charge of the collector      2s. 2d..

12. William Foxe holds freely there various lands and pays for this at the feasts aforesaid equally per annum:
viz: in the charge of the collector      2s. 10d.

13. Reginald Gibbone holds freely a meadow called Stogis meadewe and pays for this at the feasts aforesaid per annum:
viz: in the charge of the collector, 6d. and
for 'mooteffee' 1½d.      7½d.

14. The aforesaid Reginald Gibbone holds another meadow called Olffrey medowe containing by estimate one acre and pays for this at he feasts aforesaid:
viz. In the charge of the collector      2d.

15. John Barkeley holds freely during the lifetime of his wife Margaret, formerly the wife of Robert Calle, a shop (4d.) there and three roods of lying near le Wilde Hey and pays for this per annum at the aforesaid feasts:
viz. in the charge of the collector      6d.

16. Francis Pulham holds freely there certain lands and pays for this per annum:
viz in the charge of the collector      9s.

17. The same Francis holds freely certain (lands) there formerly Stogies (6d.) and a barn (4d.) there formerly Sayes and for lands formerly Lokkingtons (8d.) and pays for this at the aforesaid feasts in total per annum equally:
viz: in the charge of the collector      18d.

18. Matthew Harman holds freely (7s. 2d.) a tenement called Richers tenement

with various lands called (2s. 4d.) Hell Broks formerly John Fulmerstones and various lands (17d.) formerly Kegills and three shops (12d.) in Framlingham market-place, and for certain lands(2d) lying in the said market-place and a certain barn called Trussis Berne (3d.) and for lands formerly John Trussis (5s. 5d.) and pays for this at the aforesaid feasts equally per annum, total:

viz: in the charge of the collector          17s. 8d.

19. Thomas Burton holds freely certain lands (6d.) there formerly Jeffreys and various other pieces of land formerly John Wrights (2d.) lying in Melfylde once John Sayes and pays for this at the aforesaid feasts equally per annum:

    viz. in the charge of the collector          8d.

20. The aforesaid Thomas Burton holds freely various lands lying in Framlingham and pays for this at the aforesaid feasts equally per annum:

    viz. in the charge of the hayward for four hens    8d.

    in the charge of the collector          9s. 8d.

    and for motfee 10½d.

    (total)          11s. 1½d.

21. The same Thomas holds freely (4d.) a close called Yorkeclose formerly John Calle' and a tenement (4d.) calle Trues tenement formerly John Chirchhawe' and two acres (5d.) and a half of land there called wikerelle Lands and pays for this at the aforesaid feasts equally per annum:

    viz in the charge of the collector          13d.

    and for motfee          ½d.

    (total)          13½d.

22. The widow of Henry Rossington holds freely various lands (22d.) formerly Robert Alredde' and once John Paston's and various lands there formerly Buckenames (2s.) and various other lands (4d.) formerly Morfulles and pays for this per annum:

    viz: in the charge of the collector          4s. 2d. [deleted]

    and for motfee          3½d.

    (total)          4s. 5d.

23. George Calle holds freely various lands there formerly Thomas Wright and afterwards Nicholas Calle and a close called Dowe Crofte and pays for this per annum:

    viz in the charge of the collector          4s. 8¼d.

24. Anthony Russhe holds freely a close called Countes Crofte Closse and pays for this per annum:

    viz: in the charge of the collector          8d.

25. John Corrant junior holds freely a Tenement there called Bachelers Tenement and pays for this at the aforesaid feast per annum:

    viz. in the charge of the collector          2s.

26. Richard Butone holds freely a field called Carmans Felde and pays for this at the aforesaid feasts per annum:
    viz: in the charge of the collector                    2s.

27. The Rector of Framlingham holds freely various lands there and pays for this at the aforesaid feasts equally per annum:
    viz.                                                   5s. 5½d.
    and for motfee                                         11d.
    (total)                                                5s. 5d & ½ farthing.

28. Richard Sheming holds freely certain lands there and pays for this per annum:
    viz: in the charge of the collector                    9d.

29. Robert Jargafelde holds freely various lands there and pays for this per annum:
    viz in the charge of the collector                     14d.
    and for motfee                                         4d.
    (total)                                                18d.

30. Thomas Hacon holds freely by right of his wife various lands there and pays for this per annum:
    viz:  in the charge of the collector                   12d.

31. George Spalding holds freely various lands there formerly William Thatcher and pays for this at the aforesaid feasts per annum:
    viz in the charge of the collector                     12d.
    and for motfee                                         2d.
    (total)                                                14d.

32. John Balles  holds freely various lands there and pays for this at the aforesaid feasts equally per annum:
    viz: in the charge of the collector                    22d.

33. Widow Ewstas holds freely various lands there and pays for this per annum:
    viz: in the charge of the collector                    5d.

34. Anthony Wingffelde knight holds 16 acres of great-tenure land formerly let by copy of court-roll but afterwards leased to him as free land by Thomas late Duke of Norfolk as is set out more fully in the rolls of a court held on Monday next before the Feast of St Michael the Archangel in the 26th year of the late King Henry the Eighth and he pays for at the aforesaid feasts equally per annum:
    viz:  in the charge of the hayward                     10s 8d.and four hens, 8d.
    and in the charge of the collector                     3s. 4d.
    (total)                                                14s. 8d.

35. The same Anthony holds freely various other lands there and pays for this at the aforesaid feasts per annum:
    viz: in the charge of the collector                    12s. 9¾d.

78

36. Thomas Chamber holds freely certain lands there called Pinfoldes and pays for this at the aforesaid feasts equally annum:

| | |
|---|---|
| viz: in the charge of the hayward for one hen | 2d. |
| in the charge of the collector | 7s. |
| and for motfee | 2d. |
| (total) | 7s. 4d. |

37. The Master and Brethren of the Gild of Disse hold freely to the use of the gild aforesaid various lands formerly in the tenure or occupation of William Hollande and pay for this per annum:

| | |
|---|---|
| viz in the charge of the collector | 13s. 4d. |

38. The same (master and brethren) hold freely three acres of small-tenure land there formerly held by the aforesaid William per annum:

| | |
|---|---|
| viz: in the charge of the hayward | 18d. |

39. The same (master and brethren) hold freely various lands there formerly Foxes (16d.) and various lands (8d.) formerly Watlings and pay for this:

| | |
|---|---|
| viz: in the charge of the collector | 23d. |
| and for motfee | 16½d. |
| (total) | 3s. 3½d. |

40. The aforesaid (master and brethren) hold freely various lands there and pay per annum:

in the charge of the hayward for one hen and a half   3d.

41 John Brocke holds freely certain lands there and pays for this per annum:

| | |
|---|---|
| viz: in the charge of the collector | 2d. |

42. William Smith holds freely various lands there formerly Richers and pays per annum:

viz. in the charge of the hayward one hen  worth  2d.

43. John Calle holds freely an enclosure called Shortes Closse and pays for this per annum at the aforesaid feasts equally:

| | |
|---|---|
| viz:  in the charge of the collector | 2s. ½d. |

44. John Nuthill holds freely a Tenement (4s.) called Humbalds tenement by estimate 12 acres of land once John Oxe and six acres (12d.) of land of tenement Arberts and half an acre of land formerly Ralph Seman lying near Oldhey and a tenement (6s. 8d.) John Wright and pays for this per annum at the aforesaid feasts:

| | |
|---|---|
| viz:  in the charge of the collector | 11s. 9d. |

45. Thomas Rouse armiger holds freely certain lands there formerly held by the lord of Bardolph and pays for this per annum at the aforesaid feasts equally:

| | |
|---|---|
| viz: in the charge of the collector | 2½d. |

| | |
|---|---|
| Total of all the Free Tenants in Framlingham | £8  7s. 3¼d. |
| whereof in the charge of the hayward for rent | 2s. 2d. |
| and for thirteen and a half hens | 2s. 3d. |
| in the charge of the collector for rent | £7  8s. 2¾d. |
| for motfee | 4s. 8d. |

Memorandum that the tenants above mentioned are bound to no other service but to sute of Courte onlye.

Free tenants of the Burgage Tenements by custom of the manor of Framlingham aforesaid.

46. Katerina Chamber widow holds freely by custom of the manor five burgages and a half, viz., two burgages formerly Perrys, two other burgages called Cranes, three quarters of another burgage formerly John Arnolds, three quarters of another burgage called Bareffotts, and pays for this viz for each burgage 5d. to be paid at the feast of the Annunciation of the Blessed Mary the Virgin and St. Michael the Archangel equally per annum in total: viz: all in the charge of the collector          2s. 3½d.

47. Robert Colles holds freely  by custom of the manor one burgage there and pays for this at the aforesaid feasts per annum at the aforesaid feasts equally: viz: in total in the charge of the collector          5d.

48. William Foxe holds freely by custom of the manor two burgages there and pays for this per annum at the aforesaid feasts equally: viz: in total in the charge of the collector          10d.

49. Reginald Gibbon holds freely by custom of the manor five burgages and three-quarters lying in Framlingham aforesaid from which two burgages and a half were formerly Matthew Harmanne' and two other burgages and a quarter were formerly John and William Irelonde's and one other formerly Thomas Cade's and pays for this per annum at the aforesaid feasts: viz: in total in the charger of the collector          2s. 3¾d.

50. Richard Saverne holds freely by custom of the manor one burgage and three-quarters of a burgage there and pays for this per annum by paying at the aforesaid feasts equally:
    viz: in the charge of the collector                    8¾d. [deleted],
    and for motfee                                          ¾d. [deleted].
    (whole entry struck through and note added ' because afterwards').

51. John Barkeley holds freely by right of his wife Margaret one burgage and three quarters of a burgage lying in Framlingham aforesaid by custom of the manor and pays for this at the aforesaid feasts equally per annum: viz. in total in the charge of the collector          8¾d.

52. Francis Pulham holds freely by custom of the manor two burgages there formerly Wulnaughes and pays for this for each burgage 5d. in total paying at

the feasts per annum:
viz: in total in the charge of the collector      10d.

53. John Nuthille holds freely by custom of the manor four burgages lying in Framlingham aforesaid and pays for each burgage 5d. by paying in total at the aforesaid feasts per annum:
viz. in the charge of the collector      20d.

54. Thomas Burton holds freely one burgage there by custom of the manor and pays for this at the feasts aforesaid per annum:
viz. in total in the charge of the collector      5d.

55. Anthony Russhe holds freely by custom of the manor two burgages lying in Framlingham aforesaid and pays for each burgage 5d. by paying at the aforesaid Feasts:
viz. in total in the charge of the collector      10d.

56. Margaret Jolye formerly the wife of Richard Lawter holds freely by custom of the manor two burgages there and pays for this per for each burgage 5d. by paying at the aforesaid feasts per annum:
viz in total in the charge of the collector      10d.

57. Anna Hille widow holds freely by custom of the manor two burgages there and pays for this for each burgage 5d. paying at the feasts aforesaid equally per annum:
viz. in total in the charge of the collector      10d.

58. Thomas Hacon holds freely by custom of the manor in the right of his wife one burgage and a quarter of a burgage and pays for this at the aforesaid feasts per annum:
viz. in total in the charge of the collector      6¼d.

59. George Spalding holds freely by custom of the manor two burgages there and pays for each burgage 5d. paying at the aforesaid feasts equally per annum:
viz. in total, in the charge of the collector      10d.

60. John Spinke holds freely by custom of the manor one burgage there and pays for this at the feasts aforesaid equally:
viz in total in the charge of the collector      5d.

61. Richard Johnson holds freely one burgage there by custom of the manor there and pays for this at the feasts aforesaid per annum:
viz. in total in the charge of the collector      5d.

62. Peter Bradshawe holds freely by custom of the manor two burgages there formerly John Pulham junior and pays for each burgage 5d. paying at the aforesaid feasts per annum in total:
viz in total in the charge of the collector      10d.
Bod: 'now Griffinus Bradshaw.'

63. Robert Lawter holds freely one burgage there formerly Robert Corbolde by custom of the manor and pays for this at the aforesaid feasts per annum: viz. in total in the charge of the collector          5d.

   Bod: 'William Michell, and Nicholas Michell (d.1625) and Thomas Michell(1625) and they hold in three separate parcels. The aforesaid Robert holds the feeding of le Castell Banks and pays for this per annum 4d paid totally in the rent of the collector 4d.

   memorandum thys ys natt chargyd in the [.........]'.

64. Widow Smithe formerly the wife of William Smyth holds freely by custom of the manor a burgage there and pays for this at the aforesaid feasts equally per annum: viz. in the charge of the collector          5d.

   Bod: 'now Edmund Smythe.'

65. John Hersham holds freely by custom of the manor three quarters of a burgage there formerly in the tenure of William Hanham and before that John Michell and pays for this at the aforesaid feasts equally per annum: viz. in the charge of the collector          3¾d.

   Bod: 'now the said Edmund Smythe.'

66. John Hering holds freely one burgage and a parcel of another burgage there by custom of the manor and pays for this at the aforesaid feasts equally per annum: viz. in the charge of the collector          7d.

   Bod: 'now Robert Cole'

67. Robert Alden holds freely by custom of the manor one burgage there and pays for this at the aforesaid feasts equally per annum: viz. in the charge of the collector          5d.

   Bod.: 'now in the occupation of Tobias Nuthall (d.1637).

68. Edward Smythe Taylour holds freely one burgage there by custom of the manor formerly in the tenure or occupation of John Bell and pays for this at the aforesaid feasts equally per annum: viz. in the charge of the collector          5d.

   Bod.: 'now Thomas Crosse'.

69. John Bayaunce holds freely one burgage there by custom of the manor formerly the widow Warde and pays for this at the aforesaid feasts equally per annum: viz. in the charge of the collector          5d.

70. Widow Smithe of Glemham holds freely one burgage there by custom of
the manor formerly [.......] and pays for this at the aforesaid feasts per annum
equally:
viz. in the charge of the collector                           5d.

71. Thomas Fiske holds freely by custom of the manor two burgages there from
which one was formerly William Thatcher and afterwards John Sheming and
the other formerly Thomas Burton and pays for this per annum, at the
aforesaid feasts equally per annum:
viz in the charge of the collector                           10d.

72. John Calle holds freely by custom of the manor three burgages there and pays
for this at the aforesaid feasts for each burgage 5d. in total per annum:
viz in the charge of the collector                           15d.

73. The Rector of Framlingham holds freely there by custom of the manor seven
burgages and pays for this at the aforesaid feasts equally per annum:
viz. in the charge of the collector                           2s. 11d.

74. Widow Smythe formerly the wife of Thomas Smith holds freely there by
custom of the manor one burgage and a parcel of another burgage and pays
for this per annum at the aforesaid feasts:
viz in the charge of the collector                           7d.

75. Widow Brydgis holds freely there a parcel of a burgage by custom of the
manor and pays for this per annum at the aforesaid feasts equally:
                                                             4d.

76. Widow Dedham holds freely one burgage there by custom of the manor and
pays for this per annum at the aforesaid feasts equally:
viz in the charge of the collector                           5d.

77. Thomas Crispe holds freely one burgage there by custom of the manor and
pays for this at the aforesaid feasts equally per annum:
viz in the charge of the collector                           5d.

78. Richard Savage (deleted) Saverne holds freely by custom of the manor two
burgages there and pays for this at the aforesaid feasts per annum equally:
viz. in the charge of the collector                           10d.

79. John Garrard holds freely one ( deleted) three quarters of one burgage there
by custom of the manor and pays for this per annum at the aforesaid feasts
equally:
viz in the charge of the collector                           3¾d.

80. The Inhabitants of the town of Disse viz. the Brethren of the Gilde of Disse
hold freely by custom of the manor one burgage there and pay for this per
annum at the foresaid feasts per annum:
viz. in the charge of the collector                           5d.

83

81. Thomas Rouse armiger holds freely by custom of the manor two burgages and a quarter burgage there and pays for this per annum:
viz. in the charge of the collector         11¼d.

The total rents of the free burgage tenants there   28s. 6½d.
viz. totally in the charge of the collector, from rents 27s. 9¾d.
for motfee                           ¾d. (deleted).

Memorandum that every Tenaunte is bownde by this holde according to the Custome of this mannour to doe certayne Custumarye worke in making the Kings majestie haye in the meadowe Called Hall Meadowe That is to saye after the grasse is Tedde of the Tenaunts of the Small holde Then are they bownde to turne over and putt in the seyde grasse redy to the Cocke and then others of the Kings majestie tenaunts of the Coliar holde are bownde to Cocke itt.

Free Rents in both Framlingham and Saxted called Woodyche silver

82. from John Torner for his free rent there called woodyche sylver formerly received from William Gilbert per annum paying at the feast of St. Michael the Archangel term:
viz. in the charge of the collector             8d.

83. from Godfrey Irelonde for his free rent there woodyche sylver deriving from various lands formerly John Bachelers (1d.) and William Irelonde (2d. three farthings) and pays for this at the aforesaid feast per annum:
viz. in the charge of the collector             3¾d.

84. from John Warner for his free rent there called woodyche sylver formerly in the tenure of Richard Warner and pays for this at the aforesaid feast per annum:
viz. in the charge of the collector             4d¼d.

85. from the 4d. recently received from the lord of the manor of Okenhilhall for his rent called woodyche sylver per annum this is not received on the grounds that the aforesaid rent is now being extinguished on the grounds that the said manor is now a manor belonging to the lord King:
viz in this charge,                   nothing.

Total 16d  All in the charge of the collector
Memorandum thes tenaunts above mencioned are bownde to noo other service butt to sute of Courte onlye.
Free tenants of le Coliar Lande by custom of the manor lying both in Framlingham and Saxted

86. William Dowsing holds freely by custom of the manor 8 acres of land of le Coliar holding of which 4 acres and a half are from tenement Younghusbandes and three acres and a half from tenement Cranes and pays at the feasts of the Annunciation of the Blessed Mary the Virgin and St. Michael the archangel equally per annum:

viz in the charge of the collector         20d.

87. Katerina Chamber widow holds freely by custom of the manor six acres of the le Coliar holding of tenement Prests and pays for this per annum at the aforesaid feasts equally per annum:
viz. in the charge of the collector         15d.

88. John Smyth of Herbesawgrene holds freely by custom of the manor three roods of Coliar Lande of tenement Buttes and pays for this at the aforesaid feasts equally per annum:
viz. in the charge of the collector         1¾d. and ½ a farthing.

89. William Foxe holds freely by custom of the manor three acres of Coliar holding of tenement Honyes formerly Thomas Burtons and pays for this at the aforesaid feasts equally:
viz., in the charge of the collector         7½d.

90. Thomas Shemyng ad Montem holds freely by custom of the manor four acres and a half of le Coliar holde of tenement and pays for this per annum at the aforesaid feasts equally:
viz., in the charge of the collector         11¼d.

91. Reginald Gibbon holds freely by custom of the manor one acre of land of le coliar holding of tenement Cranes and pays for his per annum:
viz in the charge of the collector         2½d.

92. The widow of Henry Rossington holds freely by custom one acre of Le coliar holding of tenement Smythes and pays for this at the aforesaid feasts equally:
viz. in the charge of the collector         2½d.

93. Thomas Brothers and John Banham and Katerina Manbye hold freely by custom of the manor thirteen acres and three roods of le Coliar holding of which eleven acres and three rods are from tenement Forthes and two acres from tenement Younghusbondsand pay for this at the aforesaid feasts per annum:
viz., in the charge of the collector         2s. 10¾d.
and for motfee         4d.

94. Anthony Russhe holds freely by custom of the manor two acres and one rood of le Coliar holding from tenement and pays for this at the aforesaid feasts equally per annum:
viz. in the charge of the collector         5½d. and ½ a farthing.

95. Margareta Goodwine widow holds freely by custom of the manor eleven acres and a half of land of Le Coliar holding from which two acres and a half are from tenement and nine acres and a half from tenement Whitings and pays for this at the aforesaid feasts equally per annum:
viz. in the charge of the collector         2s. 3¾d.

96. Thomas Cooles holds freely by custom of the manor one acre and three rods of land of tenement Whitings and pays for this per annum:
viz in the charge of the collector        4¼d and half a farthing.

97. John Nuthille holds freely by custom of the manor twenty one acres and one rood of land of le Coliar holding from which eight acres are from tenement Yonghusbonds and thirteen acres and one rood from tenement Cranes and pays for this at the aforesaid feasts equally per annum:
viz. in the charge of the collector       4s. 5¼d.

98. Elizabeth Sterne holds freely during the minority of Matthew Harman son and heir of John Harman deceased by custom of the manor twenty nine acre and one rood of le Coliarholding  from which four acres and one rood are from tenement Smythes, thirteen acres one rood from tenement Yonghusbonds, seven acres and three roods from tenement Cranes and three roods from tenement Weylonds and three acres and one rood from tenement Whitings and pays for this at the aforesaid feasts per annum:
viz. in the charge of the collector       6s. 1¾d.

99. Thomas Burton holds freely by custom of the manor twenty five acres and one rood and half a rood of land of le Coliarholding from which three acres are from tenement Smythes eighteen acre and one rood from tenement Forthes [deleted] Buttes, two acres and half a rood from tenement Forthes and three acres from tenement Weylonds and pays for this per at the aforesaid feasts equally per annum:
viz. in the charge of the collector       5s. 3d.

100. Robert Jargafelde holds freely by custom of the manor 20 acres of land of Coliar Lande from tenement Prests and pays for this for each acre 2½d. paying at the aforesaid feasts equally per annum: 4s. 2d.

101. John Balles holds freely one acre of Coliar Lande of tenement by custom of the manor and pays for this at the aforesaid feasts equally per annum:
viz. in the charge of the collector       2½d.

102. Robert Wingfelde knight holds freely by custom of the manor nine acres and a half of land of Coliar holding of tenement Whitings and pays for this for each acre 2½d in total paying at the aforesaid feasts equally per annum:
viz. in the charge of the collector       23¾d.

103. John Calle holds freely by custom of the manor, seven acres and one rood of Coliare Lande from which seven acres are from tenement Honyes and one rood from tenement Weylonds formerly in the tenure of Thomas Burton and pays for each acre 2½d. in total paying at the aforesaid feasts per annum equally:
viz. in the charge of the collector       18¾d.

104. Robert Balles holds freely by custom of the manor thirteen acres and a half a
rood of land of le Coliar holding of which twelve acres and the half rood are
from tenement Forthes and one acre from tenement Whitings and pays for
this at the aforesaid feasts equally per annum:
viz. in the charge of the collector          2s. 8¼d. and half a farthing.

105. John Sheming holds freely ad Montem holds seventeen acres of land of
Coliar holding from tenement Waylonds and pays for this at the aforesaid
feasts equally per annum:
viz. in the charge of the collector          3s. 4d.

106. John Revett holds in right of Elizabeh his wife fifteen acres of Coliar Lande
from tenement Honies and pays for this at the aforesaid feasts equally:
viz. in the charge of the collector          3s.1½d.

107. Katerina Chamber, John Revett or Robert Colles hold freely by custom of
the manor three acres and a half of land of tenement Cranes formerly in the
tenure or occupation of Robert Wrighte and once in the tenure of Thomas
Harfrey and pay for this at the aforesaid feasts equally per annum:
viz. in the charge of the collector          8¾d.

108. The Rector of Framlingham holds freely by custom of the manor three roods
of land of Le Coliar holding from tenement Honies and pays for this at the
aforesaid feasts equally per annum:
viz. in the charge of the collector          1¾d. and half a farthing.

109. Richard Shemyng holds freely by custom of the manor four acres of
land of Le Coliar holding from tenement Preysts and pays for this at the
aforesaid feasts equally per annum:
viz. in the charge of the collector          10d.

110. Richard Johnson holds freely by custom of the manor four acres (and three
roods-deleted) of land of Coliar holding of which one acre and one rood are
from tenement Honyes, two acres and three roods from tenement Buttes
formerly in the tenure or occupation of Thomas Burton and pays for at the
aforesaid feasts equally per annum:
viz. in the charge of the collector          10d. (7¾d. and half a
                                              farthing deleted).

111. The Master and Brethren of the Gilde of the Blessed Mary the Virgin in
Framlingham aforesaid hold freely twenty seven acres and a half of land of
Coliar holding from which eighteen acres from tenement (honies-deleted)
Smiths, two acres and one rood from tenement Butts, five acres from
tenement Waylonds and three acres and one rood from tenement Whitings
and pays for this at the aforesaid feasts equally per annum:
viz. in the charge of the collector          5s. 7¼d.

112. Concerning the 4¼d. formerly received from John Capon for his rent issuing from one acre and three roods of Coliar holding from which three roods are from tenement Yonghusbondes and one acre from tenement Cranes aforesaid, he does not answer for this because it was afterwards granted to the same John by copy of the court for 14d. and by paying all the other services and customs touching the same as in the same copy is more fully set out: viz. in the charge of this (collector) here          nothing.

113. Nor does he (the collector) answer for the 5d. formerly received from Thomas Cooles for rent of three acres of land of Coliar holdyng from tenement Whitings on the grounds that it was granted afterwards to the aforesaid Thomas Cooles by copy of the Court for a greater sum viz. for the rent 8d. per annum over and above all the other services and customs owed: viz. in the charge of this officer here          nothing.

114. Nor does he answer for the 7½d., formerly received from John Shemyng de Monte for the rent of three roods of land of Coliar holding from tenement Smithes per annum on the grounds that it was granted to the aforesaid John Sheming by copy of Court for a greater sum viz. for the rent of 12d. per annum over all the other services and customs owed: viz. in this charge here          nothing.

115. Nor does he answer for the 3¾d. formerly received from John Revett for the rent on one acre of land and a half of Le coliar holding from tenement Yonghusbondes per annum, on the grounds that it was granted to the aforesaid John Revett afterwards by copy of court for a greater sum viz. for the rent of 12d. per annum over all the other services owed and customs: viz. in the charge of this officer here          nothing.

116. Nor does he answer for the 2s. 5¼ d. and half a farthing issuing or growing from the twelve acres of land and three roods of Le Coliar Lande of which five acres are from tenement Butts, three acres from tenement Honies, three roods of tenement Smitheis three roods from tenement Forthes and two acres and half of tenement Whitings per annum on the grounds that all these lands are enclosed within the park of the lord King of Framlingham: viz. in the charge of this officer          nothing.

The total of the rents of tenants of Le Coliar Lande:
viz. in the charge of the collector- in rents:          52s. 1d. and a ½ farthing.
in motfee          4d.
(total)          52s. 5d. and a ½ farthing.

Memorandum. That the Tenaunts of this sayed holding are bownde every one of theyme by the Custome of the Same to do certeyne worke in the Kings meadowe called Halle meadow in making the haye of the Same, That is to saye, after that the Tenaunts of the Smalle holde have tedde the grasse of the Same and the tenaunts of the burgage holde have turned and putt itt in redie to the cocke, then the sayued Tenaunts of the coliar holding are bownde to Cocke it in grasse cockes.

Item the sayed Tenaunts of this holde Called the Coliar holding are bownde
likewise by the same to bere the office of the Collector both to gather and levy
and collecte the Kings majesties rentes in Framlingham and Saxted aforeseyd
to that office apparteyning and belonginge. And it is charged to gather of
every acre of great holde 2½d. over and besides 8d. of the same acre in the twoe
hawardes Charges of Framlingfham and Saxted aforeseyed. And to levye all rents
arising of diverse landes that is to saye of mollande, increased londe, burges holde,
Coliar holding, Free rents, woodiche silver and mootefee And is Charged with
the proffitts arising of the boroughe Courte kepte in Framlingham aforeseyd
and to make accompt thereof yerely before the kings majesties auditor and
receyver thereof withowt any Fee And there is in Nombre 270 acres and a half
of the sayed Coliar Lande charged for the bering of this office and is elected
and Chosen att the courte kepte in Framlingham after michelmas yerely And
is devyded into nyne heades and every heade conteyneth 30 acres And the
principall or firste manne of the same heade is bownde to bere the office And
hath nott in his owne handes the full nombre of 30 acres but hath the helpers
to that nombre And every helper payeth to the heade thereof for every acre 16d.
and onse in nyne yere every acre of the same holde is charged therewith And
the kings majestie doth likewise allowe 6d. of every acre when the hede falleth
on any of the Lande that is nowe enclosed with in the parke of Framlingham
aforeseyd And the sayed office of the Collector standeth yerely charged with
the rente of Ashe iuxta Campsey and to accompte thereof yerely as before is
mencioned.

Custumary Tenants in Framlingham aforesaid

117. Robert Fletewoode holds by copy of the Court by custom of the manor
one Small tenement (2d.) called Alleyns with half an acre (5¼d.) of native
land of the great tenure, which was formerly Nicholas Fayerwether's as
appears by the same copy dated the Saturday next after the Feast of the
Annunciation of the Blessed Mary the Virgin in the 27th year of the reign of
the late King Henry 8th, and pays for this at the feasts of Annunciation of
the Blessed Mary the Virgin and St. Michael the Archangel equally per
annum:

| | |
|---|---|
| viz. in the charge of the hayward | 7d., one hen worth 2d., half a mowing-work worth 1d.. |
| in the charge of the collector | 1½d. |
| (total) | 10¼d. |

118. William Dowsing holds by copy of the Court by custom of the manor one
acre of land with a pightle (13¼d and half a farthing) of native tenure
containing one acre and one rood once Thomas Brodey's then Richard
Grene's and afterwards Edward Rous' as appears by the same copy dated the
Tuesday on the feast of St. Thomas in the 33rd year of the said late king
Henry 8th and pays for this at the aforesaid feasts equally per annum:

| | |
|---|---|
| viz. in the charge of the hayward | 10d. and one hen and a half worth 3d. |
| (subtotal) | 13d. and one egg. |

89

| | |
|---|---|
| in the charge of the collector | 3d. and a half a farthing. |
| for motfee | 7½d. |
| (total) | 23½d., half a farthing and an egg. |

119. Nicholas Stebbyng holds for him and his heirs by custom of the manor by copy of Court, four acres (3s. 6d.) of land of the great tenure of tenement Willmots, formerly Thomas Reymer's and afterwards Richard Harvye's and then George Stebbing's, father of the aforesaid Nicholas Stebbing as appears by the same copy dated Monday the day before St. Thomas the Martyr in the 25th year of the same late king Henry 8th and pays for this at the aforesaid feasts equally per annum:

| | |
|---|---|
| viz. in the charge of the hayward | 2s. 8d., and four eggs. |
| in the charge of the collector | 10d. |
| and for motfee | 1½d. |
| (total) | 3s. 7d.. 4 eggs. |

120. John Chamber holds for him and his heirs by custom of the manor by copy of the Court from the surrender of Katerina Chamber and William Chamber, one acre and a half (9d.) of land from the demesnes of the manor formerly in the tenure of William Baker lying next to the lord's park as appears by the same copy dated Friday next after Passion Sunday in the 31st year of the reign of the late King Henry 8th and pays for this at the aforesaid feasts per annum equally:

| | |
|---|---|
| viz. in the charge of the reeve | 9d. |

121. The same John Chamber holds for him and his heirs by custom of the manor by the surrender of Katerina Chamber formerly the wife of Richard Chamber deceased and William Chamber her son, a pightle called Keyttyspyttell containing by estimate two acres (2s. 2d.) lying in Framlingham aforesaid, as appears by copy dated Wednesday next after the feast of the Nativity of the Blessed Mary the Virgin in the 31st year of the reign of the late King Henry 8th, for which he pays at the aforesaid feasts equally per annum:

| | |
|---|---|
| viz, in the charge of the hayward | 2s. 2d. |

122. The aforesaid John Chamber holds for him and his heirs by custom of the manor seven acres and one rood of land (6s. 3d. and a half-farthing), parcel of a native tenement called Kegills alias Grimes containing per estimate fourteen acres in Framlingham aforesaid formerly held by Fineta the widow of John Tendourslove and Giles her son and afterwards by Anthony Rous as appears by the same copy dated Thursday on the feast of St. Thomas in the 34th year of the reign of the late King Henry 8th and pays for this at the aforesaid feasts equally per annum:

| | |
|---|---|
| viz. in the charge of the hayward | 4s.10d. and one hen worth 2d., 5s.and 7 eggs. |
| in charge of the collector | 18d.and a half-farthing. |
| | (total) 6s. 7d. one farthing and seven eggs. |

123. Katerina Chamber and John Chamber hold for them and their heirs by custom of the manor two acres (21d.) of great-tenure land, an acre and a half (10d.) of petiferme, three acres of (18d.) of smaller-measure, four acres (3s. 8¾d.) and one rood of land parcel of tenement Herfreys, and three (3s. 3¼d. and half a farthing) acres and three roods parcel of the aforesaid tenement lying in Framlingham aforesaid as appears in the 18th year of the late King Henry 7th, and a close of pasture (4s.) called Maggis containing eight acres which were recently John Seman's as appears by the same copy dated the Tuesday on the vigil of St Matthew in the 33rd year of the late King Henry 8th, and pays for this at the aforesaid feasts equally per annum:

| | |
|---|---|
| viz. in the charge of the hayward | 12s.6d., a hen worth 2d., 13s.1d. and ten eggs. |
| in the charge of the collector | 2s.1¼ d. |
| and motfee | 5½ d. |
| (sub-total) | 2s. 6½ d. |
| (total) | 15s. 7½d. and ten eggs. |

124. The aforesaid Katerina Chamber holds to her and her heirs by custom of the manor five acres of land (4s. 4½d.) of great-tenure parcel of tenement Mawgtells in Framlingham aforesaid formerly John Nichols as appears by the same copy dated Monday the day after the Conversion of St. Paul in the 19th year of the reign of the late King Henry 7th and pays for this at the aforesaid feasts equally per annum:

| | |
|---|---|
| viz. in the charge of the hayward | 3s. 4d. and 5 eggs |
| in the charge of the Collector | 12½d. |
| and for motfee | 2½d. |
| (subtotal) | 15d. |
| (total ) | [ ... d.] and 5 eggs. |

125. The aforesaid Katerina Chamber holds for her and her heirs by custom of the manor, one acre (10½d.) of native land of great tenure and an acre and a half of native land (10d.) of small tenure formerly Robert Wright' as appears by the same copy dated the Friday in Whit-week in the 18th year of the reign of the late King Henry 7th and pays for this at the aforesaid feasts equally per annum:

| | |
|---|---|
| viz. in the charge of the hayward | 17d. and one egg. |
| in the charge of the collector | 2¾d. |
| and for motfee | ½d. |
| (total) | 20d. and one egg. |

126. The aforesaid Katerina Chamber holds for her and her heirs a piece of land from the demesnes of the manor containing (7s. 6d.) fifteen acres parcel of Haleffelde formerly leased to John Stoffer after the surrender of Thomas Smith as appears by copy dated Tuesday before the feast of St Michael the Archangel in the 16th year of the reign of the late King Henry 7th and pays for this at the aforesaid feasts equally per annum:

viz.                                    [ MS. blank]

127. The aforesaid Katerina Chamber holds to her and her heirs a parcel
of pasture (2d. and half a farthing) of native land containing one rood
in Framlingham aforesaid near Lettehaughstrette parcel of tenement Jervis
formerly William Dernforth' as appears by a copy dated on the feast of the
Invention of the Holy Cross in the 22nd year of the reign of the said late
King Henry 7th by paying at the feasts equally per annum:

| | |
|---|---|
| viz. in the charge of the hayward | 2d. |
| in the charge of the collector | ¾d. |
| (total ) | 2½ d  and half a farthing. |

128. The aforesaid Katerina Chamber widow and John Chamber hold to them
and their heirs by custom of the manor one piece (20d.) of land or garden,
parcel of tenement Lokkingtons and it lies within the borough of
Framlingham formerly John Stogys as appear by a copy of the court held on
Friday after the feast of St. Matthew in 19th year of the reign King Henry
7th and pays for this at the aforesaid feasts per annum:

| | |
|---|---|
| viz. in the charge of the hayward | 20d. |

129. Anna Hill widow holds for her and her assigns for as long as she lives by
custom of the manor fourteen acres (7s.) of land from the demesne of the
manor called Halefelde formerly Thomas Hill's and previously Joan Hill his
mother's as appears by copy dated Wednesday in the third week of Lent in
the 34th year of the late King Henry 8th and pays at the aforesaid feasts
equally per  annum:                                     [blank].

130. John Smith holds for him and his heirs by copy of the court by custom
of the manor, three acres of native land called Fisks in Framlingham aforesaid
by services and rent of 2s. 8d. per annum, and ten acres of native great-tenure
(8s. 9d.) land of tenement Ahereds in Framingham aforesaid formerly
Robert Smyth's as appears by copy dated Thursday next after Dominica
in Albis in the 22nd year of the late King Henry 8th and pays for this at the
aforesaid feasts equally per annum:

| | |
|---|---|
| viz. in the charge of the hayward | 9s. 4d., three hens worth 2d., one reaping work worth 2d.. |
| (subtotal) | 10s. and ten eggs. |
| in the charge of the Collector | 2s. 1d. |
| and for motfee | 5d. |
| (subtotal) | 2s. 6d. |
| (total) | 12s. 6d. and ten eggs. |

131. The same John Smith holds for him and his heirs by copy of court by
custom of the manor one acre (10½d.) of native land of tenement Canes
parcel of nine acres (2s.) of land formerly in the tenure of Thomas Foxe and
previously of John Smith his father as appears in the same copy dated Sunday
on the feast of St. Thomas in the 31st. year of the reign of the late King
Henry 8th and pays for this at the aforesaid feasts equally per annum:

| | |
|---|---|
| viz: in the charge of the hayward | 8d. and one egg. |
| in the charge of the collector | 2½d. |
| (total) | 10½d. and one egg. |

132. Robert Cooles holds for him and his heirs by copy of court by custom of the manor two acres of native great-tenure (21d.) land formerly occupied by Alice Cowper and afterwards by Reginald Irelond as appears by the same copy dated the Saturday next before Christmas in the 18th year of the reign of the late king Henry 8th and pays for this at the aforesaid feasts equally per annum:

| | |
|---|---|
| viz: in the charge of the hayward | 16d. and two eggs. |
| in the charge of the collector | 5d. |
| (total) | 21d. and two eggs. |

133. The aforesaid Robert Cooles holds for him and his heirs by copy of the court by custom of the manor one acre (15¾d.) and a half of tenement Watlings of great-tenure in Famlingham aforesaid formerly Richard Sutton' and three acres (3¾d.) and a half of land of the tenement of William Dise and one acre of land (15¾ d.) and a half formerly Thomas Childe' and half an acre of land by increment by the service of one farthing per annum, and half an acre of meadow (5¼d) of great-tenure of tenement Semans formerly John Wright' and four acres (3s. 8½d.and half a farthing) and one rood parcel of tenement Harfreis formerly Robert Wright' and three acres three roods (3s.3d. and half a farthing) of land parcel of the said tenement Harfreys and one piece of demesne land containing six and a half acres (4s. 3d) lying in Grimes Crofte formerly John Fulmerstone' and nine acres of great-tenure land (5s. 3d.) of tenement Semans and four and a half acres (3s 6¼d.) and three roods (6¾d. and half a farthing) of land of the same occupation and an enclosure of pasture containing by estimate ten acres (2s.) called Hattons once Nicholas Calle' formerly John Saye' and Margery his wife as appears by the same copy dated Thursday next after the feast of St. Barnabas in the twelfth year of the reign of the late King Henry 8th and pays for this at the aforesaid feasts equally per annum:

| | |
|---|---|
| viz: in the charge of the hayward | 9s.6d., for three and a half chickens 7d., for two mowing works 1d. |
| (subtotal) | 20s. 2d, 26 eggs. |
| in the charge of the Collector | 5s.5¾d. and half a farthing. |
| in the charge of the reeve | 3s. 3d. |
| (Total) | 33s. 4¾d., half a farthing and 26 eggs. |

134. George Stebbing holds for him and his heirs by copy of court by custom of the manor three acres (18d) of land parcel of tenement Broks with appurtenances in Ketilberghe by petty farm formerly John Pulham senior' as appears by copy of court held on Tuesday the second day of April in the 29th year of the reign of the late King Henry 8th and pays for this at the aforesaid feasts per annum:

| | |
|---|---|
| viz: in the charge of the hayward | 18d. |

135. Thomas Foxe holds for him and the heirs of his body legitimately procreated by copy of the court by custom of the manor six acres native land of tenement Canys, three acres of native land from William Buck's tenement called Athereds lying in six pieces held by the fee farm of 8s. per annum and suit of court, and a cottage with a rood of land from increment called Carters formerly John Dring' and six acres of land from tenement Lokkingtons, 6s. 8d., rent there which were formerly John Foxe' his father as appears by copy dated Wednesday next before the feast of the Nativity of the Blessed Mary the Virgin in the 31st year of the reign of the late King Henry 8th and pays for this at the aforesaid feasts equally per annum;

| viz: in the charge of the Hayward | 13s.8d., and one hen priced at 2d., |
| (total) | 13s. 10d. |

136. John Caponne holds one acre (10½d.) of native land of tenement Alen formerly William Jervis' held by service and custom, and 12 acres of native land, meadow and pasture of tenement Canishill formerly John Caponne' held from the lord by the fee farm of 6s. per annum, a tenement called Heffd formerly containing a messuage and 14 acres of land by estimate from which 13 acres and one rood of native land (11s. 7d. and half a farthing) and three roods (6d.) of Coliarlande are held from the lord by service and custom of the manor, and two acres of native land (21d.) of tenement Harfreis are held from the lord by the custom and service aforesaid, and one acre of Coliar Lande of tenement Parkilds held by the service of 8d. rent over the services and customs, and four acres of greater-measure native land (3s. 6d.) of tenement Kenewes formerly John Gerrards and five acre of native great-tenure land (4s. 4½d.) of tenement and one acre of native land of great-tenure of tenement Cances in four pieces formerly Robert Wright' and 2 acres of native great-tenure land (21d.) of tenement Lion formerly Nicholas Ellett' and Joan his wife before that John Capon' by customary services, and 26 acres of demesne land (13s) called Grimscroft held from the lord by fee farm of 13d per annum , and two acres of native land of tenement Baddis (21d.) of great-tenure with appurtenances in Framlingham aforesaid, and one acre and a half of native great-tenure land of tenement Braddis formerly John Wright' held by the service and custom aforesaid, formerly in the tenure or occupation of his father a native tenant by blood as appears by copy dated Monday the day after Passion Sunday in the 13th year of the reign of the late King Henry 8th and pays for this at the aforesaid feasts equally per annum:

| viz: in the charge of the hayward | 27s. 2d., 1 hen worth 2d., two mowing-works |
| (subtotal) | 27s. 8d. and 31 eggs. |
| in the charge of the Collector | 7s. 9¼d.and half a farthing. |
| in the charge of the reeve | 13s. |
| (total) | 48s. 5¼d., half a farthing and 32 eggs. |

137. The same (John Capon) holds by copy as it is said one acre and a half of great- tenure land formerly John' (15¾d.) and two acres of the same measure formerly Joan Cook's and pays for this per annum:

| | |
|---|---|
| viz: in the charge of the hayward | 2s. 4d. |
| in the charge of the collector | 8¾d. |
| (total) | 3s ¾d. and three eggs. |

138. Ed(war)d Smythe holds by copy of court by custom of the manor, 4 acres (2s.) of demesne land of the manor abutting on le Stubbing, formerly in the tenure of [……] Smithe his father as appears by the same copy dated Thursday on the feast of St. Thomas in the 23rd. year of the reign of the late King Henry 8th and pays for this at the aforesaid feasts equally per annum:

| | |
|---|---|
| viz: in the charge of the reeve | 2s. |

139. Thomas Shemyng ad Montem holds by copy of the court by custom of the manor a pightle containing half an acre (2d.) called Cokks pightle, one acre (2d) abutting on Canes Weye, one acre (2d.) of land by increment abutting also on the same way, one acre (2d.) of land by increment formerly Thomasine Athered' held by the services and custom of the manor, and tenement Athereds (15s.) containing by estimation fifteen acres by the fee farm of 15s. per annum with appurtenances in Framlingham formerly Walter Shemyng' his father as appears by the same copy dated the Wednesday in the third week of Lent in the 34th year of the reign of the late King Henry 8th and pays for this in rent at the aforesaid feasts equally per annum:

| | |
|---|---|
| viz: in the charge of the Hayward | 15s. 4d., one and a half hens worth 3d. |
| ( subtotal) | 15s. 7d. |
| in the charge of the collector | 4d. |
| and for motfee | 4d. |
| (subtotal) | 8d. |
| (total) 16s. 3d.. | |

140. Reginald Gebonne holds for himself and his heirs by copy of court by custom of the manor one tenement and various native lands with appurtenances there viz., 17 acres and one rood (15s.1d. and half a farthing) of greater-tenure native land of tenement Jervis, one acre of native land with a messuage (6d.) of lesser-tenure, three roods of native land (4d.) of the tenement Roger atte Hill' held from the lord for the fee farm of 4d. per annum, one (6d.) acre of tenement Harfreys held for the fee farm of 6d., and various pieces of land held by fee farm (2s. 4d.) 2s. 4d. per annum with appurtenances in Framlingham aforesaid formerly Reginald Derneforde' as appears by the same copy date Monday next before Michaelmas in the 34th year of the reign of the late King Henry 8th and pays for this in rent per annum at the aforesaid feasts:

| | |
|---|---|
| viz: in the charge of the hayward | 15s., for two hens 4d., and 17 eggs, one mowing-work 3d. |
| (subtotal) | 15s. 9d. |

95

| | |
|---|---|
| in the charge of the collector | 3s. 7d. and half a farthing |
| and for motffee | 8½d. |
| (subtotal) | 4s. 3d. and half a farthing |
| (total) | 20s. ½ d., half a farthing and 17 eggs. |

141. The aforesaid Reginald Gebonne holds for himself and his heirs by copy of the court by custom of the manor, two pieces (8d.) of native land containing one acre and one rood of native small-tenure land with appurtenances in Framlingham aforesaid formerly the said Reginald Dernforde' as appears by the same copy dated the Monday next after the feast of St. Michael the Archangel in the 28th year of the reign of the late King Henry 8th and pays for this at the aforesaid feasts equally per annum:
viz: in the charge of the hayward           8d.

142. Richard Saverne holds for himself and his heirs by copy of court by custom of the manor one parcel of land lying between his free lands and the common river, containing in length 98 feet towards the north and in the middle of the parcel 7 feet and at the southern end 3 feet, with appurtenances in Framlingham aforesaid held by the service and custom of the manor, formerly in the tenure of Elizabeth Hastings as appears by the same copy dated Wednesday in the second week in Lent in the 33rd year of the reign of the late King Henry 8th and pays for this at the aforesaid feasts equally per annum:
viz: in the charge of the reeve           1d.

143. The said Richard Saverne holds for himself and his heirs by copy of court by custom of the manor a piece of demesne land there parcel of a certain close called Stabell yerde formerly William Saverne his father' held by the service and custom aforesaid as appears by copy dated Thursday next after the feast of St. Michael the Archangel in the 18th year of the reign of the late King Henry 8th and pays for this at the aforesaid feasts equally per annum:
viz: in the charge of the reeve           7d.

144. Robert Gilberte holds for himself and his heirs by copy of court by custom of the manor, one piece of land pasture recently empty and wasted on the road leading from Framlingham towards Soham and Dennington on which piece of ground there was once a house called le harmitage which fell to the ground a number of years ago, and recently in that place the said Robert has built for himself another house enclosed with a ditch and a hedge containing in length six yards and in the middle of the same piece of ground three yards and it lies next to the causeway called Framlingham caucey and the cross called Curteis Crosse on the west of the same causeway and cross, as appears by the same copy dated Friday next before the feast of the Exaltation of the Holy Cross in the 27th year of the oft-quoted late King Henry 8th and pays for this at the aforesaid feasts equally per annum:
viz.: in the charge of the reeve           4d.

145. Richard Coole and Margery his wife hold for them and their heirs of
Richard himself, a messuage and eleven acres of native land (9s. 7½d.) and
meadow by the greater-tenure of tenement Forthes plus another acre of the
same tenement in the tenure of Thomas Burton, and one acre (15d,) of land
by increment called Spadehaste and one acre of increment (15d.) lying in a
close called Allonde Crofte once in the tenure of Thomas Wright, Clerk and
half an acre of land (7½d.) and meadow part of an acre of land from
increment lying in Framlingham aforesaid next to the highway formerly
Richard Coole his father' as appears by copy of court dated Wednesday in the
third week of Lent in the 34th year of the oft-quoted King Henry 8th and
pays for this at the aforesaid feasts equally per annum:

| | |
|---|---|
| viz: in the charge of the hayward | 7s.4d., two hens worth 4d., one mowing-work 1d. |
| (subtotal) | 7s. 9d. and eleven eggs. |
| in the charge of the collector | 5s. 5d. |
| and for motfee | 4d. |
| (subtotal) | 5s. 9d. |
| (total) | 13s. 6d. and eleven eggs. |

146. Thomas Coole holds for him and his heirs by copy of court by custom of
the manor, six acres of native land (5s. 5d.) of tenement Mists, and one acre
(10½d. ) of tenement Hosseis, two acres by increment (8d.) of Coliar Land
from a tenement called Murdocks with appurtenances in Framlingham
aforesaid, and a piece of enclosed land called Theverslond (8d.) containing
two and half acres formerly John Brodey' and afterwards , father of the
aforesaid Thomas as appears by copy dated Wednesday in the third week
of Lent in the 20th year of the late King Henry 8th and pays for this at the
aforesaid feasts equally per annum:

| | |
|---|---|
| viz: in the charge of the hayward | 4s. 8d., and for 1 hen 2d. |
| (subtotal) | 4s.10d. and 7 eggs. |
| in the charge of the collector | 3s. 1½d. |
| and for motfee | 3d. |
| (subtotal) | 3s. 4½d. |
| (total) | 8s. 2½d. and seven eggs. |

147. John Barkeley holds by right of his wife Margaret, previously the wife
of Richard Calle, for the term of the said Margaret's life, by copy of court,
by custom of the manor, one piece of native land of tenement Bresis
containing three acres formerly William Inglonde' with appurtenances in
Framlingham aforesaid held from the lord by the fee farm of 3s. 2s rent per
annum as appears by the same copy dated Monday the day after the Nativity
of the Blessed Mary the Virgin in the 13th year of the reign of the said late
King Henry 8th and pays for this at the aforesaid feasts per annum:

| | |
|---|---|
| viz: in the charge of the hayward | 3s. 2d. and for one hen price 2d., |
| (total) | 3s. 4d. |

148. The aforesaid John Barkeley holds by right of his aforesaid wife term of her life by copy of court by custom of the manor a tenement (16d.) inside the borough of Framlingham aforesaid called Lokkingtons formerly Nicholas Calle' held by the service and custom aforesaid as appears by the same copy dated Wednesday next after the feast of the Exaltation of the Holy Cross in the third year of the reign of the said late King Henry 8th and pays for this at the feasts aforesaid equally per annum:
viz: in the charge of the collector                    16d.

149. Thomas Alrede son and heir of William Alrede deceased holds for him and his heirs, four acres of land from the demesnes of the manor lying in Mapledale with appurtenances in Framlingham aforesaid held from the lord King by the fee farm of 2s. rent per annum, and five acres, half a rood (2s. 7d.) and four perches of native land by estimate with appurtenances in Framlingham aforesaid formerly Geoffrey Irelonde' formerly in the tenure of the aforesaid William Alredde as appears by the same copy dated Thursday next after the feast of Corpus Christi in the first year of the reign of the present King Edward 6th and pays for this for rent at the feasts aforesaid equally per annum:
viz: in the charge of the reeve                    4s. 7d.

150. Alexander Gilbert holds for him and his heirs the site of a wind-mill called le Mille Hill on which two houses have recently been built by the same Alexander enclosed with ditches, and two small pieces of land or pasture outside, adjacent and annexed to the said ditch, of which one piece lies to the seouth of the said site and contains in length six yards and in breadth at its northern end next to the said site three yards, and at the southern end ten human feet, and the second piece contains nine yards in length and in breadth both at the eastern end and western end twenty-four 24 human feet and there lies on the northern side of the said site just as each piece separately is separated with bounds and ditches, a certain road called a dryfte waye clearly marked out, as appears by copy of court dated Friday next before the feast of the Exaltation of the Holy Cross in the 27th year of the late King Henry 8th, and pays for this at the aforesaid feasts equally per annum:
viz: in the charge of the reeve                    13d.

151. John Irelonde holds for him and his heirs an enclosure once called Ketillberghe Wente from the demesnes of the manor containing by estimate thirty-six acres held by the fee farm of 18s. per annum by copy of the court by custom of the manor, one messuage and thirty-five acres (35s. 7½d.) of native greater-tenure of tenement Bailes and two and a half acres (2s. 2¼d.) of native land of tenement Willimotts, and various lands (16d.) and tenements held by increment, except for one enclosure containing by estimate ten acres called Redings now in the tenure of John Sheming and formerly held by John the father of John Ireland as appears by the same copy dated Monday next after the feast the Crucifixion of the Lord in the 15th year of the late King Henry 8th and pays for this at the aforesaid feasts per annum:
viz: in the charge of the hayward                    25s.

| | |
|---|---|
| for two hens 4d., and for two mowing-works | 4d.. |
| in the charge of the collector | 9s. 1¼d. |
| in the charge of the reeve | 18s. |
| (total) | 52s. 9¾d. and 37 eggs. |

152. Geoffrey Moyle holds by right of his wife Elizabeth by copy of the court by custom of the manor three acres and a half (3s ¾d.) of great-tenure land of tenement Brodis, seven acres (6s. 1½d.) of tenement Grimes of the same tenure, and one acre of land of mollond (6d.) of the same tenement with appurtenances in Framlingham aforesaid formerly Katerina Chambers' as appears by the same copy dated Wednesday in Lent week in the 33rd year of the reign of the said late King Henry 8th and pays for this at the aforesaid feasts equally per annum :

| | |
|---|---|
| viz: in the charge of the hayward | 7s. and 10 eggs. |
| in the charge of the collector | 2s. 8¼d. |
| and for motfee | 5d. |
| (subtotal) | 3s. 1¼d. |
| (total) | 10s. 1¼d. and ten eggs. |

153. The same Geoffrey Moyle holds by right of his wife term of the life of the same Elizabeth by copy of the court by custom of the manor, five acres of land by increment (2s. 6d.) formerly Richard Warner' and one Ed(war)d Rome' with appurtenances in Framlingham aforesaid formerly in the tenure of the aforesaid Katerina Chamber as appears by the same copy dated Thursday on the feast of St. Thomas in the 34th year of the reign of the said late King Henry 8th and pays for by rent at the aforesaid feasts equally per annum:

| | |
|---|---|
| viz: in the charge of the collector | 2s. 6d. |

154. Robert Balles holds for him and his heirs by copy of court by custom of the manor, one acre of native greater-tenure land of tenement Pratts formerly Mariona Gerard' with appurtenances in Framlingham aforesaid, two acres one rood and ten perches lying in four pieces of which one acre (14d.) is from tenement Pennyngs held by the fee-farm of 14d. per annum, one acre formerly John Pynote' by the fee farm (12d.) of 12d., one acre of land by increment (6d.) formerly Thomas Godowine', one acre by increment formerly Robert Dringe', one acre by increment formerly John Gerard' and half an acre of land of tenement att Hill with appurtenances in Framlingham aforesaid formerly Alice' the wife of Richard Suttonne as appears by copy dated Thursday in the fourth week of Lent in the 36th year of the late King Henry 8th and pays for this at the aforesaid feasts per annum:

| | |
|---|---|
| viz: in the charge of the hayward | 6s. 10d., and two hens 4d. |
| in the charge of the collector | 2½d. |
| and for motfee | 6d. |
| (Total) | 5s. 3½d. and one egg. |

155. The aforesaid Robert Balles holds for himself and his heirs by copy of court by custom of the manor, a native cottage (plot) formerly built-upon (2½d. and half a farthing) containing one rood of greater-tenure of tenement Hosseis with appurtenances Framlingham aforesaid formerly Richard Coole'

99

as appears by the same copy dated the Friday next after Sunday in Passion in the 31st year of the late King Henry 8th and pays for this at the aforesaid feasts equally per annum:

| | |
|---|---|
| viz: in the charge of the hayward | 2d. |
| in the charge of the collector | ½d. and half a farthing. |
| (total) | 2½d. and half a farthing |

156. The aforesaid Robert Balles holds for him and his heirs by copy of the court by custom of the manor one ace (3d.) of land from increment next to Ravenesdowne and half an acre (3d.) of small-tenure land lying next the messuage of Roger Smith and the lands formerly John Wingfelde' knight, with appurtenances in Framingham aforesaid formerly Roger Smithe' as appears by the same copy dated Friday next after the Sunday in Passion in the 31st year of the late King Henry 8th and pays for this at the aforesaid feasts equally per annum:

| | |
|---|---|
| viz: in the charge of the hayward | 3d. |
| in the charge of the collector | 3d. |
| for motfee | 1½d. |
| (total) | 7½d. |

157. Thomas Button holds for himself and his heirs six and half acres of land (3s. 3d.) by estimate from the demesnes of the manor lying in the Field called Stubbing next to the lands of John Irelonde with appurtenances in Framlingham formerly in the tenure of Richard Button his father as appears by his copy dated Monday next after the feast of the Holy Cross in the 35th year of the reign of the said late King Henry 8th and pays for this at the aforesaid feasts per annum:

| | |
|---|---|
| viz:  in the charge of the reeve | 3s. 3d. |

158. Francis Pulham holds for him and his heirs by copy of court by custom of the manor, one piece of native land of tenement [blank] containing by estimate eighteen acres called Devislonde, four acres of land and pasture called Mysts formerly Thomas Baylyff' with a green road adjacent, one small piece of native land of tenement Lokkingtons containing by estimate three roods more or less lying in the same field  recently leased to John Pulham senior  for 16s. 8d. per annum, and nine acres of native land called Moriotts Londe recently in the lease of the same John for the rent of 18d. per annum which the same John took with other lands in the tenure of George Stebbing as appears by copy dated Friday on the feast of St. Thomas in the 35th year of the said late King Henry 8th and pays for this by rent at the aforesaid feasts equally per annum:

| | |
|---|---|
| viz: in the charge of the hayward | 13s. 6d., and for two hens 4d. |
| (total) | 13s. 10d. |

100    159. John Shemyng de Monte holds to him and his heirs by copy of court by custom of the manor, three roods of native land (6d.) of small farm with appurtenances there formerly Robert Foxe' as appears by his copy dated

Thursday the penultimate day of March in the 27th year of the reign of the said late King Henry 8th and pays for at the aforesaid feasts equally per annum:

viz: in the charge of the hayward                    6d.

160. The aforesaid John Sheming and Olive his wife hold for them and their heirs by copy of court by custom of the manor, one acre (6d.) of native small-tenure land which John Foxe alienated to the said John Sheming, and two acres of land (21d.) parcel of tenement Atherydsche with appurtenances there formerly Robert Sheming' and also ten acres of land (2s. 1d.) by increment as it lies between the land of Thomas Sheming called Banyarde Closse on the part of the east and a certain wood called Bullishhedge woode on the part of the west, of which the southern headland abuts on the land of Robert Smith in part and the lands of the said Thomas Sheming, and the northern headland upon the close of the said Thomas Sheming called Henmereclosse with appurtenances in Framlingham aforesaid, and also three acres of Coliar land formerly Adam Smith' with appurtenances in Framlingham aforesaid as appears by the same copy dated Thursday next after Sunday in Albs in the 22nd year of the reign if the said late King Henry 8th and pays for this at the aforesaid feasts equally per annum:

| | |
|---|---|
| viz: in the charge of the hayward | 22d. for four hens 8d. |
| (subtotal) | 2s. 7d. and two eggs. |
| in the charge of the collector | 3s. 6d. |
| for motfee | 14½d. |
| (subtotal) | 4s. 8½d. |
| (total) | 8s. 2½d. and two eggs. |

161. The above said John Sheming holds for him and his heirs by copy of the court by custom of the manor one acre (6d.) of land parcel of tenement Lokkingtons lying between the lands of the same John towards the east and the land of John Irelond towards the west of which the southern headland abuts onto the Town Weye and the northern headland abuts onto the lands of the said John Irelond with appurtenances of Framlingham aforesaid formerly John Sheming' his father as appears by the same copy dated Thursday next after the feast of Corpus Christi in the first year of the reign of the present king Edward the 6th and pays for this by rent at the feasts aforesaid equally per annum:

viz: in the charge of the collector            6d.

162. John Revett holds for him and his heirs by copy of court by custom of the manor, a close from the demesnes of the manor called Greate Stubbing containing by estimate forty-four acres (22s.) with appurtenances in Framlingham aforesaid held from the lord by the fee-farm of 22s. per annum formerly Robert Revett' his father as appears by the same copy dated the Thursday the penultimate day of March in the 27th year of the reign of the said late King Henry 8th and pays for this at the aforesaid feasts per annum:

101

viz: in the charge of the reeve            22s.

163. Nicholas Joly holds for him and his heirs, one piece of waste ground with a house (3d.) lately built on it by John Coubbe lying in the public roadway leading towards Countesse Crosse and the aforesaid piece of land contains in length 88 feet, in breadth on the east side 51 feet, in breadth on the west side 63 feet, formerly Margaret' the wife of the said John Coubbe, leased to him by copy of the court by custom of the manor as appears by the same copy date Tuesday on the day before St Matthew in the 33rd year of the said late King Henry 8th and pays for this at the aforesaid feasts equally per annum: viz: in the charge of the reeve                                                3d.

164. John Nuthille holds for him and his heirs by copy of the court by custom of the manor, 14 acres (11s. 8d.) of land from the demesnes of the manor at Watlings, four acres (2s.) of land from the demesnes with le mille mounte, three acres (2s. 7½d.) of greater-measure land from three separate tenements viz. from tenement Jervis, from tenement Roger Wrytte' and John Wrytte' lying next to Wrenne Parke, one acre (10½d.) of greater-tenure land from the tenement John Cooke formerly Brodeys, three roods (1½d.) of land from increment once Alice Messenger' formerly Edward Balle', a close called wheteclose containing 7 acres of greater-tenure land (6s. 1½d.) from tenement Curteis', and four acres (3s. 6d.) of greater-tenure land from tenement Harffreis, and one piece of land from the demesnes containing by estimate 5 acres (2s. 6d.) lying in Hallefelde held by the rent per annum of 2s. 6d., and one piece of waste land (2d.) on which of late a barn has been built and it lies on the highway through the close formerly Richard Fulmerstone' held at the fee farm of 2d. rent per annum formerly William Nuthille' his father as appears by the same copy dated Thursday next after the feast of Corpus Christi in the first year of the present King Edward 6th and pays for this at the aforesaid feasts per annum:

| viz: in the charge of the hayward | 10s and for two hens 4d. |
|---|---|
| (subtotal) | 10s. 4d and 15 eggs. |
| in the charge of the collector | 3s. 3d. |
| and for motfee | 10d. |
| (subtotal) | 4s. 1d. |
| in the charge of the reeve | 16s. 4d. |
| (total) | 30s. 9d. and 15 eggs. |

165. Elizabeth Sterne now the wife of Richard Sterne, formerly the wife of John Harman, holds for her and her assigns during the minority of Matthew Harmanne son and heir of the said John Harmanne by copy of the court by custom of the manor, one piece of land parcel of Grimescrofte containing by estimate 13 acres lying next to Megris, held from the lord by the fee - farm of 6d. per annum, one acre and a half of native land of tenement Nichols formerly John Atthill' held by the fee-farm of 8d. per annum, and one acre and a half of great-tenure lying in le Newecrofte in the town of Framlingham aforesaid formerly Matthew Harmanne' as appears by the same copy dated Wednesday next before the feast of the Nativity of the Blessed Mary the Virgin in the 31st year of late King Henry 8th and pays rent for this at the aforesaid feasts:

| | |
|---|---|
| viz: in the charge of the hayward | 20d. and for two and a half hens, 5d. |
| (subtotal) | 2s. 1d. and one egg. |
| in the charge of the collector | 3¾d. |
| and for moote fee | 10d. |
| (subtotal) | 13¾d. |
| in the charge of the reeve | 6s. 6d. |
| (total) | 9s. 8¾d. and one egg. |

166. Thomas Burton holds to him and his heirs by copy of court by custom of the manor, one acre of land and pasture from increment called Pratts of Coliar Lande formerly John Avelin', and two acres and one rood of land from increment parcel of ten acres of land from increment parcel of fourteen acres with appurtenances in Framlingham aforesaid held by the service of 7½d. per annum, formerly Robert Wright' alias Goodwyne' as appears by the same copy dated the Wednesday next before the Nativity of the Blessed Mary the Virgin in the 31st year of the oft-quoted late King Henry 8th and pays for this at the aforesaid feasts per annum:
viz: in the charge of the collector        7½d.

167. The aforesaid Thomas Burton holds for him and his heirs by copy of court by custom of the manor, one acre of native greater-measure land of tenement Fords held from the lord by the service and custom formerly Richard Coole' as appears by the same copy dated Wednesday next before the feast of the Nativity of the Blessed Mary the Virgin in the 31st year of the reign of the said late King Henry 8th and pays for this at the aforesaid feasts per annum:

| | |
|---|---|
| viz: in the charge of the hayward | 8d and one egg. |
| in the charge of the collector | 2½d. |
| (total) | 10½d. and one egg. |

168. The above-said Thomas Burton holds for him and his heirs by copy of court by custom of the manor two acres of arable land with appurtenances in Framlingham aforesaid as they lie in le Sande Felde alias Le Fairfelde, containing by estimate five roods of small farm, formerly Thomas Michell', held from the lord by the fee-farm of 10d. per annum, formerly Christine Calle', as appears by the same copy dated the Friday next after the Sunday in Easter in the 31st year of the reign of the said late King Henry 8th and pays for this at the aforesaid feasts per annum:
viz: in the charge of the hayward        10d.

169. The above-said Thomas Burton holds for him and his heirs by copy of court by custom of the manor, three acres of native land (6d.) once Robert Pistre' with appurtenances in Framlingham aforesaid formerly John Chirchehawe' as appears by the same copy dated Thursday in the first week of Lent in the 32nd year of the reign of the said late King Henry 8th and pays for this at the aforesaid feasts equally per annum:
viz: in the charge of the hayward        6d.

103

170. The widow of Henry Rossington holds for her and her assigns during the
minority of the son and heir of the said Henry Rossington by copy of court
by custom of the manor, all those things, lands and tenements which are
called Lokkingtons and Bucks with appurtenances which were once William
Lounde', viz., three acres of land (2s. 7d.) parcel of tenement Lokkingtons
and a close of native land containing by estimate three acres of small-tenure
land (22½d.) called Bucks with appurtenances in Framlingham aforesaid
and a certain parcel of land containing in length fifty-four regular feet and in
breadth twelve regular feet parcel of the common called Harboldshall grene
on which a grange has recently been built, held by the service of 1d. rent per
annum formerly Robert Alredde' as appears by the same copy dated the
Friday after Sunday in Easter in the 31st year of the reign of the said late
King Henry 8th and pays for this per annum at the aforesaid feasts equally
per annum:

| | |
|---|---|
| viz: in the charge of the hayward | 7s. 10½d and for two hens 4d. |
| (subtotal) | 4s. 6½ d and three eggs. |
| in the charge of the collector | 7½d. |
| and for motfee | 1½ d. |
| (total) | 4s. 11½d. and three eggs. |

171. The aforesaid widow of Henry Rossington holds to her and her assigns
during the minority of the aforesaid [blank], son and heir of the said
Henry by copy of court by custom of the manor, one messuage and seven
acres of native land (6s. 1½d.) of tenement of great-tenure with
appurtenances in Framlingham aforesaid formerly Francis Stebbing' as
appears by the same copy dated theWednesday in the second week of Lent
in the 33rd year of the reign of the said late King Henry 8th, and pays for this
at the aforesaid feasts equally per annum:

| | |
|---|---|
| viz: in the charge of the hayward | 4s. 8d., for two hens 4d., for 1 mowing, 2d. |
| (subtotal) | 5s. 6d. and seven eggs. |
| in the charge of the collector | 17½ d. |
| and for motfee | 4d. |
| (subtotal) | 21½d.) |
| (total) | 6s. 11½d. and seven eggs. |

172. John Hille holds to him and his heirs by copy of court by custom of the
manor, one piece of land from increment containing by estimate three roods
lying in Framlingham aforesaid in the Field called Sande Felde held from the
lord by the service of 1d. rent per annum formerly Robert Wright' as appears
by the same copy dated the Wednesday next before the feast of the nativity of
the Blessed Mary the Virgin in the 31st year of the reign of the oft-said late
King Henry 8th, and pays for this at the aforesaid feasts per annum:

| | |
|---|---|
| viz: in the charge of the collector | 1d. |

173. Thomas Brothers by right of his wife Margaret, John Baynhame by right
of his wife Joan, and Katerina Manbye, hold to them and their assigns during

the natural lives of each of Margaret, Katerina and Joan, a Field called Halffelde from the demesnes of the manor lying next to Sewterwente with appurtenances in Framlingham aforesaid as appears by the same copy dated the Wednesday next after the feast of St. Michael the Archangel in the 32nd year of the reign of King Henry 8th and pays for this at the aforesaid feasts equally per annum:

viz: in the charge of the reeve                     13s. 4d.

174. [refers to a property in Rendlesham.]

175. George Calle holds to him and his heirs by copy of court by custom of the manor, twelve acres (11s. 6d.) of native land of tenement Granger' and Warren', four acres and a half of native land (3s. 6d.) of tenement Stubbes, four acres and a half of native land (3s. 11½d.) with a messuage of tenement Stubbes and one acre (10½d.) of native land of tenement Cancis formerly Richard Sutton' once Thomas Wright' with appurtenances in Framlingham aforesaid formerly Christine Calle' widow, as appears by the same copy dated the Friday next after Sunday in Easter in the 31st year of King Henry 8th and pays for this at the aforesaid feasts equally per annum:

| | |
|---|---|
| viz: in the charge of the haward | 18s. 8d., for four hens, 8d. |
| (subtotal) | 19s. 4d.and six eggs. |
| in the charge of the collector | 13¾d. |
| and for motfee 18d. | |
| (subtotal) | 2s. 7¾d. |
| (total) | 21s. 11¾d. and six eggs. |

176. Anthony Russhe gentleman holds to him and his heirs 27 acres (23s. 7½d.) of great-tenure land lying in a close called Southawes with appurtenances in Framlingham aforesaid formerly John Pulham' as appears by the same copy dated the Friday on the feast of St. Thomas in the 35th year of the reign of the said late King Henry 8th and pays for this at the aforesaid feasts per annum equally.

| | |
|---|---|
| viz: in the charge of the hayward | 18s. and three hens 6d. and for two mowing-works, 4d. |
| (subtotal) | 18s. 10d. and 27 eggs. |
| in the charge of the collector | 5s, 7½d. |
| and for mootefee | 12½d. |
| (subtotal) | 6s. 8d. |
| (total) | 25s. 6d. and 27 eggs. |

177. William Verdon holds for him and his heirs by copy of court by custom of the manor, a messuage and one rood of native land, two acres (2¼d.) of land from increment parcel of nine acres from increment just as they are enclosed and lie in Framlingham aforesaid within the land of Thomas Burton formerly John Pulham Junior' on the part of the north, and a pightle of the said Thomas called Litte Hermers on the Part of the south with the eastern headland abutting on the close of the said Thomas called Hermers and the western headland abutting on the public road, formerly in the tenure of

105

Robert Goodwine, as appears by the same copy dated the Monday next
before the feast of St. Michael the Archangel in the 38th year of the oft-said
late King Henry 8th and pays for this by rent at the aforesaid feasts equally
per annum:

| | |
|---|---|
| viz.: in the charge of the collector | 2¼d. |

178. John Calle holds for him and his heirs by copy of court by custom of the
manor, a piece of land from the demesnes of the manor containing by
estimate 16 acres lying to the west of the highway leading from Framlingham
towards Mikilhounde held by the fee-farm of 8s. rent per annum, and one
acre of great - tenure land (10½d.) formerly John Jeffrey' once Alice Graunte'
lying to the west of the causeway next to the lord's park with appurtenances
in Framlingham. And a close (8s. 8d.) called Sex Acres lying next to the lord's
park, with one headland abutting on the lord King's Park there as in the same
copy dated the Tuesday on the vigil of St Matthew in the 33rd year of the
reign of King Henry 8th and pays for this at the aforesaid feasts equally per
annum:

| | |
|---|---|
| viz: in the charge of the hayward | 8d. and for one hen 2d. |
| (subtotal) | 10d. and one egg. |
| in the charge of the collector | 8s. 10½d. |
| in the charge of the reeve | 8s. |
| (total) | 17s. 8½d. and one egg. |

179. Joan Bradshawe recently the wife of Peter Bradshawe holds for herself and
her heirs by copy of court by custom of the manor, one piece of land formerly
part of the demesnes of the manor, a close called Sowterswente containing by
estimate ninteen once leased to John Stonley lately leased to Thomas
Murdocke with appurtenances in Framlingham aforesaid as in the same
copy dated the Wednesday next before the feast of St. Michael the Archangel
in the first year of the reign of the present king Edward 6th and pays for this
per annum at the aforesaid feasts equally-

| | |
|---|---|
| viz: in the charge of the reeve | 19s. |

180. John Pulham holds for him and his heirs by copy of court by custom of the
manor, one piece of land containing by estimate fifteen and a half acres of
land, and another piece of land containing ten acres by estimate and another
piece of land containing seven acres by estimate with a small piece of land
and a way lying to the east of the said ten acres and seven acres as it lies in
Framlingham in a certain field called le Faireffeld from the demesnes of
this manor by the rent of 35s. 2d. per annum as appears in the same copy
dated the day and year above said and pays for this at the aforesaid feasts
equally per annum:

| | |
|---|---|
| viz: in the charge of the reeve | 35s. 2d. |

181. Margaret Goodwynne widow holds term of her life for her and her heirs
by copy of the court by custom of the manor, four acres (8d.) of native land
by increment once John (Kin)ghous', one acre (2d.) of land from increment
once John Brodhey' with a cottage built on it, and one rood of native of

tenement Caneys and half a rood land from increment (2½d. and half a farthing) formerly Richard Stonehame', one rood of native land (2½d. and half a farthing) with a cottage formerly Richard Stube and one acre of native land of tenement Warrens held by the fee-farm of 8d. per annum, and one acre of great-tenure land (10½d.), one acre (6d.) of small tenure. And also two acres (6d.) and three roods and a half of land from increment with appurtenances in Framlingham aforesaid held from the lord by for ½d from increment per annum formerly Robert Goodwinne' as appears by the same copy dated the Monday next after the feast of the conception of the Blessed Mary the Virgin in the 28th year of the reign of the said late king Henry 8th and pays for this at the aforesaid feasts per annum:

| viz: in the charge of the hayward | 2s.2d., and for three hens, 6d. |
| (subtotal) | 2s. 8d. one egg. |
| in the charge of the collector | 19¾d. |
| and for mooteffee | 8d. |
| (subtotal) | 2s. 3¾d. |
| ( total) | 4s. 11¾d. and one egg. |

182. The same Margaret Goodwinne holds by copy of court by custom of the manor, a meadow containing by estimate two acres with appurtenances in Parham as it lies there, and one piece of land containing by estimate two acres with appurtenances in Parham lying in a certain field called highfelde held from the lord together at the fee-farm of 9s. 4d. per annum formerly in the tenure of as appears by the same copy dated the Monday next after the feast of the conception of the Blessed Mary the Virgin in the 28th year of the said late King Henry 8th and pays for this at the aforesaid feasts per annum:

| viz: in the charge of the hayward | 9s. 4d. |
| in the charge of the collector for motfee | 3d. |
| (total) | 9s. 7d. |

183. John Driver holds by right of his wife Katerina during the minority of Thomas Derneforde, one piece of land from increment parcel of three acres from increment parcel of nine acres containing two and a half acres and it lies in Framlingham aforesaid between the lands of Anthony Wingffelde knight called Clarbolds on the east and lands of the said Anthony once Rivers on the west and the northern headland abuts on the highway leading from Framlingham to Parham And also a piece of land from increment containing half an acre parcel of three acres in Framlingham aforesaid and it lies at Lampett broke with a highway there formerly in the occupation of Paul Dernefforde as appears more fully in the same copy dated the Wednesday next before the feast of the Nativity of the Blessed Mary the Virgin in the [blank] year of the late King Henry 8th and pays for this at the aforesaid feasts equally per annum:

| viz: in the charge of the collector | 14d. |

107

184. William Rousse holds for him and his heirs by copy of court by custom of the manor, a close of pasture called Mapledale with appurtenances in

Framlingham aforesaid containing by estimation sixteen and a half acres (8s. 3d) of land from the demesnes of the manor, and one acre of great-measure meadow (10½d.) from tenement Brothers formerly in the tenure of Reginald Rousse with appurtenances in Saxted and afterwards in the tenure of Anthony Rousse knight as appears more fully in the same copy dated the Monday next before the feast of St. Michael the Archangel in the 38th year of the said late king Henry 8th and pays for this at the aforesaid feasts equally per annum:

| | |
|---|---|
| viz: in the charge of the hayward | 8d. and one egg. |
| in the charge of the collector | 2½d. |
| in the charge of the reeve | 8s. 3d. |
| (total) | 9s. 1d. and one egg. |

Common Fine there:

185. From the Inhabitants of the town of Framlingham aforesaid for a common fine there paid from antiquity on the feast of St. Michael the Archangel viz: in the charge of the hayward   6s. 8d.

Total of all rents paid by Custumary Tenants with customary works in Framlingham aforesaid   £29 10s.7¼d. half a farthing and 259 eggs, of which,

| | |
|---|---|
| in the charge of the Hayward | |
| from rent     £14  4s. | for a common fine 6s. 8d. |
| | for 51 hens |
| | for 11 mowing-works 22d. |
| | and 260 eggs. |
| in the charge of the collector from rent | £4  0s. 5½d. |
| for motfee | 13s. 3½d. |
| In the charge of the reeve from rent | £9  10s  3d. |

Memorandum that the Tenaunts of the greate holde in Framlingham is Charged therby to finde yerely the Offic off the haywarde to Gather and Levye the Kings maiesties rents in Framlingham aforesais to that office appurteyning and bolenginge and to make accompte therof yerely before the Kings maiesties auditor and Recevour without any manner of fee. And the haywarde is Charged to receyve of every acre off greate holde 8d. and one Egge over and besides 2½d. of the same acre in the Charge of the Colltor and to gather all rents growing and arising off the Small holde, Fee ferme, Sithes and hens. And likewise he is bounde too see the Kings maieties haye fellyd and to give Knowledge to the Tenaunts there to make itt and to see it doune accordinglye. Item there is a Courte and a lete ther Kepte yerely and the proffitts therof arising is likewise in the Charge of the sayed hayward. Item there is in Framlingham aforeseyd two hundred and sixty one acres of the greate holde in the occupacionne of the sayed Tenaunts, and is dyvded into 21 hendes or offices and twelve acres is a hende berith the office for one yere and onse in 21 yere every acre is Charged therwith. And yf he that is the hende therof have nott in his owne holding the nombre of twelve acres then hath he helpe of some other folowing in the same hende to make upp the nomber of twelve acres, and the helper to paye for every acre therof to the hende 12d. and therby the seyd helper is discharged of gathering of the seyd rents And the hende takith the charge holy upon him.

Item The tenaunts of this holde aforeseyd is bounde likewise to bere the office of the Reve whoo is the officer both off framlingham and Saxted and is Charged only with the gathering of the demaynes is bounde And to make his accompte as before is mencioned withowte any Fee. And is chosen in like manner as the hawardes is And is Charged butt on yere in Framlingham and two yeres in Saxted and twelve acres of the seyd towne berith the office.

186. The Common in Framlingham aforesaid.
From a certain profit arising from the common there called Harboldshall Grene by estimate eight acres per annum, he does not answer because there was no profit arising from this except the 6s. 8d. above under the title of a common fine charged:
viz. in this charge                                   Nothing.

187. The Common in Saxted aforesaid.
Nor does he answer for a certain profit arising from the Common of Saxted aforesaid containing by estimate 30 acres per annum, on the grounds that no profit arose from it except the 3d. charged afterwards in the common fine and on the grounds that by ancient custom it was granted to the township of Saxted aforesaid:
viz:  in the charge of the                               Nothing.

Tenants at the will of the lord Framlingham aforesaid of parcels from the demesne.

188. Robert Appleyard gentleman holds at the will of the lord a wood called Offerey Woode containing by estimation fifty acres and three acres of pasture adjacent to the same wood lying towards the east, and also three acres of arable land lying in Framlingham aforesaid and pays for this at the feasts of the Annunciation of the Blessed Mary the Virgin and St.Michael the Archangel equally per annum:
viz: in the charge of the reeve                          40s..

189. Reginald Gibbonne holds similarly at the will of the lord a pasture called Botenhawe containing by estimate thirty-five acres with the pasture of a wood adjacent to it and pays for this per annum at the aforesaid feasts per annum:
viz: in the charge of the reeve                          £7.

190. Thomas Sheming holds similarly at the will of the lord a pasture there called Bradelhawe containing by estimation thirty-two acres, a pasture of the wood adjacent to it called Bradelhawe Woode containing by estimate twenty-six acres and pays for this per annum at the aforesaid feasts equally
                                  53s. 4d.

109

191. The lease of a Fair held there at the feast of St. Michael the Archangel
and Tolls of the market-place there held on Saturday every week viz. from
the revenues of the same from year to year paid at the feast of St. Michael
the Archangel per annum:
viz:  in the charge of the bailiff                                    13s. 4d.


Total of the rents arising as well from the Tenants at will as from the profits of
the Fair there                                                    £12  6s.  8d.,
viz: in the charge of the Bailiff                        17s.  2d
in the charge of the reeve                               £11  13s. 4d.

192. Grazing of the Park
Nor does he answer for any profit arising annually from the grazing of the
lord King's park of Framlingham aforesaid, on the grounds that no revenue
arose on the oath of Robert Appleyarde gentleman and parker or keeper of
the aforesaid park and on the oaths of various men loyal to the lord King.
viz: in the charge of the                              nothing
                                                       in the office bailiff.


Memorandum that the seyde parke adionith to the Castell of Framlingham and
conteyneth by estimacion 400 acres and every acre is worth to be letten
                                         20d. yerely.

193. Item in the seyd parke is a faire Lodge Newly [see also Text 3, p14] buylyd
with a garden and
divers houses of offices therunto adioyning and conteyning in it self half an
acre where in nowe the seyd Robert Appleyarde keper of the seid parke
dwelleth in, who hath the going or sending of 16 heade of neate and on bulle
with two horses over and besides his Fee hereafter mencioned.

194. Meadows there
Nor does he answer for any profit arising or growing from a meadow lying
within the parke aforesaid called Hall meadowe containing by estimate ten
acres per annum on the grounds that it is reserved for the sustenance of the
lord King's wild animals in winter-
viz: in the charge of the                              nothing
in the office of the
bailiff.

195. Nor does he answer for any profit arising or growing from another meadow
there lying within the aforesaid park called Newe Meadowe containing by
estimate twelve acres per annum, on the grounds that eight acres of the same
meadow are submersed with the water or lake there called Le mere so that no
profit came from it  and the remainder of it is reserved for the sustenance of
the lord King's wild animals of Framlingham aforesaid:
viz: in the charge of the                              nothing
in the office of the bailiff.

196. Nor does he answer for any profit arising from the fishery of the lake or water aforesaid called le Mere lying in Le Newe meadowe aforesaid within the park aforesaid per annum on the grounds that the fishery of the same is totally reserved for the use of the lord King:

viz: in the charge of the                  nothing
in the office of the bailiff.

197. Nor does he answer for any profit arising from a barn and two stables with a pightle adjoining them called Le Stabell yarde containing by estimate three acres, lying next to the aforesaid park per annum, on the grounds that the aforesaid barn and the aforesaid stables are reserved to store the lord's hay in winter for the sustenance of the lord's wild animals in winter, and the profits arising from the aforesaid pightle from antiquity are granted to the aforesaid bailiff Robert Appleyarde the lord King's bailiff there by virtue of his office:

viz: in the charge of the                  nothing
in the Office of the bailiff.

Memorandum that the sayed meadowes above mencioned are severally made as herafter foloweth. First the sayd meadow called Hall meadow the tenaunts are bownde to doo ther service in making if the same as upon every holde above is mencioned and the King is charged butt with mowing, carying and Innyng of the same. And the other meadowe called Newe meadowe is made holye att the King's majesties charge. And the hey coming of them both is Inned and mowed in the barne and stabelles above seyd for the sustentacion of the dere in the winter by the bayly. And the baylye hath the going of one horse in the parke of Framlingham aforeseyd.

Item, every acre of the seyd meadowes is worth to be letten          3s. 4d.

198. Pasture of a wood there called Newhawe woode
For anything arising from the grazing or pasture of a wood called Newe hawghe woode containing by estimate 50 acres, per annum, he makes no answer because the profit coming from this was granted from antiquity to the aforesaid bailiff by virtue of his office:

viz: in the charge of the                  nothing
in the office of the bailiff.

199. Site of the Castle of Framlingham aforesaid
Nor does he answer for any profit arising from the site or precinct of the said lord King's Castle there with all and singular the gardens, apple-orchards and other Empty grounds within the precinct of the Castle lying and being there, per annum, on the grounds that the profits coming or growing from this source were granted from antiquity to Thomas Sheminge Keeper of the same Castle by virtue of his office:

viz: in the charge of                  Nothing          111
in the office of the bailiff.

Memorandum the sayed Castell is adioyning to the Towne of Framlingham very strongly walled and dyched and with owte the dyche of the same is a faire garden and certayne voyde groundes and conteyneth in itt selff with the garden and voyde groundes and other house by estimacion 5 acres. And many of the houses of the same Castell is in great decaye and diverse of theme is like to falle downe onlesse they be shortly repaired And one Thomas Sheming is keper of the same and hath the iestmente of 2 kyne in the parke of Framlingham aforeseyd over and besides his fee hereafter mencioned.

Memorandum that the Towne of Framlingham is a markett Towne and hath a Libertie that the Sheriffe shall nott execute or serve any processe within the Libertie upon any manne but deliver itt to the baylye and the baylye to have the execution therof and also there is Framlingham one parysshe Churche and in Saxted another and be a myle distante the one from the other and one Rowland Cotton Clerke is parsom there and is butt one benefice and hathe bene parfson there by the space of 4 yeres and hadde it of the gyfte of Thomas late Duke of Norffolk and is worth yerely £40 and hath a faire mancion housse to dwelle in adioyning to the Chirche yarde of Framlingham aforeseyd Furthermore the Chancell of the seyd Churche with the Iles of the same was plucked downe by the sayed late Duke of Norfolke and is nott as yett all buylded upp againe Also there is certayne leade whiche was taken of the seyd Churche with glasse bourdes and Tymber appurteyning to the seyd Churche lying in the Castell aforeseyd and much of the seyd tymber is redy framed for the use of the same Churche.

Free tenants of certain lands there by custom of the manor bearing the office called Le Woodwarde office for maintaining the pale of the lord King's park viz. of Framlingham.

200. Tenement Verdons

From a certain profit arising from twelve acres of land there in the tenure of Robert Jargafelde per annum, he answers nothing on the grounds that the aforesaid twelve acres of land were granted to the said Robert Jargafelde from time beyond the memory of man without paying anything for it in rent except the services below specified and declared:

viz: in the charge of the here,                    nothing
in the office of the bailiff.

201. Tenement Haywards

Nor does he give and answer for any profit arising from twelve acres of land there now in the tenure or occupation of Godfrey Irelond, John Nuthill and John Warner per annum on the grounds that the reason above said in the nearest particular precedent is recited:

viz: in the charge of the                    nothing
in the office of the bailiff.

112    202. Tenement Canes

Nor does he answer for any profit arising from twelve acres and a half of land. There now in the tenures or occupations of John Dorrant, Nicholas Sutton,

John Helwis and Godfrey Irelond per annum, because the above-said in the second nearest precedent is recited:

viz: in the charge of the                            nothing
in the office of the bailiff.

Memorandum that these three Tenements above mencioned are bownde by the Tenure of there Lande to maynteyne and upholde the King's maiesties park pale of Framlingham and to kepe the reparacion therof yerely every one in his parte. And they to have tymber mete and necessarie for the same att the King's maiesties officers' appointment  And the seyd Tenaunts are bownde likewise to fell, carye, bind and sett uppe the same at ther owne proper costs and charges And also to bere all other charges therunto belonging  Excepte the rale to be sawen att the Lordes charge   And likewise they to have the olde payle And all windfalles falling upon the seyd payle And moreover the seyd payle is devyded to thes three heades and to every tenemente likemmuche  And the contente therof is abowte by estimacion three miles with the Scite of the Castell  Also they have the Goyng of three horses in the seyd parke every Tenemente one.

Total of the complete valuation of this domain of Framlingham aforesaid with its members:

| | |
|---|---|
| viz: in the charge of: | |
| the hayward of Framlingham from rent | |
| | £14 16s. 10½d. |
| from a common fine there | 6s. 8d. |
| from 64 ½ hens | 10s. 9d. |
| from customary works | 22d. |
| from 260 eggs worth | 12d. |
| (subtotal) | £15 17s 1½d. |
| the hayward of Saxted from rent | £15 0s 8½d. |
| from a common fine there | 3d. |
| from various customary works | 6s. 2d. |
| from the rent of 65 hens | 10s. 10d. |
| from 365 eggs 18¼d. | |
| (subtotal) | £15 19s. 5¾d. |
| the collector of Framlingham and Saxted from rent | £30 3s. ½d. |
| from a common fine of Ashe | 2s. |
| from mooteffee | 35s. 4¼d. |
| (subtotal) | £32 0s 4¼d. |
| the reeve of Framlingham and Saxted from rent | £25 7s 2d. |

113

£26 18s 9d.

the bailiff from the profits of a fair with
tolls of market 17s. 2d.

(total)                                              £84 0s. 17d.
from which:
In the Rentall the …ys… £31   10s 9¼d and half a farthing besides extr … ys
made by the auditor boke 64th att London. To ask to make the accorde to the
rental for itt so chargys in the audit

Rents Paid Out

203. In rent paid out Master Louth, gentleman, to the 21d. per annum to be paid
at the Feast of St.Michael then per annum:
viz: in the office of collector                    21d.

204. In a similar rent paid to the manor of Cranes Hall to the 12d. per annum
payable at the aforesaid feast then per annum:
viz: in the office of collector                    12d.

205. In a similar rent paid put to the heirs of Matthew Harmanne to the 16d. per
annum payable at the aforesaid feast per annum:
viz: in the charge of the collector                16d.

206. In a similar rent paid out to the manor of Ketelberghe to the 12d. per
annum payable at the aforesaid feast then:
viz:  in the office of the collector               12d.

Total of Rents Resolute          5s. 1d.

Fees and Wages.
207. In the fee of Robert Appleyarde gentleman the lord King's bailiff there at
2d. per day granted by reason of the execution of his office from year to year
paid at the feasts of the Annunciacion of the Blessed Mary the Virgin and St
Michael the Archangel equally per annum:
viz in the allowance of                            60s. 10d.

208. In the fee of the said Robert Appleyarde keeper of the lord King's park of
Framlingham aforesaid granted to him by reason of his execution of his
office from year to year at 100s. per annum paid at the aforesaid feasts
equally:
viz. in the allowance                              100s.

209. In the fee of Thomas Sheminge keeper of the lord King's Castle of
Framlingham granted by reason of the execution of his office at 100s. per
annum from year to year paid at the aforesaid feasts equally:
viz, in the allocation of                          100s.

210. In money paid to the rector of Framlingham aforesaid for the tithes coming
as well from the park of the lord King of Framlingham as for various
meadows there reserved for the sustenance of the said lord King at 20s. 4d.
per annum paid to him from antiquity:
viz. in the allocation of                                    20s.4d.

                        Total                        £14  0s. 14d.

Bondmen of bloode Regardaunte to the seyd lordshippe off Framlignham
aswelle dwelling within the seyd lordshippe as without.

211. John Capon of Framlingham husbandmanne of the age of 56 yeres having
8 children, Robert, John, Luke, John, Agnes, Kathrine, Joan and Alice, and is
worth in goods                                £66 13s. 4d.

212. Roberte Athered of Framingham aforeseyd Tyler (?) of the age of 50 yeres
having 5 children, John, William, Roberte, Lyonell and Elizabeth and is
worth in goods                                nothing.

213. William Capon off Parham husbandmanne in the Countie off Suffolk of
the age of 50 yeres having 5 Children, Roberte, William, Thomas, Margarett
and Alice and is wortth in goods              £10.

214. William Capon of Glemham carpenter of the age of 29 yeres having noo
childen nor yett goods but in Copye holden of the manor of Soteton and is
of the clere yerely valewe off                20s.

215. William Capon of Dersham carpenter of the age of 68 yeres having two
children Phillippe and Roberte is worth in goodes
                                               £20.

216. John Capon of Glemham husbandmanne of the age off 36 yeres having
twoe children, Roberte and Margerye and is worth in goodes
                                               £30.

217. Richarde Wyarde of Erle Soham off the age of 52 yeres having 9 children,
William, Randolff, Roberte, John, Nicholas, Humffrey, Margarette, Joan and
Denise is worth in goodes                     £40.

218. Robert Wyarde of Erle Soham off the age of 52 (22) yeres having noo is in
revercione after the deceasse of his mother of certen Copye holde of the clere
valewe off 60s and is worth in goods
                                               £6  13s. 4d..

[in rough- draft later hand]
219. Roger Alen of Elwerton by Boxford of the age of 50 ther a belongeth
bound to Framlingham [   ]f or [   ]    for [   ] to Stoke [   ] to but [   ] valor          115

## Comments

In putting the data contained in the survey to practical use, whether backwards in time towards a reconstruction of the medieval town or forwards for 'house-history' research, chapters 16-20 (pages 342-388 inc.) of Robert Loder's History of Framlingham are virtually indispensable. Published in 1798, Loder in effect made available to a wider readership for the first time the work of Robert Hawes (1665-1731) previously seen only by the owners of the three, possibly four, exquisite, hand-written copies of his History of Framlingham. Another highly capable local historian, the printer Richard Green, stated in his History of Framlingham published in 1834 (footnote p. 11) that Robert Hawes was engaged in writing and copying his MS volumes between 1712 and 1724. The earlier of these dates may be singularly pertinent. It coincides with Hawes' appointment as Steward of Framlingham by Pembroke College. It also marks the point at which he ceased compiling tenancy-histories of many of the properties described in the surveys of 1547 in order, presumably, to complete his magnum opus. A marginal note in the MS Bod. (fol. 14) bears the date 1711 in what appears to be one of Hawes' informal hands, suggesting that he probably had access to both versions of the survey.

CHAPTER 9

# The Inventory of Framlingham Castle 1606

## Preface

Most inventories encountered by researchers are those which originally accompanied the wills of the recently deceased in order to facilitate the distribution of goods and chattels according to his or her last wishes. Framlingham's grandest such 'probate inventory' was certainly that of 1524 compiled after the death of Thomas the 2nd Duke. At the other end of the income-scale, several 17th -18th century examples of the inventories drawn up by the parish overseers of the few worldly possessions left by the poorest of the poor can be found in Framlingham's excellent collection of Parish Records (ref. Suffolk Record Office, Ipswich, FC101).

Another circumstance necessitating the production of an inventory was a change in the ownership of a property or the departure by death or otherwise of the officer in charge of it. A spectacular example in the former category is the collection of inventories in the National Archive concerning the contents of Kenninghall Palace after the forfeiture of the 3rd Duke in 1547. It is unfortunate that no companion volume for Framlingham Castle appears to have survived.

Inventories have a number of different applications. On the one hand, the typical probate inventory compiled by neighbours as soon as practicable after a death had occurred can be a rich source of dialect and of information fuelling the standard-of-living debate. Individual artefacts and objets d'art listed in the inventories of the wealthy, on the other hand, readily open up new avenues of research. One such project which may prove worth initiating concerns the fate of the tapestries described and valued in the Inventory of 1524, especially the History of 'Arcules'.

Perhaps the most useful feature of any inventory is the order in which the various rooms, corridors and outbuildings are listed: it is possible in many instances to recreate the route taken by the valuers through a typical 16th century Suffolk farmhouse, for example. It is precisely this application which makes the newly-discovered inventory of Framlingham Castle in 1606 a valuable resource. With the execution of Thomas the 4th Howard Duke in 1572 for his involvement in

117

the Ridolfi Plot to replace Elizabeth on the throne of England by Mary Queen of Scots, the last chance for Framlingham Castle to be returned to its full glory finally disappeared. Thomas had intended to make Framlingham the family home again. For the next thirty years, the Castle was again in royal ownership and leased to what Richard Green in 1834 chose to call 'a plebeian race of tenantry'.

In 1603, The Framlingham estate was returned to the Howards by James 1st: it was, however, divided into two moieties but neither of the inheriting Howards, neither uncle nor nephew, was interested in renovating the castle. The nephew, Thomas Howard, was in that same year created Earl of Suffolk and landed one of the most financially rewarding posts in the realm, the office of Lord Chamberlain. It was also the year in which, with the assistance of the uncle Henry Howard Lord Northampton, he began to build Audley End, the largest privately-owned house in England. Framlingham Castle was again put out to lease and it was a change of lessee from Edward Shemyng to Thomas Fuller which occasioned the inventory of 1606.

This manuscript is one of a small gathering of documents which strayed from the main collections into the archive of the Henniker Estate at Thornham. Because successive historians of Framlingham, including Hawes, Loder and Green, seem not to have known of its existence, an early-to-mid 17th century date for its 'disappearance' appears likely. It is not in good condition and was clearly a draft in the first instance: deletions by the clerk are here entered in italics. It is now located in the Ipswich branch of the Suffolk Records Office, as part of MS. ref. S.R.O.I., HD88/6/1.

### TEXT 9

An Invetory of sutche things as were left in the Castle at Framlynghan by Edward Shemynge unto Thomas Fuller the 27th of September anno domini 1606.

First of all, in the **Dynyng Chamber**, one longe Table of furre, 2 longe Tables, Three Formes, one other short Forme.

In another **Chamber by the Dynyng chamber**, 2 lokes one to [ … ] with a cable.

Item in the **longe Entery**, one forme.

Item in the **great hall**, 3 Tables, 3 shorte formes, 3 longe Ashen shoores, 2 pecces for a (Crune).

Item in the **Buttery**, 4 Beere stalles, one Table with a locke one the doore and one Table.

In the **Pantery** one Breed Binge with 3 several roomes and 3 shelves.

*Item in the Pantery one beere stall*

Item in a **Chamber over the longe entery**, one Beere stall.

Item in **a chamber over the Panetry,** one levry table, *Locke and* a key.

In the **Pantery** one locke and a key.

In the **Skollery,** one Payer of musterd quearnes, twoe shelves and one Bouldting tub with 2 sevrall romes.

In the **inner kitchen** 2 plankes for dresser *Boordes.*

Item in the **prevy kitchen** 2 iron Rackes with 2 stall.

In the **Commen Kitchen,** 2 Boylinge leds and a marble Stone in the Grownde, one longe dresser Boorde.

In the **Pastery,** 3 mowlding Boordes and a planke hanging up.

In the **Gate chamber** one levry Table one ould dubill shelfe to sett pewter one.

In the **seller next the Porters lodge** 2 beere stalles.

Item **over the Buttery** one levery table.

In the **Brewhowse** 3 Fattes one (n..olynge) board and a troffe.

In the **mellhowse** 3 stones a hopper and a trundle and a horse myll.

In the **Wyne seller,** one Beere stall.

In the **Chapple chamber** 2…(.rei...) of Iron of the **great gunne** one (..) key to the doore.

*In the Chaple chamber 2 lok keyes to the doore.*

In the Chaple one aulter stone.

Item in the **Burgony stayers** one Great Copper.

Item 2 ladders.

Item in the **Burgo**[….].

Item 2 ladders.

## Comments

The Castle appears to be unfurnished and uninhabited, although this inventory could have belonged to the type which listed only the rooms within the building and the fixtures within them. This would explain the presence of tables still in place in the Dynyng Chamber and the Great Hall. Some of the ancillary buildings, notably the brewery, continued in use for

119

another forty years or more. The spectre of a vigorous asset-stripping exercise in 1603 will not disappear, however, and the possibility that the two Howards removed the remaining furniture and furnishings between 1603 and 1606 appears very real. The tradition repeated by Richard Green, that the Hercules Tapestry was removed from Framlingham to Audley End, gives some support to this hypothesis, as does the entry for October 8th 1667 in Samuel Pepys' Diary: ' there was not one good suite of hangings in all the house (Audley End), but all most ancient things, such as I would not give the hanging up of in my house'.

The 'Hercules' saga continued with the story that during a visit to Audley End by William 3rd (1694-1702), the said king so admired the tapestries that he removed them to one of his (unspecified) palaces in Holland. For any researcher attempting to bring 'Arcules' back to Framlingham Castle, if only on loan for a temporary exhibition, the Dutch connection does seem to be the best starting-point. It is equally possible, however, that some of the Framlingham tapestries were un-pegged from the walls and taken to Kenninghall Palace soon after 1524 where they were described in the Inventories of 1547 (above), or that the widowed Duchess Agnes sold some and transferred others to her residence in Lambeth. Indeed, the inventory of Henry VIII's tapestries in his Palace of Greenwich catalogued after his own demise in 1547 included '9 peces sorting late bought of tholde Duchesse of Norfolk'. This last fragment of information comes from an abridged version of Henry VIII's inventory and clearly the entire original document would have to be searched for further items of the same provenance.

For architectural historians, this inventory poses as many questions as it answers. There are glaring omissions. No mention is made of, for examples, the garderobe (storage-room for large items), the stables, well or armoury even though the office of Armour-Keeper was still in existence in 1611. The 1524 inventory counted three dining areas and fourteen 'chambers'. In 1606, only five chambers were identified and the dining-rooms had been reduced to two. On the other hand, this appears to be one of the very few references to the 'The Long Entry', linking the Dining Chamber and the 'Great Hall': to confuse still further any attempt to visualise the interior of the Castle before the demolition really began, the Entry had a chamber 'over'. It could have occupied the space below the present Lanman Museum through which the household staff delivered food and drink to the former State Chamber eastwards and southwards to the Great Hall. One alternative interpretation among many could be that it was an internal service corridor running east to west along and integrated within the block of rooms crossing the court seen by the local historian Matthew Leverland between 1653 and 1679.

Difficulties with the Long Entry notwithstanding, those who drew up the 1606 inventory progressed anti-clockwise round the inside of the curtain-wall. There is no mention of the block of high-quality chambers against the east wall of the Castle (e.g. 'My lord's chamber in 1524). A possible explanation for this omission may be that Schemyng and then Fuller resided in it. The presence of part of the 'Great Gunne' in the Chapel Chamber is, at the very least, intriguing: Fuller was, however, holding the offices both of Bailiff and of 'Armour-Keeper' in 1611. The presence of the 'Great Copper' on the 'Burgony stairs' is similarly puzzling. This reference to the Burgony (allegedly a corruption of 'Barbican' or watch-tower) could be significant. The exceptionally high Tower Six in the curtain wall is located where the 1606 inventory infers a Burgony was situated, near or, in this case, above the chapel. Alternatively, this 'Burgony' referred to the tower in the Dungeon block, in which, according to a 15th century account-roll, an oratory or private chapel existed.

# CHAPTER 10

# A Thriving Market Town
## The Rental of Framlingham Market c. 1610

## Preface

Provided that the names of the rent-paying tenants have not been arranged in alphabetical order, a detailed rental can be of considerable assistance to the historical reconstruction of a village, manor or township: this applies also to other types of documents, for example Subsidy (Tax) Returns, Muster Rolls and Extents. This Market-Rental from the closing decades of the Howard era demonstrates vividly that Framlingham's economy was in good fettle and provides useful evidence for the lay-out of the space occupied by the shops and stalls on market-days.

The market complete with Toll-House was fully operational by 1270, according to one of the early Extents. An early 13th century date for its inception is extremely likely. Both it and its partner the borough appear to be 'seigneurial' in origin, established by one or other of the Bigod lords of the manor as an entrepreneurial venture to generate income from rents and tolls. Quite when the freely held properties abutting onto the market-place, Bridge Street and Church street were granted self-regulating borough status is difficult to ascertain. The 'Burgh' was not mentioned in 1270 and the account-roll for 1279-1280 ominously refers to the Tax of the Town (ville'), not of the Borough ('burgi'). The account for 1301-2 confirms its existence then and the immensely important roll of 1324-5 adds that the 'seventeen' properties formerly described as 'sub villa' (suburbs) were then called the 'seventeen messuages in the borough'. Tenants of the shops, inns and a few private residences within the borough were known as 'burgesses', their properties as 'burgage tenements'. According to White's Directory of Suffolk in 1844, about seventy burgage-holders still existed then.

The original manuscript transcribed below is the only example of its type discovered so far in the Framlingham archive. Catalogued as Pembroke College Cambridge MS. L8, it is undated, but matching the shop and stall-holders with the burials in

Framlingham Parish Registers has caused a change in its estimated date from the late 17th century to *c.*1610.

## TEXT 10

| | | |
|---|---|---|
| John Powes, glover, | for a shop, | 10s. |
| William Smyth, shoemaker, | for a shop, | 10s. |
| Richard Goodwyn, butcher, | for a shop, | 10s. |
| John Bucher, butcher, | for a shop, | 10s. |
| George Hewet, sadler, | for a shop, | 10s. |
| John Cooper, pewterer, | for a shop, | 10s. |
| Thomas Smythe, barber, | for a shop, | 10s. |
| George Sawier, [MS. defective.] | for a shop, | 10s. |
| Anthony Church, barber, | for a shop, | 10s. |
| Robert Duckling, chapman, | for a shop, | 10s. |
| | | |
| Franciscus Balie, chapman, | for a stall, | 5s. |
| Marie Church, | for a stall, | 5s. |
| Richard Lowndy, butcher, | for a stall, | 4s. |
| John Blyeth, butcher, | for a stall, | 4s. |
| Robert Spaldyng, butcher, | for a stall, | 4s. |
| John Girlinge, butcher, | for a stall, | 4s. |
| Richard Goodwyn, butcher, | for a stall, | 3s. 4d. |
| John Sarlet, butcher, | for a stall, | 6s. 8d. |
| George Burch, butcher, | for a stall, | 3s. 4d. |
| William Johnson, butcher, | for a stall, | 3s. 4d. |
| Edmond Sarle, butcher, | for a stall, | 3s. 4d. |
| Thomas Girlinge, butcher, | for a stall, | 3s. 4d. |
| James Dene, butcher, | for a stall, | 3s. 4d. |
| Barnaby Gibson, butcher, | for a stall, | 3s. 4d. |
| William Spaldyng, butcher, | for a stall, | 3s. 4d. |
| Thomas Bucke, chapman, | for a stall, | 2s. 6d. |
| John Cornishe, chapman, | for a stall, | 2s. 6d. |
| Margaret Horsin, | for a stall, | 2s. 6d. |
| Eliha Balie, peddler, | for a stall, | 2s. 6d. |
| William Coppyng, mercer, | for a stall, | 2s. 6d. |
| John Dye, chapman, | for a stall, | 2s. 6d. |
| John Archer, chapman, | for a stall, | 2s. |
| John Archer, chapman, | for a stall, | 2s. 6d. |
| Thomas Bulleyne, weaver, | for a stall, | 2s. |
| Robert Saterne, weaver, | for a stall, | 2s. |
| William Smythe, weaver, | for a stall, | 2s. |
| Robert Romsye, weaver, | for a stall, | 2s. |
| John Wyard, | for a stall, | 2s. |
| Robert Nunne, weaver, | for a stall, | 2s. |
| Edmonde Cricke, chapman, | for a stall, | 2s. 6d. |
| Robert Cole, shomaker, | for a stall, | 16d. |
| William Smyth, shomake, | for a stall, | 16d. |
| William Shemynge, shomaker, | for a stall, | 16d. |

| Thomas Mosse, shomaker, | for a stall, | 16d. |
|---|---|---|
| Robert (Curdise), smyth, | for a stall, | 16d. |
| Edward Shemynge, cobler, | for a lytle shope, | 2s. |

## Comments

Attention is drawn immediately to the block of ten which heads the list of thirty-six holders of shops or stalls. Without question, these match in number the shops situated at ground-floor level in the Market-Cross or Toll-House, their shop-fronts sheltered by a portico. The south-easternmost shop-space served as an overnight clink for much of its history but was replaced later in the 17th century by a parish cage close-by in the market-place called 'the goose-house'. The upper storey, in which the 18th century schoolroom was later located, was divided into two, the one half being reserved for the use of the borough court and the other for the storage of stalls between market and fair days. Certainly of 13th century origin or earlier, this large, presumably stone, building was a prominent feature of the market-place until *c*.1789 when it was considered unsightly. Those towns-men who persuaded Pembroke College to allow its destruction most certainly deprived the modern tourist industry of Framlingham's third, if not second, best historical attraction. Not one contemporary representation of it, in pencil, ink, paint or print has yet been identified.

For those contemplating its 'virtual reconstruction', the market-house at New Buckenham in Norfolk may prove a useful model in the first instance. Placing Framlingham's toll-house within the market area solely from documentary sources is remarkably difficult. The first edition of the Ordnance Survey Map covering the area was drawn up between 1816 and 1820 and shows, when suitably magnified, that the two sites currently occupied by the Prince of India Restaurant and the single-storey, lightly-built block of three shops were both in existence then. This casts serious doubt as to whether the Toll-house despised by those 18th century property-owners who thought it spoiled the general view of their prestigious, newly-fronted properties was fully demolished. The broadly north-south orientation of the above restaurant's roof leads to the conclusion, until proven otherwise, that the Toll-house occupied the space now taken by both these two buildings: it may not be entirely coincidental that the three shops are sited where they are.

Because the borough courts were not consistent in their function as land-registries and only seldom gave details of property-boundaries, tracing the history of the inns and shops abutting the market-place is a thankless if not impossible task. What clearly emerges from the available documentary evidence is that the large majority of properties on the east side of the market-place and of Church Street were at some time or other inns, eating-places or beer-houses. The first extant list of licensed premises in Framlingham was compiled between 1617 and 1620 when the corrupt M.P. Giles Mompesson, collected £5 per licence on behalf of the crown before absconding with the takings:

| | |
|---|---|
| Beare | George Stockdale |
| Bell | Edmond Crosse |
| Crosse Keyes | Thomas Fuller for his Inne |
| Swann | Bartholomew Jackson |
| White Hart | Tobias Nuttall |
| White Horse | George Stockdale |
| White Lyon | Francis Driver |

Five of the above hostelries can be identified with confidence. The Bell, for which a probate inventory exists, stood at the west gate to the churchyard at the top of Church Lane: it was part of the church glebe and one of the few messuages in the Manor of Framlingham Rectory. The Swan was located in the south-eastern corner of the market-place, now a hairdressers' salon and stationery shop. The White Hart is now the Crown and Anchor. The White Lyon, now a restaurant and solicitors' office, stood at the bottom of Church Street facing the White Hart across White Hart Lane, now Crown and Anchor Lane. Neither the Beare nor the Crosse Keys have been identified. Of the two obvious omissions, the Griffin, now Bridges & Garrards plus Carley & Webbs, was first mentioned by name in a court-roll of 1620 and the Crown in a churchwarden's account of 1635. It should be stressed that all these properties had almost continuously functioned as inns or beer-houses for three hundred years and more before the above dates. The Griffin lent its name to the gate at the eastern end of Crown and Anchor Lane. The Griffin Gate is one of the few documentary references available for suggesting Framlingham may, at a much earlier point in time, have been a walled town. The name of one of the medieval inns may have survived in a surname of *c*.1381, 'Le Cock': its site has yet to be ascertained.

Given the perennial enthusiasm of the more bibulously inclined local historians to collect the names of inns and alehouses, a list is provided below of those premises in Framlingham which, although of post-Howard date, were licensed between 1712 and 1715 by the licensing magistrate Devereux Edgar together with the names of their keepers. Two additional pubs from the Framlingham Tithe Book of 1716 are here added for good measure:

| | | |
|---|---|---|
| Crown | John Newson | 1712 |
| White Lion | John Ribbons | 1712 |
| Shoulder of Mutton | Mary Letherland | 1712 |
| Black Swan | Edward Kell | 1712 |
| White Hart | Elizabeth Morgan | 1712 |
| Bird in Hand | Joshua Gardiner | 1712 |
| Griffin | John Slea | 1712 |
| Dove | Thomas Doughty | 1712 |
| Stair House | Thomas Kemp | 1712 |
| Bell | Thomas Meane | 1712 |
| Marlborough's Head | Anne Newman | 1712 |
| White Horse | John Kemp | 1712 |
| Two Potts | Nicholas Malster | 1713 |
| Black Horse | Thomas Doughty, *jun.* | 1715 |
| Bush | Thomas Grey | 1716 |
| Blue Boar | Edward Kell | 1716 |

Returning to the Rental, the clusters of butchers, chapmen, and weavers within the open market area strongly indicate that in *c*.1610 separate zones had been set aside for the different groups of traders. By contrast, the barber-surgeons both operated indoors. There were, again, inexplicable omissions such as the fishmongers and bakers. Butchers were particularly numerous as were the complaints in borough and manor courts concerning the way they conducted their business. Blood from animals slaughtered out in the market-place or in the shops flowed out onto the pavements. The disposal of unwanted animal parts was evidently a problem: it should have been no surprise that, during the recent construction of the Solar supermarket, a large pit of bovid's skulls was found opposite the present Post-Office. For the butchers at least, the pronounced slope in the market-place brought a positive benefit. Their industrial waste trickled down Queen's Head Alley towards the river, an arrangement which continued well into the mid-20th century, according to oral tradition.

Unlike Bungay and Ipswich, Framlingham market-place appears not have had a bull-stake to which the animals were tethered before being tormented by dogs: this allegedly enhanced the flavour of the meat. In clearing away the stalls after each market, encroachment onto the market space first by permanent stalls and then by lightly-built shops was prevented. Saxmundham market allowed both these developments, the results of which can still be seen complete with alleys between the different zones. That the stalls for use in Framlingham's fairs were also stored upstairs in the Toll-House may be evidence that the fairs also were usually held in the market-place and not in Fairfield, which was originally arable land belonging to the demesne. That Fairfield was used for certain official community uses was attested in a notable 16th century land dispute, however.

CHAPTER 11

# Constructing the Tomb of
# Henry Howard the Poet Earl

Griffith's Memorandum to Mr. Fuller, 1616.

## Preface

Although not equal in reputation to the three other tombs in the Howard Chapel (i.e. the chancel) in Framlingham church, the tomb of Henry Howard 'The Poet Earl' is nevertheless one of the monuments which attracts many visitors to the town. Any new source of information concerning its specifications and construction is therefore of considerable interest.

The document transcribed in Text 11 below was found in the same recently discovered gathering of miscellaneous notes as the inventory of 1606 in Suffolk Record Office Ipswich MS. HD88/6/1.

### TEXT 11

*28th July 1616*

To take order presently before the Tumbe maker comes downe to bricke up the doore and to new plaster with lyme and haire the two pillers against which the tumbe is to be erected and withal to whiten them and to close up the cracke in the (fr)ame of the windowe.

To give the Tomemaker when he comes his best directions and helpe in furtherance of the worke and now and then to caste his Eye upon him to see it be well followed and Artificiallie wrought and that accordinge to covenaunt and by articles between him and me all the materials be eyther Touche [Raynske-after Rennes in Brittany] or Allabaster and that he use noe wood eyther for crest or anythinge else. And to take a precise noate of the daie he beginns to sett up the Tumbe.

To inclose with boardes the place wheare the Tombe ys to be sett up that both the Tumbemaker maie more precisely folowe his labure and that he worke yt selflye (safely) not open to be defaced by any or other idle persons that comes into the church whiles that is in doeinge.

To agree with ioyner to make a grate about the Tumbe suitable to that of the two dutchesses, likewise with a smyth for iron pickes to be sett upon the Toppe of the grate.

To sende to Mr Shepherde for money as he shall have cause to to use yt for performance of these thinges with whom I will take order to supplye him.

To hearkene for a perpetuall rent of fortye shillings per annum to be purchased neare Framlyngham for the keepeinge the tombe and mayntenance in repayre of that parte of the Chapel over yt.

To wryte unto me in the beginninge of September to what estate the worke is and to convey yt unto me by Mr. Shephearde.


John Griffith.

## Comments

This small document appears to make a disproportionately large contribution to the bank of information concerning the Howard Chapel and tombs. Reminiscent, perhaps, of the army of workmen employed by Henry VIII in 1538 to raze the entire village of Cuddington in Surrey for space to build his 'Nonesuch' Palace, Thomas the 3rd Duke's men had flattened, in 1545, the medieval chancel of Framlingham to accommodate family tombs including those previously at Thetford Priory. The Survey of 1547 (see Text 8) compiled after Thomas' execution in that year confirmed that the rebuilding work was not then completed:
'Furthermore the Chancell of the seyd Churche with the Iles of the same was plucked downe by the sayed late Duke of Norfolke and is nott as yett all buylded upp againe  Also there is certayne leade whiche was taken of the seyd Churche with glasse, bourdes and Tymber appurteyning to the seyd Churche lying in the Castell aforeseyd and much of the seyd tymber is redy framed for the use of the same Churche.'

Entries in the churchwardens' accounts for 1557 and 1558, suggest that, thanks to money-raising sales of church ornaments and a modest donation from the deceased Edward VI 'towards the reparation of the church', the work of restoration was then virtually finished. An extent of 1589 in the National Archives (ref: E164/46, fol. 272) introduces an element of doubt as to how thoroughly the work had been conducted:
'That the Iles of both sides of the chauncel of Framlingham have always been repaired by the said late Erle (Philip of Arundel) and his auncestors and is now utterlie decaied, the charges of repairing whereof will amount unto about forty shillings. And the reparacion of the said Castle, Iles (and) of the (Mille-) bridge are veere needful to be done'.

The reference in the very first paragraph of Griffiths' Memorandum to patching up the crack in the window-frame casts doubt as to whether the repair works had ever been fully completed to a high standard. It invites speculation also that the chancel had been extended at the cost of building on unstable ground, the lip of a late-Saxon or early medieval defensive ditch.

The decision to site the Poet Earl's tomb where it necessitated bricking up a door and plastering over both it and the two pillars next to it was extraordinary: hair-line cracks in the plaster over the door are visible in 2009. It begs the question as to why the Poet Earl's new tomb had not been placed in the South Aisle on the plot taken 20 years later by the monument to Sir Robert Hitcham. The 'Hitcham' plot was, perhaps, already occupied in 1616 or had been reserved for the tomb of another member of the Howard family not yet deceased. Because the Poet Earl's remains had been sent from London to Framlingham in 1614, it is feasible that a temporary tomb had been stationed in the South Aisle while arrangements were made for the construction of his permanent monument. If the plot were indeed reserved, the Poet Earl's own son, Henry Howard, Earl of Northampton (d.16th June 1614) would be one leading candidate and another, his grandson, Thomas the First Earl of Suffolk and builder of Audley End (d.1626). It appears only a very remote possibility that the fragmented tomb of Thomas the 2nd ('Flodden') Duke was still at Framlingham in storage at the Castle in 1616 with the intention that it would eventually be restored and erected next to that of Thomas the 3rd Duke and his wife.

The precautions taken for the safety-at-work of the anonymous tomb-maker, thought to be William Cure (al. Cuer) 2nd son of William Cure 1st (both master-masons of Dutch extraction in the employ of James 1st.), and the construction of spiked iron cages round both the Duchesses' tomb and that of the Poet Earl, seem to add to the evidence for local disaffection towards the Howard regime.

# CHAPTER 12

# *The Beginning of the Demolition*
## The Stones Account, 1656.

## Preface

Theophilus Howard, the 2nd Earl of Suffolk inherited the Framlingham estate and a mountain of debt in 1626. His father Thomas had expended £200,000 (*c.* £25m.) on building and furnishing Audley End and Theophilus the ' able-bodied nonentity' proved almost his equal in profligate spending. A 'fire-sale' became inevitable and Framlingham was sold eventually to lawyer Robert Hitcham in 1635 for £14,000 (*c.* £1.75m). Hitcham died 15 months later leaving a will riddled with 'ambiguities' and a sting in its tail that if Pembroke did not obey his wishes Framlingham was to be given to Emmanuel College instead.

A short probate inventory of Hitcham's goods 'In the Castle' in 1636 (Pembroke College MS. D11, fols. 22-3) underlines the impression given by the Inventory of 1606 that the physical condition of the Castle had deteriorated further:
'In the Castle.
Item one Iron Gunne and a chamber ten shillings.
Item one Mill price fifteene shillings.
Item in the Brewhouse Yard thirty shillings.
Item tymber in the Courte yard thirty shillings.
Item tymber in the Maultinge house and Lead in the Queenes Lodgeinge five pounds and tenne shillings.
Item Tymber in the Seller at the Halls end five shillings.
Item Tymber in the Plumbers Chamber thirty shillings.
Item twenty five Bunches of Lathe and newe Boards there fortie shillings.
Item twoe Ladders in the long Entry six shillings eight pence.
Item tymber in the kitchin and back Yard one pound and five shillings.
Item ould Bricks Tyles and Stone fiftie shillings.
        Summa seaventeene pounds Eleven shillings and eight pence'.

The references to building timber and to 'old' bricks, tiles and stone, suggest the

Castle was being used as a store and that piecemeal demolition had already begun. If it can be assumed, despite the much reduced number of interior buildings listed, that the valuers again proceeded anti-clockwise from a point on the west side of the court, the Queen's Lodgings were, as tradition maintains, on the east side. This seems to be a reference to Queen Mary's 12-day visit to the Castle in July 1553. It again appears to be the case that the Long Entry linked the cluster of high-quality chambers against the east wall to the 'workhouse' block against the west wall. The Back Yard seems identifiable with the former Inner Court. It should be born in mind that the brewery itself and some of the other buildings were in the hands of tenants in 1636 and that their contents were not the property of Sir Robert Hitcham. It has to be assumed that the formerly 'prince-like' Chapel was empty but still standing.

As late as 1644, Theophilus' son James, the 3rd Earl of Suffolk, petitioned the House of Lords to annul the sale of Framlingham to Hitcham on the grounds that his father sold it under its real value when he (James) was only fourteen years old and that Sir Robert Hitcham had 'craftily resorted to Recoveries and a Writ of Error to bar his claim'. The dispute was apparently settled in 1649 when Pembroke Hall paid James the sum of £2000 (*c.* £180.000). Fresh disputes had arisen meanwhile, several of them involving the steward of the manor Edward Alpe.

The order to begin the demolition of the Castle interior is therefore attributable not to Pembroke Hall but to a clause in Hitchams' will:
'Item, I will that presently after my decease, all the Castle, saving the stone building be pulled down....'
It took the Ordinance of Lord Protector Oliver Cromwell dated March 20th 1653 to break the various legal log-jambs and confirm sole ownership of the estate on Pembroke. Bricks recycled from buildings inside the first court of the castle were to be used for the construction of Hitcham's almshouses: the building specifications for this work still survive. Demolition of stone buildings began in 1655.

Of the five batches of stone the highway surveyors of Framlingham parish purchased in that first year, the largest by far was entered against 'Mr. Alpe': this was for 'nine days' work and for stone, £3 15s 0d.'. Among the properties Alpe held was the estate now known as Framlingham Hall which included 'Bird's Meadow' (its 19th century name) on the north bank of the River Wincknel abutting at its eastern end onto the Roman road listed in Vol.1 of I.D. Margary's '*Roman Roads in Britain*' as 34B. In 1964, high-quality carved stone fragments were excavated there by a local enthusiast Anthony Moore. Other pieces had previously been given to Ipswich Museum by the tenant farmers. By kind permission of the present farmer, Mr. John Wall, further work was undertaken in 2008 by the Deserted Medieval Settlements Archaeological Team. More carved stone was retrieved from the footings of a 17th century hovel. Specialists from English Heritage are of the opinion that the stone is from a tomb or tombs dated 1370-1440. The most likely origin of these sculptured fragments is the chapel within the Castle, courtesy of Edward Alpe, 1655.

1656 was certainly the busiest year in this phase of demolition to the extent that the Highway Surveyors of Framlingham parish created what amounts to an appendix at the end of their annual account to record the removal of stone. This document survives as Suffolk Record Office Ipswich, FC101/A3/6/59, fol. 4.

## TEXT 12

*The Accounte of the Stones*

| | |
|---|---|
| Payde to Mr. Sampson for 125 lodes of stones | £05-08-08 |
| Payde to Mr. Storland for 5 lodes of stones and for a Tree for a Truncke | £00-11-08 |
| Payd to John Draper for 40 lodes of stones | £01-13-04 |
| Payd to Robert Mooer for 12 lodes of stones | £00-12-00 |
| Payd to John Sater for 38 lodes of stones | £01-18-00 |
| Payd to James Criknell for 1 lode of stones | £00-01-00 |
| Payd to Poll Dade for 6 lodes of stones | £00-06-00 |
| Payd to Thomas Tabell for 1 lode of stones | £00-01-00 |
| Payd to Jaremey Raymer for 6 lodes of stones | £00-06-00 |
| Payd to Thomas Fisher for 3 lodes of stones | £00-06-00 |
| Payd to S(del) Mr. Goultey for 5 lodes of stones | £00-05-00 |
| Payd to Mickell Spurlling for 8 lodes of stones | £00-08-00 |
| Payd to John Weber for 12 lodes and a halfe of stones | £00-12-06 |
| Payd to John Shaperi(n)..for 4 lodes of stones | £00-04-00 |
| Payd to Thomas Kell for 3 lodes of stones | £00-03-00 |
| Payd to Thomass Clarcke for 3 lodes of stones and a halfe | £00-03-06 |
| Payd to John Blanding for 1 lode | £00-01-00 |
| Payd to Thomas Boldrey for 15 lodes and a halfe of stones | £00-15-06 |
| Payd to John Moorise for 2 lodes of stones | £00-02-00 |
| Payd to John Mayes for 6 lodes of stones | £00-06-00 |
| Payd to John Shimonge 41 lodes of gravell at 2d. the lode and for the Trespies for feching of the gravell | £00-08-02 |
| Payd to Thomas Stimson and John Skiner and Jones Spincke for bring on up of 16 lodes of stones upon the Casell hilles | £00-16-00 |
| Payd foor a plancke for a brige and for 1 stolpes for to laye the planckeone and for the mending its the mending it | £00-03-06 |
| Payd for a brige mending in the Casell Brockes | £00-01-00 |
| Payd to Rycherd Smythe for newe hamyer for to breake downe the Casell Walle in woyte of it eleven pounds at 4d. the pounde | £00-03-08 |
| Payd to Richerd Smythe for a picke layinge | £00-01-04 |
| Payd to John Dowsing for the Ordinance | £00-00-08 |
| The Totell Sume of the Desbursments | £52 07 10. |
| | (*c.* £10,000) |

| | |
|---|---|
| Thomas Fisher | John Blomfild |
| Thomas Clarke | Mihell Spruling |
| Thomas Peare | Thomas Baker his marke |

## Comments

That Mr. Sampson was the leading supplier of stones adds credibility to his statement concerning the fate of the chapel recorded in his History of Framlingham (*c.*1663):
'In the same court also was a neat chappell now wholly demolished, anno 1657, and transported into the highways'.

In 1657, Henry Sampson, rector of Framlingham (above) during the 'Usurpation' 1650-1660, had removed a further 12 loads of stone. His total of 137 loads was approached only by that of the deposed rector 'Mr. Golty', at 109 loads. These priests were therefore not only eye-witnesses to and leading perpetrators of the Chapel's demise, but appear also to have profited from it. Golty's role in the demolition is particularly intriguing, given that he was carrying out the orders of a regime he presumably did not support politically.

The garden of Framlingham Rectory, whether in the care of either Sampson or Golty, abutted at its high, eastern end onto the Castle Hills from which 16 loads of stone were also taken (above). This entry in the account therefore brings valuable evidence to bear on whether a defensive outwork had been located there, outside the Castle moats, in an earlier period: it would make an ideal position from which a hostile force could bombard the lower court of the castle with downward cannon- or ballista-fire. There is also the possibility that if Framlingham had ever been a walled town, this would be the logical place to secure its north-eastern corner with a fortified watch-tower.

It follows that under the road-surfaces of modern Framlingham lie tons of carved stone not only from the chapel but also from the other stone buildings abutting onto the inside of the curtain wall of the Castle (excluding the Hall on the site of the workhouse). The road to Dennington seems to have caused particular trouble in the 16th and 17th centuries and may have been the main beneficiary, If some of the stone-pickers named above and in the other extant accounts 1655-8 followed the example of Edward Alpe and diverted cart-loads from filling holes in the roads to other uses, some buildings in Framlingham may contain, as at Bird's Meadow, 14th century body-parts of late-medieval lords and ladies from the Castle carved in soft Norfolk 'clunch' (limestone). The only positive documentary evidence that stone was put to such other use is to be found in the 1657 account, when John Draper tipped 50 loads into a slough in 'le Faierfield, against John Shymyng's land'. That deposit, if not damaged by the waterlogged ground, is presumably still in situ.

# Bibliography

**Printed Sources.**

British Library, Catalogue of the Arundel MSS, London, 1829.

Brown, M., Framlingham Castle, Suffolk - Survey Report, for English Heritage, 2002.

Chamberlin, R., *Audley End*, English Heritage, 1986.

Crawford, A., *Howard Household Books*, Alan Sutton, 1992.

Dymond, D., *The Register of Thetford Priory*, The British Academy and The Norfolk Record Society, 1995.

Given-Wilson, *The Parliament Rolls of Medieval England*, The National Archives (CD).

Green, R., *The History, Topography and Antiquities of Framlingham and Saxted*, London, 1834.

Kilvert, M.L., *A History of Framlingham*, Bolton and Price, 1995.

Loder, R., *The History of Framlingham*, Woodbridge, 1798.

MacCulloch, D., *Suffolk and the Tudors*, Clarendon Press, Oxford, 1986.

Martin, T., *The History of the Town of Thetford in the Counties of Norfolk and Suffolk*, London ,1779.

Oxford Archaeology Unit, for English Heritage, 'Framlingham Castle', Suffolk Conservation Plan, 2003.

Raby, F.J., & *Framlingham Castle Suffolk*, HMSO, 1959.
Reynolds, P.K.,

Ridgard, J.M., *Medieval Framlingham*, Suffolk Records Society, Vol. XXVII, 1985.

Robinson, J.M., *The Dukes of Norfolk*, Phillimore, 1995.

Stratford, Jenny, *The Bedford Inventories*, Society of Antiquaries, London, 1993.

Smedley, W.,     'A newly Discovered fragment of a Daily Account Book for Framlingham Castle, Suffolk', in *PSIAH* (41), 2005.

Thomson, W.G.,   *A History of Tapestry*, Hodder and Stoughton, 1930.

Williams, N.,     *A Tudor Tragedy*, Barrie & Jenkins, 1964.

**Manuscript Collections Consulted.**

Arundel Castle Archive -  MS A1610.

Bodleian Library, Oxford - MS Gough Suffolk 2.

British Library -  Add. Ch. 16554
Add. Ch. 27451
Add. Ch. 16555
Add. Ch. 17745
Add. Ch. 24688
Add. Ch. 76202
Lansdowne 106 no. 45.
Lansdowne 406.

College of Arms- MS Arundel 49.

The National Archives- LR2/113-117
E164/46, f.271-3

Norfolk and Norwich Record Office - MS. Rye 74.

Pembroke College Cambridge Archives - Framlingham L 17.

Pembroke College Archives, Framlingham L theta.
Pembroke College Archives, Framlingham D11.

Pembroke College Archives, Framlingham Court Rolls I for the year 1520 and passim.

Pembroke College Archives, College MS. Framlingham Lz (zeta).

Pembroke College Archives, College MS. Framlingham L theta.

Pembroke College MS. 300.

Suffolk Record Office, Ipswich Branch - FC101/A4/1/1.
HD88/6/1
FC101/A3/6/59
FC101/E2/31 and passim.

*NOTE: Readers are advised to check all three indexes if they want a profile of any particular individual or place-name.*

**INDEX 1**

# *Keeper's Account*
**CHAPTER 4**

People and Places

Aldered, Robert  25
Aldred, Roger  33
Antonye, Mastyr  30
Any's, lady  22
Appilleyarde, Roger  47
Arendelle, lady  51
Arnedelle, lady  48
Arundelle, lady  21
audyt  21, 24
audyte  32, 33, 41
audytyr  44
Awdeley, Sir John  35
Awdeley, Syr John  23, 38
awdyt  28, 30, 36
awdyte  33, 34
awdyter mastyr  24
Aylmer  30
Aylmer, mastres  50, 52
Aylmer, Robert  25
Aylmer, Thomas  24
Aylmere, Sir Roger  53
Ayschfelde, Jorge  19

Bacon, Dam Margery  29
Bacone, mastres  51
Badingham, parson of  51
Badyngham  31
Badyngham, parson of  37, 41
Bakar, Jeorge  43
Baker, George  52
Bakone, Thomas  48

Baldre, mastres  52
Baldre, Thomas  30, 43
Baldrye, Thomas  39
Banyerd, Thomas  24
Barbor  45
Barker, John  32
Barnes, lady  43, 50
Barnes, lord  25, 31
Bedynfeld, Edmond  22
Bedyngfeld, lady  29
Bedyngffylld, master  47
Belynforyth, Thomas  48
Belyngeford, master Sir  52
Benet, Thomas  36
Berey, abbot of  40
Berneys, lady  37
Berry  24, 26, 42
Berry, abbot of  26, 42,
Berrye, selerer of  39
Bery, Abbot of  33, 35, 49, 51
Bery, prior of  52
Berye, Sellerer of  31
Betson, Syr John  25
Blaksalle, parsone off  47
Blaksalle, parson of  43, 49
Blander Hasset, lady  50
Blanderharsete, mastress  52
Blaxshalle, parson of  37
Blenerhasset, Dame Margaret  43
Blenerhasset, John  23
Blyant, Watyr  29

135

Boleyne, Sir Edward 52
Bongey 36, 43
Bongey, prioress of 26
Bongey, pryoress of 23
Bongey, townschyp of 27
Bongeye, towne of 32
Bonggey, townshepp of 24
Booleyn, Sir Thomas 39
Boreman, John 52
Borneman, John 49
Borowe, parson of 41
Bothe, Sir Philip 51
Bouser, lady 44, 47, 51
Bowse, Sir John 36
Bowser, lady 20, 30, 32, 36
Boyeth, lady 47
Brame, lady 23, 26
Brandon, Sir Robert 31
Brandon, Syr Robert 24
Breget, Syr Doctyr 25
Brewse, Robert 32
Brewsse, mastrys 43
Brewsse, Robert 22, 23
Brisyard, abbas of 47
Broket, Edward 43
Bromhill, prior of 52
Brosyard, Abbas of 20
Brosyarde, abbas of 40
Brosyerd, abbas of 26, 42
Brosyerd, abbes of 29
Brosyerd, abbess of 45
Brosyyerd, abbas of 23
Brosyyrd, Abbas of 35
Brown, Robert 22
Browne, Robert 36
Bryan, *mastyr Chasy ys clarke* 20
Bryant, mastyr 45
Bryaunt 37
Brysyarde, abbas of 51
buck 18, 48, 53
Buckler, William 20
Bucknam, Willyem 29
Bucus, Willyam 48
buk 19, 21, 22, 23, 24 25, 26, 27, 28, 29, 30,
31, 32, 33, 34, 35, 36, 38, 39, 40, 41, 42, 43,
44, 47, 48, 50, 51, 52
Buknom, Jeorge 37
Bukynham, Jorge 31

Bulleyn, Sir Thomas 44
Bungey, towne of 40
Burdy, Mastyr 22
Burels, Thomas 50
Burton, Mastrys 26
Butley, Prior of 51
Butley, prior of 35, 47
Butley, Pryor of 20
Butley, pryor of 24
Butleye, prior of 40
Buttley convent of 26
Buttley, prior of 37, 41, 49
Buttley, Pryor of 27
Buttley, pryor of 24, 29, 31
Buttley, pryoy of 28
Byrsschope, lord 38
byschope of Norwyche 27

Calle, Doctor 35, 48
Calle, Nicholas 24, 37, 38, 43, 44, 49, 49, 51
Calle, Nocoles 47
Calle, Robert 23
Calle, Nycholas 31, 36, 41, 45
Cally, Nycholas 37
Cally's, Nycholas wyffye 34, 37
Callys, Nycholas 34
Caltheprope, Sir Fraunces 49
Caltherope, Sir Phillipe 50
Calthorpe, Frances 37
Calthorpe, Fraunces 41, 47
Calthorpe, Frauncys 40
Calthorpe, Fraunsys 45
Calthorpe, lady 37
Calthorpe, Sir Fylype 37
Caltrolpe, Edward 41
Caltrope, Fransis 51
Campsey, Priores of 49
Campsey, prioress of 24, 26
Campsey, pryoress of 35
Camsey, Pryores of 22
Camsey, Pryoresse of 21
Candelmas 34
candelmes 34
candyllmes 34
candylmaes 34
candylmes 38
Cansey, priores of 47, 51
Cantrell, Ralff 52

Capele, lady 39
Car, Doctor 50
Cardenalle, lord 44
Carleton, mastyr of 43
Carlton, mastyr of 26
Castlaker, prior of 43
Catesby, lady 40
Catyr, Robert 31
Catysbe, lady 37
Catysbe, ladye 32
Caundysche, Rychard 26
Caundysche, Syr Rychard 32
Cawndyshe, Sir Rychard 35
Cawnedysche, Rychard 29
Chafy, mastyr 20
Chafy, Mr. 20
Chamber, Richard 18
Chamber, Rychard 31
Chambre, Rychard 42, 47
Chambyr, Rychard 21, 25, 29, 30, 33, 34, 38
Chananer 23
Chancerey 35
Chase, Mastyr 32
Chaumber, Richard 50
Chauncy (Chasye), mastyr 36
Chauncy, mastyr 37
Cheek, Robert 28
Cheeke, Robert 22, 24
Cheeke, Syr Robert 22
Chek, mastyr 25
Cheke, John 33
Cheke, mastyr Robert 37, 38
Cheke, obard 47
Cheke, Robard 51
Cheke, Robert 30, 32, 35, 43, 45
Cheke, William 19
Chelisworth, parson of 51
Chyrete, John 49
Clopton, Syr Wyllyem 27
Clowthe, Wylyem 27
Cole, Simon 53
Collanes, lordship of 52
Collnes, Lordschipe off 47
Collome, Roger 48
Colton 35
Colveeke 23
Colvylle, Robert 20
Colvylle, Rychard 26

Comissarie, Master 47
commysary, mastyr 35
comyssarye, Mastyr 29
Cook, Herry 23, 44,
Cooke 29
Cooke, Herry 39
Coole, Thomas 36
Coolle, Doctor 31
Cornwalese, Edward 22
Corpus Christi Gylde of Norwych 31
corrector, mastyr 34
Corrector, mastyr 31, 37
Corsome, lord 47
Corsoun, lord 40
Cosyn, Thomas 30
course 19
Crane, master 47
Crane, William 36
Crispe, John 49
crist cherche, pryor of 23
Cristichurche, prior of Ipswiche 47
Cristismas 49
Cryst Churche, pryor of 19
cryst chyrche, prior of 37
Crystechurche, prior of 51
Crystmas 20
Cursom, lord 38
Cursome, lord 50
Curson, Syr Robert 29
Cursonn, lord 35
Cursum, lord 27
Cursunn, Dame Anne 26

Dacres, lord 39
Dallyng, Geffrey 36
Danyelle 25, 30 32
Danyelle, John 32
Danyelle, Syr Jamys 30
Dawnde, Edmonde 23
Dawndye, mastyr 28
daye, Lady 50
deane of her chapell 52
deane of his chapell 52
Debnom, lady 21
Debnom, vicar of 19
Demok, Sir Lyonelle 34
Dennington 53
Denyngton 42

137

Denyngtone 50

Denys, Mary 29

Derham, Abbot of 22

do 20, 21, 33, 36, 37, 44

Dod Nysch, pryor of 26

Dodnysche, pryor of 23

Dodreysche, pryor of 19

doe 19, 37, 50

dog 21, 25, 36, 49

Done, Humfrey 27

Donwich, Toune 47

Donwyche, prior of the black fryers 38, 42

Donwyche, towne of 22 32, 40

Donwyche, town of 44

Downewich, towne of 51

Dowty 29

doys 20, 21, 24, 25, 28, 29, 30, 31, 32, 34, 36, 37, 38, 41, 42, 44, 45, 46, 47, 49

Draper, John 35

Drure, mastrys 19

Dune, Humfrey 48

Dychyngham 49


Echyngham, John 29

Echyngham, John *and Edward hys sonne* 29

Echyngham, lady 44

Edmond, lord 39, 44

Ele, prior of 47

Ely, poor of 28

Ely, Prior of 51

Ely, pryor of 29

Elye, prior of 35

Elye, pryor of 32

Elyzabethe of Boleyne, lady 23

Erle Soham, parsone of 50

Ersham Parke 34

Everard, Herry 27

Everard, Rafe 31

Evered, Herry 20

Everord, Herry 24

Everton 31

Everton, Humfrey 22, 23, 24, 26, 36

Evertone, Humfferey 52


fallow deer 18, 19

138  Fastale, masteres 47

Fastalle, masteresse 50

Fastalle, mastrys 26, 33, 43

Fastalle, Thomas 24

Fastoff, Thomas 52

Fastolfe, mastres 51

Fastolfe, mastrys 40

Fastolle, mastyr of Pettow 43

faunyngetyme 48

fawn 19

fawnyngtyme 31, 34, 38, 42

fawnys 20, 21, 25, 28, 29, 31, 34, 38, 42, 44, 45, 46, 47, 50

fawynyngtyme 19

Fayerweyther, Thomas 49

Fayrechillde, John 52

Feast of Corpus Christi. 53

Filstoue, prior of 47

Flexton, prioress of 32

Flyxtone, pryoress of 23

Forthe, Robert thelder 35

fownyngetyme 50

Fox, John 34

Foxe, John 42

Foxe, Marget 41

Framlingham, parson of 39

Framlingham, Survey of 15, 17, 75, 77, 79,

Framlyngham 34, 47, 50

Framlyngham Gylde 48

Framlyngham gyllde 43

Framlyngham Parke 33, 46, 50, 53

Framlyngham, parson of 22, 23, 24, 27, 28, 30, 32, 33, 35, 45, 49

Framlyngham, parson of for his tythe 35

Framlyngham, parson of for hys tythe 33

Framlyngham, parson of for tythe 30, 45

Framlyngham, parson of for tytthe 49

Framlyngham, servaunts and sowgyors at 32

Framymgham, Syr Jamys 29

Framyngham, Sir James 35

Fraunceys, Robert 50

Fwatyr, lords 40

Fylstow, prior of 41, 42

Fylstow, pryor of 23, 27

Fylstowe, prior of 40

Fylstowe, pryor of 37

Fyncham, John 44

Fyncham, mastyr Thomas 36, 39

Fynchome, John 52


Game, Nycholas 31

Ganelle, Thomas 26
Gardener, William 52
Gardener, Wylliam 45
Gardyner, William 49
garget 19, 32, 41, 44, 48,
gargett 32
Garland, John 43
Garlond, John 35
Garlonde, John 51
Garlunde, John 49
Garnyche, John 49
Garnyshe, mastyr 25
Garnyssche, John 45
Garnysshe, John 27
Garnysshe, Mastyr 31
Garrson, herry 21
Geldyngham, Mastyr 32
Gelgate, Edmond 19, 47, 47
Gelgate, Edmunde 51
Gelgate, mastyr 40
Gelgatt, Edmond 35
Gelone, Reynold 52
Geney, Syr Edmond 23
Germyn, John 41
Germyn, mastrys 24
Gernard, John 26
Gerningham, Mary 48
Gernyngham, Edward 27
Gernyngham, (Mary) 48
Glemham, John 22, 24, 25 35, 40, 51
Glemham, Sir John 35, 51
Glemham, Syr John 40
Glemham, towne of 32, 49
Godfferey, Thomas 52
Godsalf, master 52
Goldyngham, John 20, 27
Goldyngham, mastyr Goldyngham 32
good Fryday 25
Gosnalle, Robert 43
Gosnold, Robert 49
Gosnolde, Robard 52
Gray, John 27
Great Lodge 53
Great Rising of 1381 53
gres 19
gresse 19
Grey, Elizabeth 48
Greye, Elizabeth 48

Grymston, Edward 23, 26
Grymston, Houg 25
Grymston, Thomas 37
Guylde of Framlyngham 27
gyld of Framlyngham 35
Gylde of Framlyngham 23
gylde of Framlyngham 32, 39
Gylforthe, Sir Herry 38
Gylgate, Edmund 30
Gyrlyng, Houg 39

Hadley 33
Halle, Thomas 25
Halle, Wyllyem 23
Hallsworthe, baly of 50
Hamerton 26
Hamerton, mastrys 44
Hamerton, Reyner 23
Hansard, Antonye 29
Hansart, Anthony 31
Hansart, Antony 21
Hansert, Sir Anthony 35
Hanserth, Anthony 37, 40
hare 42
Hare, doctor 52
Harleston, towne of 19, 36
Harlston 23
Harlyston, townshepe of 30
Harlystone, towne of 43
Harman, Cristofer 19, 26, 28, 33, 40, 49, 51,
Harman, Matthew 19, 33, 40
Harman, Cristover 47
Harman, Crystofer 24, 35, 37, 40, 45,
Harman, Matthew 31, 37, 43, 47, 49
Harmane, Matthew 33
Harvye, Robert 45
Haryson, Mastyr 32
Hasseet, mastyr 24
Hasset, Marget 40
Hasset, masteres 47
Hasset, mastres 40
Hasset, mastrys 25
Hasset, mastrys Marget 36
Hastyngs, Syr Rychard 22
hawdite 49
Haylmer, Robert 31
Hedge, Syr Wyllyem 22
Henne, William 40

Henry VIII 18
Henyngham 42
Henyngham, George 40
Henyngham, John 19, 23, 26, 28, 45, 47, 51
Henyngham, mastyr 41
Hersham 34, 41, 46
Hersham parke 38
Hevenyngham, John 24, 30
Hevenyngham, Jorge 29
Hevertone, Humfrey 48
Hevyngham, John 35, 40
Hevyngham, Mastrys 30
Hevyngham, Syr John 38
Hewat, Crystofer 33
Hey, Prior of 35
Hey, Pryor of 20, 31, 33
Hey, pryor of 24, 26, 30
Heydon, Sir Cristofer 52
Heydon, Sir Crystofer 37
Heye, pryor of 19
Heyward, Cristofer 48
Hitcham, Sir Robert 53
Hobbard, Syr Jamys 29
Hobberd, Syr Jamys 22
Hogon, Robert 40, 52
Hogone, masteres 50
Hogone, Richard 52
Hogone, Robert 43
Holfereth 49
Holsiley, parson of 52
Holy Rood 36
Hopton, Arthur 30
Hopton, Artur 26
Hopton, Mastyr 22
Hopton, Sir Arthur 35
Hopton, Syr Arthur 40
Hoptone, Sir Artur 47, 50
Hottoffe, mastrys 25
Howard, Anne 26
Howard, Edmonde 37
Howard, Edmond 38, 44
Howard, Edmond 39
Howard, Edmund 30
Howard, lord Edmond 44
Howard, Lord 20, 21, 26
Howard, lord 22, 23, 24, 25, 28, 29, 30, 31, 33
Howard, mastyr Edmund 33
Howard's, lord servaunts 33

Howard's, lord servauntys 30
Hoxon, pryor of 19
Hubard, Waltyr 26
Hubbard, Syr Jamys 24, 27
Huggone, Sir Robard 47
Hulle, Thomas 27
Hunt, John 33
Hyham, mastyr 26
Hylle, Jamys 31
Hylle, Edmond 41
Hylly, Thomas 42

Ichyngham, John 19
Ichyngham, lady 48, 52
Ichyngham, Sir Edward 36
Ickeyngham, Sir Edwarde 51
Iechyngham, John 22
Ippwyche, towneschyp of 27
Ipswich, Towne of 51
Ipswiche 50, 51
Ipswyche, towne of 19
Itchingham, Sir Edward 47

Jackesson, Nicholas 39
Jackessone, mastyr 39
Jacob, Edmond 23
Jacob, Edmund 34
Jacobe, Edmunde 52
Jacobe, Syr John 22, 33
Jacsone, master 51
Jakson, master 48
Janney, Elizabeth 52
Jarmyne, John 48
Jeney, lady 29
Jeney, Rychard 29
Jeney, Sir Edmonde 47
Jeney, Sir Edmond 35, 42
Jeney, Sir Edmunde 49, 51
Jeney, Sir Edmund 28, 45
Jeney, Syr Edmond 40
Jeney, William 35, 40, 47
Jeney, Wylliam 42
Jenney, Edmond 19
Jenney, John 22, 23
Jenneys, Sir Edmond 41
Jenye, Willyem 28
Jermyn of Mettfeld 37
Jernyngham, Edward 22

Joly, Nicholas 33, 39, 44, 51
Joly, Richard 21

Kelsale, parson of 20, 24, 30,
Kelsalle 41
Kelsalle, parson of 26, 43,
Kemp, mastyr 39
Kempe, Elizabeth 43
Kempe, Robert 30, 31, 41
Kennyggahelle 49
Kennynghalle 28
Kent, master 51
Kent, mastyr 40, 45
ketylbere, parson of 44
ketylberggys, parson off 44
Ketylbergh, parson of 30
Ketylberghe, parson of 26
King Henry 8 31
Knyvet, Edward 43
Knyvet, Syr Thomas 29
Kook, Herry 22
Kooke, Herry 36
Kylle, Mr 21
kyng Henry the VIII 21, 29, 42, 47
Kyng Herry 33
Kyng Herry the 8 25
kyng Herry the 8th 38
kyng Herry the VIII 34, 50
kyng's celester 21
Kynge, Jamys 33

Lambethe 36, 48, 49
Lancaster, John 50
Lancastre, John 41
Lancastyr, John 27
Lane, mastyr 33, 35
Lannse, Mastyr 29
Latymer, mastyr 33
Latymer, William 19
Laxfeld 36
Laxtffylde, vicar of 49
Lege, master 52
Leistone, abot of 49
Letheringham 49
Letheringham, steward of and the prior 49
Letheryngham, prior of 37, 40, 42, 51
Letheryngham, pryor of 41
Lewes 26

Leyston, abbot of 28, 31, 33, 36, 40, 42
Leystone, Abbot of 51
London 20, 24, 28, 33, 37, 41
lorde kyng Herry the VIII 50
Loveday 26
Lovelle, Sir Thomas 35
Lovelle, Syr Thomas 39
Lowthe, mastyr 33
Lowthe, Thomas 37
Lucas, mastress 52
Lucas, mastyr 29, 36
Lucas, Thomas 39
Lucase, Thomas 48
Luce, lade 32
Lyn, Mastyr mayr of 32
Lytton, Willyam 25
Lytylprow, Regnold 36

maille 19, 42
Malbard, doctor 39
Mannok 27
Mannok, Jorge 20, 22, 23, 29
Mannok, Mastyr 32
Mannoke, mastyr 39
Mary 'the French Queen' 18
Mascalle, John 35
Mastyr Dene of the chapelle of the Felde 32
mastyr of the chapelle of the field 29
Mekylfeld, William 36
Mekylfelde, William 44
Mekylfellde, William 39
Melis, Thomas 48
Melket, John 22
Mellis, Robard 52
Mells, Robard 48
Mells, Robert 36
Mellys, Robert 41, 43
Mendham, prior of 44
Metfelde 41
Mettfeld 37
Metyngham, mastyr of 19, 24, 26, 29, 32, 35
Metyngham, the mastyr of 19, 24, 26, 35
More, Thomas 50
moren 19, 20
moreyne 34
morkyn 19, 25, 33
morkyn fawynys 33
Mowneyes 44

Mowor, doctor  52
murrain  19
my lady  20, 21, 22, 23, 24, 26, 27, 28, 29, 33, 34, 36, 37, 38, 39, 40, 43, 44, 45, 47, 48, 49, 50, 51, 52
Myche, Mastyr  32
Mychelmas  53
Mychelmes  28
Mycholmes  44
Mychyll, Johnn  30
Mychylle, John  23
Mychyllys, John  24
Mylls, Robert  50
Mylmer, Robert  23

Naunton, Thomas  50
Nauntone, Thomas  48
Nawntone, Thomas  51
Nedom  43
Newton  33
None, Herry  21, 31
None, Mastyr heery  31
Norfolk, lord of  46, 48, 49
Norfolke, lord of  34
Norwich  48
Norwich, lord of  50
Norwich, masterdyshryff off  48
Norwolde, parson of  39
Norwyche, grey fryers of  42
Norwyche  22, 24, 29, 32, 34, 40, 42
Norwyche, fryers of  40
Norwyche, Lord of  22
Norwyche, lord of  29, 32, 34, 40
Nowne, Herry  41
Nowne, mastyr Herry  29

Oldryng, Symon  37
Olyveor of the barony  21
Orforde, parson of  47, 49, 51
Orforth, parson of  32
Orforthe, parson of  35, 43
Oxforth, lord of  24, 28,
Oxforthe, lord of  30

Packe, John  51
Pak, John  44
parson for his tyethe  52
parson for hys tythe  43

parson for the tythe  41
Payton, Robert  26, 32
Peche  26
Peersys, Thomas  21
Penteney, Pryor of  31
Pentney, prior of  20, 44
Pentney, Pryor of  21
Pettaw  40
Pettawe  47
Petyte, mastrys  27
Peveralle, Rychard  31
Playter, Wyllyem  22, 23
Playtere, William  40
Poley, Houge  25
Pope, Herry  31, 39
Powlys (Paul's), dene of  22
Prat, Rychard  31
preketts  19, 21, 25, 31, 33, 34, 38, 42, 44, 45, 46, 47
privy sealle  39
*Parson* ~~Pryor~~ of Framlyngham for hys Tythe  32
Pulham, John  37, 38, 45, 49
Pullam, John the elder  42, 43, 48
Pullome, John  51

quick  19, 53

Raffe (Enyrs)  20
Rambery  21
rascalle  19, 33, 42, 45, 46
Raycleffe, mastyr Thomas  47
regis Henrici VIIIth.  34
Reve, Edward  19
Reve, Thomas  49, 52
Revet, James  26
Revet, Jamys  24, 29
Revet, Thomas  23
Reynolde, John  48
Reynowe, John  52
Robardy, Master Richard  50
Roberts, Rychard  43
Romborow, prior of  43
Rookwode, Edmond  40
Rookwood, Edmond  36
Rookwoode, Edmonde  41
Roosch, Thomas  22
Roosche, mastyr Thomas  24
Roosche, Thomas  26

root  19, 32
Rosyngton's, John *wyffe*  31
Rous, Sir Willyam  47
Rowces, Syr Willyam  49
Rows, Edmunde  52
Rows, John  51
Rows, lady  49
Rows, Regnold  31
Rows, Reynold  51
Rows, Sir William  35, 51
Rows, Sir Willyam  37
Rows, Willyam  31
Rowse, lady  45
Rowse, mastyr Willyem  33
Rowse, Regnold  44
Rowse, Sir William  42
Rowse, Sir Wyllyam  41
Rowse, Syr William  33
Rowse, Wyllyam  21, 41
Rowse, Wyllyem  22
Rowsse, lady  40
Rowsse, Syr Wyllyam  40
Rowsse, Willyam  30
Rowsse, Wyllyem  23
Rowsse, Wyllyem  25
Roysche, Thomas  32
Roysngton, John  37
Rusche, Thomas  47
Rushhe, Thomas  36
Russche, mastyr  23
Russhe, Thomas  51
Rychers, John  36

Sabeon, William  43
Sadeler, John  31
Sampson, Robert  39
Sampson, Thomas  20, 22
sargeantsfest  28
Savage, mastyr  33
Scoolle mastyr.  35
Sent Peters, pryor of  30
Sente Petris, prior of  47
Seynt Bartylmewys daye  32
Seynt Jeorge day  21
Seynt John's day  20
seynt John's daye  49
Seynt Jonis, Abbot of  51
Seynt Mark's day  42

Seynt Overas, prior of  39
Seynt Peters, prior of  44
Seynt Peters, Pryor of  24, 27
Seynt Peters, pryor of  19, 20, 28
seynt Peters, pryor of  23
Seynt Peturs, prior of  51
Seynt Petyrs, prior of  35, 37, 38
Seynt Petyrs, Pryor of  31, 32, 33
Sharpe, John  27, 28
Sipton, Abbot of  51
Siptone, abbot of  47
Smyth, Willyam  30
Smythe, John  27
Smythe, Robard  52
Snape, prior of  51
sore  19
sorell  19
Southhawys, Rychard  23
Southwelle, Robert  27
Sowolde, towne of  43
sowrells  20, 21, 25, 27, 28, 30, 33, 34, 38, 40,
42, 44, 45, 46
Sowthwolde, towne of  52
Sowtwelle, lady  21
Spoorne, Thomas  27
Sporne, Thomas  32, 36, 43
Sporre, Thomas  30
Spylman, mastyr  27
St.Petrys, prior of  49
Stannard, John  49
Steward, Mastyr  22
Steward, mastyr  28, 37
Stonham, parson of  39
Stonwey, Mastyr  26
Stooke, Mr. Chafy, *the vycar of*  20
Stooke, servaunts of  23
Stow  31
Stratbrook, Dowe of  28
Stuard, mastyr  20, 21, 23, 24
Stward, mastyr  40, 41
Stwrd, mastyr  24
Suffolke, lord of  40
Surrey, lorde of  48
Surrey, lord of  34, 41, 44, 49, 50
Surrey, lord  39
Surrey,  lord of 43, 51
Surreye, lord of  45
Surry's grome  39

143

Sypton, Abbot of   30
Sypton, abbot of   23, 28, 31, 35, 40, 42
Sypton, the vicar of   19
Sypton, vecar of   52

Talmage, Lionelle   29
Talmage, Lyonell   26
Talmage, mastyr   23
Tannington   53
Tanyngton   36
Tasborow, John   22, 23
Tayler, Robert   43
Taylor, Robert   41, 50
Taylor, Thomas   26
Taylyar, Robard   48
tegg   19
Temperley, lady   50
Temperley, Sir John   48
Tendyrlove, William   42
Tendyrlovys, John   34
Tendyrlovys, John  dowtyr   34
Terelle, Thomas   20, 27, 30
Terrelle   20
Terryman, doctor   25
Tersylle, John   19
Teye, John   31, 35, 39
Thafy, Herry   22
the gylde   51
the parsone of Framingham's Tyethe   48
the surveyor   43
Thelforthe, Mastyr Prior of   36
Thetforthe, convent of the priory of   43
Thetforthe, John   31
Thetforthe, prior of   39
Thetforthe, priory of   43
Thetforthe, pryor of   43
Thorpe   23
Throgmorton, mastrys   24
Thyrkylle, John   44
Tilney, Edmomd   48
Tompson, George   41
Toppyng, Anne   45
townys End, mastyr   22
Townysend, mastyr   28
Trymley   40
Tyllneye, mastyr   41
Tyllneye, Syr Phylyppe   36
Tylney, lady   29

Tylney, master Edmunde   52
Tylney, Mastyr   21
Tylney, mastyr   23, 27, 28, 30,
Tylney, Mr.   20
Tylney, Sir philipe   47
Tylney, Sir Phylype   44
Tylney, Syr Fylyppe   24
Tylney, Thomas   43, 47, 49
Tylneye, Edmund   43
Tylneye, mastyr   32, 33, 37, 39, 43
Tymperley, Syr John   24
Tymperley, Wyllyam   29
Tyrelle, Sir Thomas   36

Vere, lady   33, 34, 37

Walton, Towne of   40
Warner, Anes   42
Warner, Watyr   42
Warton   26
Warton, Richard   52
Warton, Rycharde   22
Warton, Rychard   29, 35, 43
Waslyngton   23
Wellebye, Syr John   37
Wentforthe, Sir Rychard   35
Wentforthe, Syr Rychard   23
Wentworth, Sir Rychard   50
Wentworthe, Rychard   40
Wentworthy, Sir Rychard   35
Wentwoyrth, Sir Rychard   47
Wherlyngworthe, parson of   26
Wilbenyghbe, lord   47
Wilbenyghbe, Sir John   47
Willoube, John   51
Wodbrege, towne of   35
Wodbryge, prior of   47, 49
Wodebrygge, prior of   51
Wodiwarde, John   50
Wodous, John   30
Wodows, Mastyr   32
Wolsey, Cardinal   18
Wolverston, Thomas   19
Wood, Geffery   21
Woodbrege, prior of   26, 35, 40, 42
Woodbrege, Pryor of   31
Woodbrege, pryor of   23, 29
Woodbrege, towschyppe of   29

Woodebrege, towne of 19
Woodows, John 26
Woodwalle, John 39
Woolpet, parson of 22, 23
Woolpete, parson of 39
Wooverstone, Thomas 26
Worlingworth 53
Worsepe 21
Worsop, John 48
Wyleby, Lord 19
Wyllebeye, lady 31
Wylleby, lady 21, 26, 26, 27
Wylleby, lord of 34
Wylleby, Lord 20
Wylleby, lord 25, 26, 28, 34, 41
Wylleby, Lord *ys brodyr law* 20
Wylleby, Masteyr Jeorge 32
Wylleby, lord 37
Wylleby, Sir John 35
Wyllebye, Cristofer 27, 31
Wyllebye, Crystofer 30
Wyllebye, lady 28, 30
Wyllebye, lord 21, 24, 28, 30, 32, 33, 36, 38, 42
Wyllebye, lady 23, 30
Wyllebye, Sir Crystofer 36
Wyllebye, Sir John 42
Wyllebye, Syr Cristofer 33
Wyllebye, Syr John 40
Wyllebye, masteyr Thomas 32
Wylloby, Crystofer 20
Wyllybyee, Sir John 41
Wylmer, Robert 22
Wyndam, Thomas 27
Wyndbusher 26
Wyndferdyng 45
Wyndferdyng parke 34
Wyndham, Sir Thomas 41, 47
Wyndham, Syr Thomas 40
Wyndome, Sir Thomas 49, 50
Wyndysssore, Andrew 40
Wyngefelde, Humfrey 51
Wyngefelde, Robard 52
Wyngfeld, Anthony 31
Wyngfeld, Antony 24
Wyngfeld, lady 24, 28
Wyngfeld, mastyr Antonye 28
Wyngfeld, mastyr Antony Wyngfelde 19, 27

Wyngfeld, Mastyr Edmond 35
Wyngfeld, mastyr Humfrey 26
Wyngfeld, Robert 24, 26
Wyngfeld, Sir Anthony 35
Wyngfeld, Syr Anthony 33
Wyngfeld, Willyem of Spexalle 22
Wyngfelde, Anthony 22, 23, 38, 42
Wyngfelde, Antonye 30
Wyngfelde, Humferey 22
Wyngfelde, lady 20
Wyngfelde, lady 20, 23
Wyngfelde, Sir Anthonye 41
Wyngfelde, Sir Anthony 38, 42
Wyngfelde, Sir Antone 50
Wyngfelde, Sir Antonye 47
Wyngfelde, Sir Antony 37
Wyngfelde, Sir Robert 44
Wyngfelde, Syr Robert 27
Wyngfelde, Thomas 29, 39
Wyngffylde, Sir Antone 49
Wyngffylld, Siyr Humferey 47
Wyngfyad, Humfrey 50
Wyseman, John 51
Wysman, John 22
Wysman, mastyr 21
Wysman, Thomas 27
Wyssman, John 26
Wython day 38
Wyythe, mastyr 43
Wyythe, Sir Thomas 36

Yarmowthe, towne of 33
Yermowthe, balys of 33
yermowthe 37
Ypswycche, grey fryers of 44
Ypswyche, balys of 35
Ypswyche 33, 44
Ypswyche, townshepe of 35
Ypyswyche 39

# The Survey of Framlingham, 1547
CHAPTER 8

Ahereds tenement 92

Alden, Robert 82

Alen tenement 94

Alen, Roger 115

Alleyns tenement 89

Allonde Crofte 97

Alredde, Robert 77, 104

Alrede, Thomas 98

Alrede, William 98

Annunciation of the Blessed Mary the Virgin 75

Appleyarde, Robert 109, 110, 111, 114

Arberts tenement 79

armiger 79, 84

Arnolds, John 80

Ashe iuxta Campsey 89

Athered, Roberte 115

Athered, Thomasine 95

Athereds tenement 94, 95

Atherydsche tenement 101

atte Hill tenement 99

atte Hill, Roger, tenement 95

Atthill, John 102

Avelin, Johnn 103

Bacheler, John 84

Baddis tenement 94

Bailes tenement 98

Baker, William 90

Balle, Edward 102

Balles, John 78, 86

Balles, Robert 87, 99, 100

Banham, John 85

Banyarde Close 101

Bardolph, Lord of 79

Barkeley, Margaret 76

Barkeley, John 76, 80, 97, 98

Bayaunce, John 82

Bayly, 111, 112

Baylyff, Thomas 100

Baynhame, John 104

Baynhame, Joan 104

Bell, John 82

Berne, Trussis 77

Boten hawe 109

Boxford 115

Bradel hawe 109

Bradshaw, Griffinus 81

Bradshaw, Joan 106

Bradshawe, Peter 81, 106

Bresis tenement 97

Brethren of the Gilde of Disse 83

Brocke, John 79

Brodey, Thomas 89

Brodey, John 97

Brodeys, 102

Brodhey, John 106

Brodis tenement 99

Broks tenement 93

Brothers tenement 108

Brothers, Thomas 85, 104

Brothers, Margaret 104

Brydgis, Widow 83

Buck, William 94

Buckenames 77

Bucks, 104

Bullish hedge  101
Burgage  80
Burton, Thomas  77, 81, 83, 85, 86, 87, 97, 103, 105
Butone, Richard  78
Buttes tenement  85, 86, 87
Button, Thomas  100
Button, Richard  100
Butts tenement  87, 88

Cade, Thomas  80
Calle, George  77, 105
Calle, John  77, 79, 83, 86, 106
Calle, Nicholas  77, 93
Calle, Robert  76
Calle, Christine  103, 105
Calle, Richard  97
Calle, Nicholas  98
Cancis tenement  105
Canes Way  95
Canes Tenement  92, 112
Caneys tenement  107
Canishill tenement  94
Capon, John  88, 94, 95, 115
Capon, John  of Glemham  115
Capon, William  115
Capon, William  of Dersham  115
Capon, William  of Parham  115
Capon, William  of Glemham  115
Carmans Felde  78
Carter, David  76
Carter,  94
Castell Banks  82
Castell of Framlingham  110
Castle of Framlingham  111
Chamber, John  75, 90, 91, 92
Chamber, Katherine  75
Chamber, Katerina  80, 85, 87, 90, 91, 92, 99
Chamber, Thomas  79
Chamber, William  90
Chamber, Richard  90
Childe, Thomas  93
Chirchehawe, John  77, 103
Churche  112
Clar bolds  107
Cokks pightle  95
Cole, Robert  82
Coliar Lande  84, 85, 86, 88, 89, 97, 101, 103

collector of Framlingham  113
Colles, Robert  76, 80, 87
Common of Saxted  109
Cook, Joan  95
Coole, Richard  97, 99 103
Coole, Margery  97
Coole, Thomas  97
Cooles, Thomas  86, 88
Cooles, Robert  93
Corbolde, Robert  82
Corrant, John  junior  77
Coterowe Rente  76
Cotton, Rowland  112
Coubbe, John  102
Coubbe, Margaret  102
Countes Crofte Closse  77
Cowper, Alice  93
Cranes  80, 84, 85, 86, 87, 88, 114,
Cranes Hall  114
Cranes tenement  84, 85, 86, 87, 88
Crispe, Thomas  83
Crosse, Thomas  82
Crosse, Countesse  102
Curteis tenement  102
Curteis Crosse  96

Dedham, Widow  83
Dernefforde, Paul  107
Derneforde, Reginald  95, 96
Derneforde, Thomas  107
Dernforth, William  92
Devislonde  100
Dise, William  93
Dorrant, John  112
Dowe Crofte  77
Dowsing, William  75, 84, 89
Dring, John  94
Dringe, Robert  99
Driver, John  107
Dryfte waye  98
Duke of Norfolke  78, 112

Ellett, Nicholas  94
Ellett, Joan  94
Elwerton  115
Ewstas, Widow  78

Fair 110
Fairfielde le 103, 106
Fayerwether, Nicholas 89
Feast of St Michael the Archangel 78
Feast of St.Michael 114
Fineta *the widow* 90
Fiske, Thomas 83
Fisks 92
Fletewoode, Robert 89
Fords tenement 103
Forthes tenement 85, 86, 87, 88, 97
Foxe, William 76, 80, 85
Foxe, Thomas 92, 93
Foxe, John 94, 101
Foxe, Robert 100
Foxes 79
Framlingham caucey 96
Free Tenants in Framlingham 80
Fulmerstone, Richard 102
Fulmerstone, John 77, 93
Fulmerstones 75

Garrard, John 83
Gebonne, Reginald 95, 96
Gerard, Mariona 99
Gerrard, John 94, 99
Gibbon, Reginald 80, 85
Gibbone, Reginald 76, 109
Gilbert, William 84
Gilbert, Alexander 98
Gilberte, Roger 96
Godowine, Thomas 99
Goodwine, Margareta 85
Goodwine, Robert 106
Goodwinne, Margaret 107
Goodwinne, Robert 107
Goodwyne, Robert 103
Goodwynne, Margaret 106
Granger and Warren tenement 105
Graunte, Alice 106
Grene, Richard 89
Grenes 75
Grimes tenement 99
Grimes crofte 93, 94, 102

Hacon, Thomas 78, 81
Haleffelde 91, 92, 102, 105
Hall Meadowe 84, 110

Halle meadow 88, 111
Hanham, William 82
Harboldshall grene 104, 109
Harfrey, Thomas 87
Harman, Matthew 76, 86
Harman, John 102
Harmanne, Matthew 80, 102, 114
Harmitage le 96
Harvye, Richard 90
Hastings, Elizabeth 96
Hattons 93
hayward of Framlingham 113
Haywards Tenement 112
Heffd tenement 94
Hell Broks 77
Helwis, John 113
Henmereclosse 101
Herfreys tenement 91, 93, 94, 95, 102
Hering, John 82
Hermers 105
Hermers Little 105
Hersham, John 82
Highfelde Parham 107
Hill, Roger *atte* tenement 95
Hill, Anna 76, 92
Hill, Thomas 92
Hill, Joan 92
Hille, Anna 81
Hille, John 104
Hollande, William 79
Honies tenement 87, 88
Honyes tenement 85, 86, 87
Hosseis tenement 97, 99
Hulver Pigthle 75

Inglonde, William 97
Inhabitants of the town of Disse 83
Irelond, Godfrey 112, 113
Irelonde, Godfrey 84
Irelonde, John and William 80
Irelonde, William 80, 84
Irelonde, Reginald 93
Irelonde, Geoffrey 98
Irelonde, John 98, 100, 101

Jargafelde, Robert 78, 86, 112
Jeffrey, John 106
Jeffreys 77

148

Jervis tenement 92, 95, 102
Jervis, William 94
John Cooke tenement 102
Johnson, Richard 81, 87
Joly, Nicholas 102
Jolye, Margaret 81

Kegills 77, 90
Kenewes tenement 94
Ketelberghe 114
Ketilberghe 93
Ketillburghe wente 98
Keyttyspyttell pightle 90
King Henry 8th 89, 90, 91, 92, 93, 94, 95, 96, 97, 98, 99, 100, 101, 102, 103, 104, 105, 106, 107
King Henry the Eighth 78
(Kin)ghous, John 106
Kings Croft 76

Lampett broke 107
Lawter, Richard 81
Lawter, Robert 82
le Coliar 84, 85, 86, 87, 88
le Coliar Lande 84
le Mere 110, 111
Le Stabell yarde 111
Le Woodwarde 112
lease of a Fair 110
Lettehaughstrette 92
Lion tenement 94
Lodge 110
Lokkingtons 76, 92, 94, 98, 100, 101, 104
Lounde, William 104
Louth, Master 114

Maggis 91
Manbye, Katerina 85, 104, 105
Mapledale 98, 107
Masons 75
Master and Brethren of the Gild of Disse 79
Master and Brethren of the Gilde of the Blessed Mary the Virgin 87
Maughtells 75
Mawgtells tenement 91
Mawgtells 91
Megris 102
Melfylde 77
Messenger, Alice 102

Michell, John 82
Michell, Nicholas 82
Michell, Thomas 82, 103
Michell, William 82
Mille Hill le 98
mille mounte le 102
Mists tenement 97
Morfulles 77
Moriotts Londe 100
Moyle, Geoffrey 99
Moyle, Elizabeth 99
Murdocke, Thomas 106
Murdocks tenement 97
Mysts 100

New hawghe woode 111
Newe meadowe 110, 111
Newecrofte le 102
Newhawe woode 111
Newmans, Edward 75
Newmarketclose 76
Nichol, John 91
Nichols tenement 102
Nuthall, Tobias 82
Nuthill, John 79, 112
Nuthille, John 81, 86, 102
Nuthille, William 102
Nutthille 76

Offerey Wood 109
Okenhilhall 84
Oldewayes 76
Oldhey 79
Olffrey medowe 76
Oxe, John 79

parke of Framlingham 89, 111
Parke, Wrenne 102
Parkilds tenement 94
parysshe Churche 112
Paston, John 77
payle 113
Pennyngs tenement 99
Peris pigthle 75
Perrys 80
Pinfoldes 79
Pistre, Robert 103
Pratts tenement 99, 103

149

Prests tenement  85, 86
Preysts tenement  87
Pulham Francis  76, 80, 100
Pulham, John  105, 106
Pulham, John *junior*  81, 105
Pulham, John *senior*  93, 100
Pynote, John  99

Ravenesdowne  100
Rector of Framlingham  78, 83, 87, 115
Redings  98
reeve of Framlingham and Saxted  113
Revett, John  87, 88, 101
Revett, Robert  101
Reymer, Thomas  90
Richers  76, 79
Richers tenement  76
Rivers  107
Roger Wrytte tenement  102
Rome, Ed(war)d  99
Rossington, Henry  77, 85, 104
Rous, Edward  89
Rous, Anthony  90
Rouse, Thomas  79, 84
Rousse, Anthony  108
Rousse, William  107
Rousse, Reginald  108
Russhe, Anthony  77, 81, 85, 105

Sande Felde le  103, 104
Savage, Richard  83
Saverne  83
Saverne, William  96
Saverne, Richard  80, 96
Saxted  84, 89, 108, 109, 112, 113
Saye, John  93
Saye, Margery  93
Sayes  76, 77
Sayes, John  77, 93
Seman, Ralph  79
Seman tenement  93
Seman, John  91
Sex Acres  106
Sheming, John  83, 87, 98, 101
Sheming, Richard  78
Sheming, Olive  101
Sheming, Robert  101

Sheming, Thomas  101, 109
Sheming, Thomas, *keper*  112
Sheminge, Thomas *keeper*  111, 114
Shemyng de Monte, John  100, 101
Shemyng, Richard  87
Shemyng, Thomas ad Montem  85, 95
Shemyng, Walter  95
Shortes Closse  79
Smith, Thomas  83, 91
Smith, William  79
Smith, John  92
Smith, Roger  100
Smith, Adam  101
Smithe, John  76
Smithe tenement  88
Smithe, Widow  82, 83
Smithes tenement  87, 88
Smyth, John  *of Herbesawgrene*  85
Smyth, William  82
Smyth, Robert  92, 101
Smythe, Edmund  82
Smythe, Widow  83
Smythe, Edward  82, 95
Smythes tenement  85, 86
Southawes  105
Sowterswente  105, 106
Spadehaste  97
Spalding, George  78, 81
Spinke, John  81
St. Michael the Archangel  75
Stabell yerde  96,
Stebbing, Nicholas  75
Stebbing, George  90, 93, 100
Stebbing, Frances  104
Stebbyng, Nicholas  90
Sterne, Elizabeth  86, 102
Sterne, Richard  102
Stoffer, John  91
Stoffers  75
Stogies  76
Stogy, John  92
Stonehame, Richard  107
Stonley, John  106
Stubbes  tenement  105
Stubbing field  100
Stubbing Greate  101
Stubbing le  95

Stube, Richard 107
Sturmyns 76
Survey of Framlingham 15, 17, 74, 75, 77, 79, 81, 83, 85, 87, 89, 91, 93, 95, 97, 99, 101, 103, 105, 107, 109, 111, 113, 115
Sutton, Nicholas 112
Sutton, Richard 93, 105
Suttonne, Alice 99
Suttonne, Richard 99

Tendisloves, John 76
Tendourslove, Giles 90
Tendourslove, John 90
Tenement Bachelers 77
tenement Humbalds 79
Tenements Bareffotts 80
Thatcher, William 78, 83
the Coliar 84, 89
the hayward of Saxted 113
Theverslond tenement 97
Torner, John 84
Town Weye 101
Towne of Framlingham 112
Trues tenement 77
Trussis, John 77

Verdon, William 105
Verdons Tenement 112

Warde, *widow* 82
Warner, John 84, 112
Warner, Richard 84, 99

Warrens tenement 107
Watlings 79, 93, 102
Watlyngs 76
Waylonds tenement 87
Weylonds tenement 86
wheteclose 102
Whitings tenement 85, 86, 87, 88
widow of Henry Rossington 77, 85, 104
Wikerelle Lands 77
Wilde Hey 76
Willmots tenement 90, 98
Wingfelde, Robert 86
Wingfelde, John *knight* 100
Wingffelde, Anthony 78, 107
Woodyche silver 84
Wright, John 76, 79, 93, 94
Wright, John *senior* 76
Wright, Thomas 77, 97, 105
Wright, Robert 91, 93, 104
Wrighte, Robert 87
Wrights, John 77
Wrytte, John 102
Wulnaughes 80
Wyarde, Richarde 115
Wyarde, Robert 115

Yonghusbondes tenement 88
Yonghusbonds tenement 86
Yorkeclose 77
Younghusbandes tenement 84
Younghusbonds tenement 85

# *General Index*

For CHAPTERS 1, 2, 3, 5, 6, 7, 9, 10, 11 and 12

accountant 70

Adrian Culterman 58

Agnes, *our wife* 2

Albrede, John 64

ale 12, 59

alehouses 124

ale-sellers 59

Alfeld, Joan 59

Alfeld, John 58, 59

Allexander, Mrs. 16

Allexanders, Mrs. Elizabeth 16

Almshowses 15

Alpe, Edward 14, 130, 132

Annunciation of the Blessed Mary the Virgin 63, 67

appells 6

Archer, John, *chapman* 122

armiger 71, 72

Armour-Keeper 120

Arundel Castle 62

Ashe 68

Ashebye William 2

Ashing Groave 15

auditor, 70, 71

Audley End 118, 120, 128, 129

Back Yard 130

Baddingham Gate 16

Baddingham quarter 14

Badingham 13, 15, 16

bailiff 63, 67, 69, 70, 72

Bakemett 7, 8

Baker, John 15

Baker, Thomas 131

bakers 8, 59

bakyd cony 6

Baldrey, Thomas 72

Baldwewyn, Thomas 58

Balie Eliha, *peddler* 122

Balie, Franciscus, *chapman* 122

Balle, Edmund 64

Banham, Roger 64

barber-surgeons 124

Barow, John 64

Battle of Bosworth Field 1

Beare 123, 124

Beart, Ralph 15

Bedford, John Duke of 61

Befe 6, 9, 10, 11

Bell 123, 124

Bence, John 16

Bendysshe, Mr. 5

Berners, John 2

Bery 6

Bigod 121

Bird in Hand 124

Bird's Meadow 130, 132

Bishop of Norwich 55

Black Horse 124

Black Swan 124

Blanding, John 131

Blenerhassett, Sir Thomas 2

Blomefield 56

Blomfild, John 131

Blue Boar 124

Blyeth, John, *butcher* 122

boars 59

Boldrey, Thomas  131
Book of Purchases  4
Borough of Framlyngham  68
Borys Hede  6
Bottar  17
Braddelhawe  64, 67
Bradhawe  64
Brandon  12
Braune  6, 11
Brawne  7, 8
Brawne pottage  6
Bray, Sir Edward  55
bread  59
Brede  6
Breghouse, Joan  60
brewers  8, 59
Brewhouse Yard  129
Brewhowse  119
Brick  67
Brickell (Brick Kiln) Close  16
Brickell Close  15
brick-kiln  73
Bricks Tyles  129
Bridge Street  121
Brittany  126
Brody, John ,  64
Browne, Nicholas  15
Bucher, John, *butcher*  122
Bucke, Thomas, *chapman*  122
Buckingham Duke of  1
Bucks, Philip  15
Bull- stake  125
Bulleyne, Thomas, weaver  122
Bungay  60, 125
Burch, George, butcher  122
Burton, Thomas  63, 71, 72
Bush  124
butchers  65, 124
Butere  16
Butley, prior of  55
Butley, Priory of  72
Butter  11
Buttery  118
Button, Thomas  71, 72
Buttons meadow  14
Buttons, Jeames  14
Bynowe, John  64
byrdys  10

Calle, Margaret  59
Calle, Nicholas  63
Calle, Robert  59
Cambridge University Library  4
Campsey, Priory of  66
Candyll  11
cannon  132
capon  6, 7, 8, 9, 10, 11
Caponn, Walter  64
Caponn, John  64
Carlisle  55, 56
Carthouse pightell  14
Carthowse Pightell  16
Castle  127
Castlelands  15
Castor, John  15
Chamber, Katerina  61
Chamber, Richard  60
Chapel  127
chapmen  124
Chapple chamber  119
Church, Marie,  122
Church Lane  124
Church Street  59, 121
Church, Anthony, barber  122
Clarck, Thomass  131
Clarck, Thomas  15
Clare Castle  17
Clarenceux  55
Clarke, Thomas  131
Clayland  14
cod,  17
Cole, Nicholas  58
Cole, Richard  63, 71
Cole, Robert, *shomaker*  122
Collector  63, 70, 71, 72
Collys, Robert  58
Common Dunghill  61
compotus  62
cony  6, 8, 10
conyse  6, 7, 9, 11
Coole, Richard  72
Cooper, John, *pewterer*  122
Coppyng William, *mercer*  122
cord  6
Corlewys  5, 9, 11
Cornishe, John, *chapman*  122
Cornwallis  13

153

Counterfet Arras 3
Coxes Lane 14, 16
crème 6
Cricke, Edmonde, *chapman* 122
Criknell, James 131
Cromwel, Oliver 130
Crosse Keyes 123, 124
Crosse, Edmond 123
Crown 124
Crown and Anchor 124
Crown and Anchor Lane 124
Cuddington 127
Curdise, Robert, *smyth,* 123
Cure, William 128
Custard 7, 8
custarde 6, 17

Debnam, Mr 5
de Brotherton, Margaret *Duchess of Norfolk* 1
de Brotherton, Thomas 1
de Mowbray, Catherine 12
de Mowbray, John 12
de Wingfeld, Sir Robert 12
Deer Park 13, 15, 17
demesne 64, 67, 70, 72, 125
Dene, James , *butcher* 122
Dennington 132
Deserted Medieval Settlements
Archaeological Team 130
Diggins 15
Dining Chamber 120
Dinnington 15
Dinnington quarter 14
Dinyngton Gate 14
Diss 16, 54, 55
Domesday 13
Doughty, Thomas *sen.* 124
Doughty, Thomas, *jun.* 124
Dove 124
dowsetts 9, 10, 11
Dowsing, John 131
doyse 5, 6
Drane, Robert 68
Draper, John 131, 132
Drewry, Alexander 65
Driver, Francis 123
Duchess Agnes 120
Duchess of Norfolk, Margaret 61

Duckling, Robert 122
Dunstons, Mr. Edward 15
Durrants Brige 14
Dye, John , *chapman,* 122
Dynyng Chamber 118, 119
dyshhes 11

Earl Soham 61
Ebbys, Robert 58
Edgar, Devereux 124
Edward III 63
Edward VI 127
eggs 5, 11, 16, 56
ells 17
elys 16
Eme, John 64
England 118
English Heritage 130
Erlond, John 63
Erlonde, John 71, 72
Ersam 6
Eward, Henry 2

Faierfield, le 132
Fair 67
Fairfield 60, 125
fairs 125
Fayrefeld 64
Fayrefelde 66
feast of Michaelmas 63
Feast of St. Andrew the Apostle 63
Feast of St.Michael the Archangel 58
Feast of the Purification of the Blessed
May the Virgin 59
Fisher, Thomas 131
fishmongers 124
Flodden 128
Fludyate, le 64
Fore Street 61
Framlingham chauncel of 127
Framlingham 1, 4, 12, 13, 14, 15, 17, 54,
59, 55, 57, 56, 58, 59, 60, 61, 62, 63, 65, 67,
69, 71 73 117, 118, 119, 120, 121, 122, 123,
124, 125, 126, 127, 128, 129, 130, 132,
Framlingham, Castle 4, 12, 17, 55, 54, 73,
117, 118, 119, 120, 121
Framlingham, church 56, 60, 126
Framlingham, Guild 60

154

Framlingham, Parish Register  122
Framlingham, Parke  14
Framlingham, Rectory  15, 132
Framlingham, Tithe Book  124
Framlingham, History of  132
Framlingham, Manor of  57
*Framlingham, History of and Saxted*  1
Framlingham, Survey of  13, 15, 17 *see also*
*Survey of 1547*
Framlyngham  2, 63, 68, 70, 71
Framlyngham, ad Castrum  63
Framlyngham, Church of  68
Framlyngham, market-place  65, 66
fretter  6
Fuller, Thomas  118, 123
Fulmerston, John  58

Gabone, John  69
garderobe  120
Gardiner, Joshua  124
Gaunte, John  68
gely  6, 7
gelyse  9
Gibson Barnaby, *butcher*  122
Gilbert, Tenement  65
Gilberts  14
Girlinge, John, *butcher*  122
Girlinge, Thomas, *butcher*  122
Glebe  15, 60
Gleve, Robert  61
Godwyn, Robert  66
Goldsmyth, Ida  59
Golty, Mr.  132
Goodwyn, Richard, *butcher*  122
Goultey, Mr.  131
Gramer Schole  61
Gravellpitt Close  14
grazing  64, 67, 68
Great Chamber  3
great gunne  119
Great Hall  118, 119, 120
Great Lodge  13, 14
Great Paddox  15
great Stable  65
Green, Richard  118, 120
Greenwich, Palace of  120
gret ele  16
grete byrds  5

Grey, Thomas  124
Griffin  124
Griffin Gate  124
Griffith, John  127
Griffiths' Memorandum  127
gromes  7, 8, 10
Grymescrofte  64
Guardians of the Guild of the Blessed
Mary  58
Guild of the Blessed Mary  60
Guildhall Yard  60
Guyldehalle  59
gyger brede  7, 8, 9
Gylbert, Alexander  66
Gylbert, Robert  66

Hakon, Thomas  58
Hallefelde  64
Hallmede, le  70
Harman  58
Harold, Margery  61
Harrow  14
hayward  63, 70, 71, 72
Hen VIII  4
Henniker Estate  118
Henry IV  61
Henry VIII  60, 120, 127
Henry VII  1
Henry VI  63
Henry V  61
Hercules  2
Hercules Tapestry  120
Herings Lane  14
Hersclose  15
Hewet, George, *sadler,*  122
Hille, Joan  58, 59
Hitcham,  56
Hitcham, Robert  129
Hitcham, Sir Robert  128, 130
Hokestowe, John  64
Holande, William  66
Holbroke, John  68
Holdyche, Robert ,  71
Holegatehille  64
Holland  120
Home Parke  14
Hommeadow  16
Horsin, Margaret  122

Howard, Thomas *the 2nd Duke of Norfolk* 1
Howard, Thomas *the 3rd Duke* 56
Howard, Thomas 1, 2, 54, 57, 118
Howard Chapel 126, 127
Howard, Henry 126, 128
Howard, Henry *Lord Northampton* 118
Howard, Theophilus 129
Hoxne 55

Inner Court 130
inns 124
Inventory of 1524 1
Ipswich 125, 126
Ireland, Francis 14, 15
Irelond, William 58, 64
Irelond, Reginald 59
Irish knights 12
Iron Gunne 129

Jackson, Bartholomew 123
James 1st 118, 128
Jenny, John 2
Johnson, William, *butcher* 122
Joly, Margaret 59
Joly, Nicholas 58, 59, 60, 63, 66, 67, 69, 72

Kell, Thomas 131
Kell, Edward 124
Kelsale 6
Kemp, Thomas 124
Kemp, John 124
Keninghale 70
Kenninghall 3, 16
Kenninghall Palace 117, 120
Kennyggale 5
Kenred, Thomas 59
Kerich, John 15
Ketylbergh 64
Ketylberghe 72
Ketylberghe Hall 68
Ketylberghe, Lord John 68
kiln 71
King Henry 7th 65, 66
king Henry 8th 66
King Henry 8th 71
King Henry VII 64
King Henry VIII 63
king's assize 59

kitchen 12, 119
kitchin 129
kychyn 10, 11

Lancaster, John of 61
Lanman Museum 120
Laughter, Robert 59
Laxfield 14
Le Cock 124
Leche 6, 7, 8, 9, 10, 11, 17
Leet 57, 68
Lemons, Mr. 14
Letherland, Mary 124
Leverland, Matthew 120
Leveryngstok 64
Little Lodge 13
Little Paddocks 16
Little Paddox 15
Loder, Robert 13
Loes Hundred 57
Lokyngton, Thomas 66, 69
Lokyngton's Mede 66
Lokyngtons 59
London 1, 3, 4, 128
Long Entry 120, 130
long Entry 129
Lord Chamberlain. 118
Lowndy, Richard, *butcher* 122
Lynge 17
lytle shope 123

Mackerell, Dr. 56
Maidston, Mr. 15
malards 5, 9, 10, 11
Malster, Nicholas 124
Maltells 14
manchetts 11
Maneryarde 66
Manor House 73
Manor of Framlingham Rectory 124
Mapledale 13
Mapuldawe 64
Margary, I.D. 130
Market 67
Market Cross 57, 123
Market-place 59, 124, 125
Marlborough's Head 124
marlyngs 5

Marshalle  10
Martin, Thomas  54, 56
Mary Queen of Scots  118
Maultinge house  129
Mayes, John  131
meadow  14, 17, 60, 64, 65, 66, 69, 70
Meane, Thomas  124
Meermeadow  15
mellhowse  119
mercer  65
Mere  13, 14, 16, 17
Mey, John  59
Michaelmas  62, 63, 65, 66, 67
Mill  129
mill  66
Mille bridge  127
Mompesson, Giles  123
Mooer, Robert  131
Moore, Anthony  130
Moorise, John  131
Morgan, Elizabeth  124
Morse, Joseph  15
Mosse, Thomas, *shomaker*  123
motton  9, 10, 11
Mounteys, le  65
Mowbray  1
mowing-work  70
Moyse, John  58
Mylbridge  15
Myllhill  66

National Archive  117, 127
Nativity of St. John the Baptist  63
New Buckenham  123
Newclose  66
Newlaidclose  15
Newman, Anne  124
Newmedew  70
Newson, John  124
Nonesuch' Palace,  127
Norfolk, Duchesse of  120
Norfolk  3, 12, 16
Norfolk, Duke of  54, 60, 62, 71
Northampton, Earl of  128
Norward  14
Norwich Record Office  16
Nunne, Robert, *weaver*  122

Nuttall, Tobias  123
Nuttalls Bottom  14
Nuttelle, William  66
Oakenhill Manor  13
Oldefreth  65
Oldefryth  69
ones Spincke  131
oppbyrds  5
Owles, Richard  66
oxbyrdys  5, 11
Oxford, Earl of  1
oysters  17

pack-horse  61
Pantery  118, 119
pantry  11
Parham  66, 69
Park Pale,  13, 71
partryches  5
Pastery  119
pasture  64, 65, 66, 67, 69
pastyse venyson  6, 7, 9
Peare, Thomas  131
Peasants' Revolt  62
pecoks  5
pecotcoke  6
peke  17
pekoke  11
Pembroke College  4, 14, 17, 58, 121, 123, 129
Pembroke Hall  130
Pepys, Samuel  120
perchys  16
Pereson, John  72
peykys  16
pigs  59, 61
Pin Meadow  60
place  17
playse  16
plovers  5, 9, 11
Plumbers Chamber  129
podryd code  17
Poet Earl  126, 128
Poll Dade  131
porage  7, 8
portars  8
Porters lodge  119
pottage  9

Powes, John, *glover* 122
Pre-Reformation 16
prevys 5
Priory, Thetford 54, 56, 127
Pulham, Agnes 59
Pulham, John *junior* 58
Pulham, John *senior* 58
Puppet theatre 60
pygge 5, 7, 8, 11

Queen Mary 73, 130
Queen's Head Alley 125
Queen's Lodgings 129, 130
quoits pitch 60

Rameshulte, William 66, 69
Ramshult, Thomas 66
Raymer, Jaremey 131
Rectory Garden 73
rede heryng 17
redeshanks 5, 6, 9, 11
reeve 63, 70, 71, 72
Regent of France 61
Rennes 126
Rettingpitclose 15
Revett, Mr. 5
Ribbons, John 124
Rice ap Thomas 56
Richard the Parker 61
Ridolfi Plot 118
River Wincknel 130
Robarrts, Mr. 12
rochys 16
Roke, George 58
Roke, Joan 59
*Roman Roads in Britain* 130
Romsye, Robert, *weaver* 122
Rost vele 7
rostyd capons 6
Rostyd vele 6, 8
Russhe, Arthur 72
Russhe, Mr 5
ryse pottage 17

salt ells 17
Salt Field 16
salt salmon 17
Saltfield 16

Saltfish 16, 17
samon trowt 16
Sampson, Mr. 131, 132
Sarle, Edmond, *butcher* 122
Sarlet, John, *butcher* 122
Sater, John 131
Saterne, Robert, *weaver* 122
Savage, William 58
Saverns, Thomas 15
Sawier, George, 122
Saxe, William 58
Saxsted 63, 70
Saxtead 60, 63
Saxted 68, 70, 72
Saxtedewente 64
Saye, John 58
Schemyng 120
Seintclere, John 3
semewys 5
Servaunts 8
Sewell Thomas 15
Shaperi(n), John 131
Shemmyng, Joan 59
Shemyng, Edward 118
Shemynge, William, *shomaker* 122
Shemynge, Edward, *cobler* 123
Shephearde, Mr. 127
Shepherde, Mr 127
Shimmyng, Thomas 71
Shimonge, John 131
Shoulder of Mutton 124
Shymmyng, Thomas 63
Shymmyng, Thomas 72
Shymmyng, John 58
Shymyng, John 132
Skiner, John 131
Skollery, 119
Skynner, Matthew 15
Slea, John 124
smale byrdys 5, 6, 7
Smock Pightell 14
Smyth William, *shoemaker* 122
smyth 127
Smyth, Edmond 15
Smyth, Martha 15
Smyth, Robert 58
Smythe, Thomas, *barber* 122
Smythe, William, *weaver* 122

Smythe, Richerd   131
Smythe, Robert   63, 71, 72
Smythe, Rycherd   131
Snell's Pightelle   71
snyttes   5
solys   16
Sowse Brawne   8
Sowterswent   64, 66, 71
Spaldyng, William, *butcher*   122
Spaldyng, Robert , *butcher*   122
Spruling, Mihell   131
Spurlling, Mickell   131
Spynke, Jones   131
Spynke, Walter   58
Spynke, John   63, 71, 72
Stableyard   15
Stair House   124
stall   122, 123
Sterkeweather, Alice   59
Stimson, Thomas   131
Stockdale, George,   123
Stoge, John   69
stoke   6
Stoke, John   65
Stoke-by-Nayland   3, 4, 12, 17
Storland, Mr.   131
Stubbyng, le   64
stuyd capon   7
Stuyd vele   7, 8
Suffolk Record Office   117, 118, 126, 131
Suffolk Records Society   1, 4
Suffolk, Earl of   55, 118, 128, 129, 130
Surrey   127
Survey of 1547   13, 127
Swan   124
swane   6, 7
Swann   123
swannes   11
swannys   5
swimming-pool   73
Symonde, Thomas   65

Tabell, Thomas   131
tanners   65
Tarte   7, 10
tarte gynger   6
Tarte of Corde   9
telles   5, 6, 7, 9

tellys   11
tenche   16, 17
Tendring   56
Tendring Hall   3
Tennis Yards   60
The Bedford Hours   61
The Book of Emptions   4
the Crown   60
the Crown and Anchor.   60
Thetford, History of   54
Thetford, Priory of   2
Thornham   118
Toll-House   65, 121, 123, 125
Tomemaker   126
town of Hoxne   55
Towndyshe   58
Towne Parke   15
trenchers   11
Two Potts   124
Tye, Thomas   58
Tyle kyllne   71
Tylney, Mr.   12

Uplands.   57
Uvedale, John   2

Vautts   9
venyson   8, 10, 11
Vyneyarde   15, 64

Waldgrave, Mr. John   16
Wall, Mr. John   130
Waller, Thomas   61
Warde, Joan   64
wardyns   6
waste land   66
watch-tower   132
Watlyngeswente   64
wax-scot   68
weavers   124
Weber, John   131
wegyns   5, 11
Whitby   56
White Hart   60, 123, 124
White Hart Lane,   124
white heryng   17
White Horse   60, 123, 124
White Lion   124

White Lyon 123, 124
White's Directory of Suffolk 121
whytyng 16
William IIIrd 120
Windham 55
Windsor 55
Winsell Meadow 16
Wolsey, Cardinal 3
Wood 67
woodcocks 5
Wyard, John, 122

Wyarde, Roger 64
Wydderleys 69
Wyne seller, 119
Wynsell 16
Wynter, John 64

yeman 10
yeomen 7, 8
Yeste 16
York, Cardinal 2
York, John 69